ANTHROPOLOGY Made Simple

John Lewis, B.Sc., Ph.D.

Made Simple Books
W. H. ALLEN London

Foreword

This book provides a general introduction to Physical and Social Anthropology, whether as a subject taken for a degree in university or technical college or by the general reader who wants to know what modern science has to say about the evolution of man. The book outlines the transition from man's precursors to man himself, the manners and customs of primitive society, and the origins and nature of religion and the moral order. All this has much relevance to many wider, but highly debatable questions in the modern world, and today's reader expects to be given not an *ex parte* judgment on these questions but the latest contribution from the experts.

Many of the topics discussed, however, are still a matter of controversy and even expert opinion is responsible for conflicting judgments. In a book which aims at 'simplicity', I have had to be drastically selective with the immense amount of material available. I have considered and carefully weighed the views of all important schools of thought, and much has had to be discarded. I have included the theories and findings of the best-authenticated judgments and avoided continuous quotation and counter-quotation. At the end of each chapter the authorities on which the exposition is based will be found in the list of suggested reading, and the student is advised to continue his study by reading those books most appropriate to his particular field of interest.

JOHN LEWIS

WHAT IS ANTHROPOLOGY?

Anthropology is the study of the way of life of primitive people as they can still be found today, or not too much altered by contact with civilization. Every primitive community presents a picture not of queer, picturesque customs and beliefs—which is how travellers used to see them—but of a surprisingly well-organized, complex pattern of social life, in most ways totally different from our own. To get to know a whole people intimately, to learn to recognize the common-sense meaning of behaviour, beliefs, strict rules of living, alien to what we feel to be normal, is a fascinating study.

It is because these societies are simple compared with ours, and *small*, so that we can grasp the whole pattern in all its interacting parts, that we study *primitive* societies. The range of social contacts, lack of developed technology, the relatively small scale of numbers and territory, give us a chance to learn a great deal about a complete, self-sustaining community.

When we do so, it quickly becomes apparent that it *is* an organized whole that we are looking at. It is not just the separate customs or beliefs that are different, but the whole *pattern* of working, living, marrying, worshipping, organizing politically, keeping order and so on. Everything is different from the way we do things because the structure, the plan and the ideas behind them, are different.

This is an educational shock. We are so accustomed to thinking, or rather *assuming*, that our European–American ways of living are universal, obviously the only conceivable ones and somehow *right*, that it is disturbing to find different ideas of right and wrong, strange but strict marriage regulations, legal and political systems which don't square with ours but nevertheless work. One of the hardest things to accept is the fact of a whole scale of values, ordinary concepts, ideas of what is rational, that is totally different from our own.

The anthropologist finds these differences in certain departments, as it were, of community life. The family, for instance: elaborate kinship relations may extend to cousins, second cousins, connexions of all sorts, and constitute a tight organization on the basis of which all economic, moral, religious and legal ways of thought depend. The anthropologist has to spend a long time living with these people, exercising much patience and industry in unravelling this complexity of personal relationships and ideas. That is why modern anthropology rests not on academic speculations at home, but on years of field-work. It is this field-work that quickly brings us to a new respect for primitive people, to the discovery that they are as intelligent, as human, as likeable and as competent in their way as we are in ours.

Let us see how the anthropologist sets about his task. Beside the job of getting to know a certain community by living with it, he has to compare it with others to see just what is particular about it and what it has in common with them; then, if he can, he finds out something about its history. This may be a difficult job, for there will be no written records, and traditions don't go far back; anyway they are not reliable. Then there are two background studies of a general kind that anthropologists have to make: the first is called **Physical Anthropology** and it deals with the anatomical types of primitive people, their races, tribes and so forth; the second study is called **Ethnology** and concerns the fundamental ground of all races, the origin and evolution of man, *Homo sapiens*, and of his extinct cousins. Ethnology includes **Pre-Historic Archaeology**, the study of fossil man and his evolutionary progenitors. With this goes a survey of the very first cultures of primitive men—their stone tools, their dwellings, their hunting, their fire-making, and anything else that can be found out—and of how the gradual transition took place to settled agricultural communities, then cities. But in sight of this last step the anthropologist stops; his province extends no farther.

Getting to know a primitive people in its own community will reveal the

> uniformities and regularities of social life, for a society must have some sort of order, or its members could not live together. It is only because people know the kind of behaviour expected of them, and what kind of behaviour to expect from others in the various situations of social life, and co-ordinate their activities in submission to rules and under the guidance of values, that each and all are able to go about their affairs, and lead their lives in harmony with their fellows.
>   (Evans-Pritchard, *Social Anthropology*.)

Anthropology can therefore be described in terms of three intersecting circles representing **Physical Anthropology, Ethnology** (prehistory, race and classification), and **Social Anthropology**. An important sub-section of Social Anthropology covers such matters as writing, art, moral codes, mythology, etc., and is separately classified by some anthropologists as **Cultural Anthropology.** There is one more aspect of primitive society which we are coming to believe is of supreme importance, and that is **social change.** This is the study not only of how such societies have come to be, or have changed within the period covered by tradition, but of how they are changing *now*, especially under the impact of the advanced peoples of the world. This brings us to our first insight—always in relation to original, primitive institutions and traditions—of the emergence of what has come to be called *The Third World*: the Asian, Pacific- and Oceanic-island communities and the South American primitive areas. It is necessary to a complete understanding of the significant social changes of our time that we should know as thoroughly as we may the social and psychological content, and attitudes, beliefs and moral rules, of the embryo world now in process of birth.

Finally let us come back to the importance of anthropology for ourselves. The study of these societies which, while primitive, are not necessarily simpler than our own in their kinship rules, throws into relief certain general features of social life, which concern all of us. We can learn something applicable to the whole of human evolution from the first true man to the races of today; we can perhaps reach conclusions that are valid for all human societies.

Do we not find in these primitive forms of social life indications of the *origins* of the basic features of our own more complex society—our religion, moral codes, social and political structure? If so, then to study these is to study ourselves. The men of all human societies are, fundamentally, organized in societies, therefore comparisons between primitive cultures and civilized societies are illuminating.

Anthropology helps us to see beyond our own ways, and our own community and nation, to those of our distant kinsmen who are facing fundamental human questions in other ways. Like this we may see ourselves in perspective—beholding our own image in the mirror of mankind.

Table of Contents

PART ONE

PHYSICAL ANTHROPOLOGY: MAN AND HIS ORIGINS

CHAPTER ONE

MAN'S PLACE AMONG THE PRIMATES

THE DESCENT OF MAN

Scientists generally accept the fact that human beings evolved from ape-like ancestors. However, they disagree about the details of the progressive changes and the dynamic causes underlying evolution.

The appearance of the first true man may have occurred half a million years ago, when the remarkable Ape-Men of South Africa, the **Australopithecus** group were replaced by *Homo erectus* (formerly known as **Pithecanthropus**) which includes the **Java Man** and **Peking Man.** While some experts doubt whether modern man is a descendant of *Homo erectus*, Le Gros Clark (the leading authority on fossil man and his antecedents) is strongly supported in his view that from this type development occurred in two directions—to the extreme Neanderthal type that became extinct, and in the other direction to *Homo sapiens*.

When the English scientists Charles Darwin and Thomas Henry Huxley first suggested man's descent from ape-like creatures, there was very little fossil evidence of the existence of these ancestral types. Today we have a considerable number of such fossils, all of them in deposits belonging to the **Pleistocene,** a period of relatively 'short' duration, covering about three million years. It was the period of the **Ice Age** in Europe, which ushered in the 'recent' deposits and changes of the last 20,000 years.

THE ERA OF NEW LIFE: THE CENOZOIC

The Pleistocene was not a period of continuous cold but one of alternating cold and warm phases—climatic factors of some importance in estimating the migrations of early man and determining his physical and cultural evolution.

The **Pleistocene (or Ice Age)** was the last period of the **Cenozoic** era, which extends from the end of the **Cretaceous** period—the period of the great chalk deposits, some 70 million years ago—to the present time. The Cenozoic era comprises the following periods: **the Eocene, the Oligocene, the Miocene, the Pliocene** and, as we have seen, **the Pleistocene,**

3

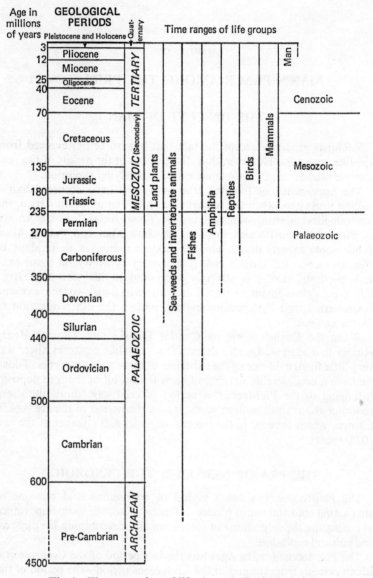

Fig. 1 The succession of life through Geological time.

THE AGES BEFORE MAN

In order that we may see this whole period during which the mammals became dominant and man was evolved against the time scale of Earth's history, let us briefly note that the **Mesozoic,** or **Middle Life era,** during which the reptiles and the great dinosaurs flourished, extended through the Cretaceous and preceding periods from about 225 million years ago. Before that the **Palaeozoic,** or **Old Life era,** went back another 375 million years to the very dawn of animal life, about 600 million years ago. The only fossil remains of the Palaeozoic era are those of the early **invertebrates,** the first clearly recognizable forms being shellfish. Undoubtedly even more primitive forms had evolved through the preceding ages when the earlier sedimentary rocks were being laid down, a period lasting for another 1,000 million years. Before that we travel back another 3,000 million years to the formation of the Earth's crust.

MAN APPEARS

In **Eocene** times—70 million years ago—small primitive mammals rather suddenly gave rise to over a dozen very different orders: hoofed animals (odd-toed and even-toed), elephants, carnivores, whales, rodents, bats and monkeys. Since that time no other orders of mammals have evolved. There have been great varieties of evolution within the orders that did appear, but strangely enough major evolution seems to have halted. Of course there have been many new species formed, but they all belong to families that appeared millions and millions of years ago. But a few million years ago a new kind of evolutionary progress began with the emergence of the hominoids and then of the man apes, the precursors of the ape men. And with the first true men—*Homo sapiens*—evolution begins again, in a new form, with the evolution of social man that is still going on today.

MAN AND EARTH HISTORY

Hominoids have existed for only a small part of Earth history; man himself is a very recent event indeed.

Perhaps the best way to appreciate the age of the Earth in proportion to the period during which life has existed, and, even more significant, in proportion to the period during which *man* has existed, is to imagine a series of photographs put together to form a film. Suppose our first imaginary picture was taken 500 million years ago, when the first evidence of life appears in the fossiliferous rock, and succeeding pictures were taken every 5000 years. We would have 100,000 negatives and the film would last an hour. At least half the rock-forming history would have already passed, during which some 32 miles of sedimentary rocks were laid down in the ocean and later raised up. During the 500 million years covered by the film another 21 miles of rocks were made. When the reel opens we see shells, jellyfish, crab-like creatures, and sea lilies. Phase by phase we see fishes, then amphibians and reptiles, and, finally, mammals. In the last *two seconds* man appears, and civilized man appears in the last tenth of a second.

THE PRIMATES

The highest mammalian order to evolve during the Cenozoic era is the **Primates**. This order shows a series of ascending levels from the little tree shrew (a mouselike creature) through the lemurs and tarsioids to the monkeys and anthropoid apes—a series in which the intervening gaps are partly filled by fossils. This does not mean that man includes types like existing tree-shrews, tarsiers and lemurs in his ancestry, for all present-day animals of these types have shown considerable specialization, which has led them away from the main line of evolution culminating in the human species.

The Primates have certain definite characteristics that are shared by all members of the group from shrew to man. Among these are the forward-looking eyes and relatively large brain (smell is becoming of less importance than vision), the flexible hands or forepaws with their five fingers, including the opposable thumb which makes manipulation possible. Then instead of claws we usually find nails, and on the underside of the fingers soft, fleshy pads.

But what is important about the Primates is that they have produced, as well as more specialized types, a line of development which has been remarkably unspecialized. The other mammalian orders are clearly distinguishable because they are hoofed or marked out in some other way. The fact that the Primates are the least specialized order makes the evolution of man possible. Even the Primates specialize to some degree—note, for example, the immense development of arms and chest in the larger anthropoids which do not run and leap along the high branches but swing from bough to bough. This degree of specialization rules out the possibility that the higher apes, such as the chimpanzee and gorilla, were the ancestors of man. For, once this degree of specialization has been reached, it cannot be reversed. Evolution in different directions can only proceed from an *unspecialized* type. It is from such a type that the anthropoid apes were evolved by a long process of specialization for swinging in the branches of trees, which we call brachiation. Man on the other hand evolved in an unspecialized direction from this common ancestor.

On Climbing Trees. The prehensile (adapted for seizing or grasping) hand and well-developed vision go with an arboreal habitat. The Primates took to the trees, but later some types came down again; and it was only from these (from *some* of them) that man could evolve.

It was life in the trees that was responsible for the evolutionary advance of this order. That life produced many improvements in sensory perception and the use of the hands, advances which led to others in the brain, which receives the information newly acquired from these sense organs, converting it into appropriate action. The emancipation of the forelimbs from the duty of always supporting the weight of the body would leave them free for exploring and manipulating the environment, thus adding to the creature's mental horizon.

The Tarsius. One of the most interesting of the early Primates which probably in some ways resembled man's oldest ancestor, is the tarsier. We have many fossils of this and one living representative, the **Tarsius** of Borneo (which is nocturnal and has great forward-looking, owl-like eyes). This, compared with the earliest Primates (the shrews), shows definite signs of the march towards the monkey form. The Tarsius has prehensile hands with disc-like expansions on the fingers. Its muzzle is reduced; its eyes are enormous; its brain is well developed, largely because the cerebrum is emancipated from the duties of a smell brain and is occupied in dealing with vision and touch, very delicately controlling the muscular responses involved in leaping from bough to bough. It was undoubtedly the change from plodding along on the ground on all fours to clambering among the branches that swung the evolution of the little insectivorous mammals towards the anthropoid direction.

The Monkey. There are some authorities who would trace man's origin directly back to a tarsioid ancestor, regarding the monkeys as a development in a different and more specialized direction. But most authorities would include in man's family tree a monkey-like (**pithecoid**) stage; though it must be understood that modern monkeys have changed considerably from the type that was the ancestral form of both man and monkeys as we know them.

It was in the **Oligocene**, 35 million years ago, that a creature lived that was more developed than a tarsier but in some ways less developed than any monkey or ape now alive—and very much less than a man. It was fully arboreal and better perfected for that kind of life than any of its own ancestors. It was in fact a monkey. Larger than the Tarsius, its increased size and weight put greater demands upon the climbing mechanism, i.e. strong, grasping hands and feet. A heavy survival value was placed on balance and distance judging, the senses and brain being developed accordingly. We also note a trend in the direction of the *upright body*, for in a tree it is easier and safer to sit or stand than it is to lie down.

The Hominoids. Although this advance first took place in the New World, there was no further progress in this hemisphere beyond the level of the New World monkeys. But in the Old World this new type developed not only into the Old World monkeys, but gave rise to a progressive branch which advanced from the pithecoid or monkey stage to the *hominoid* stage. This is 'man-like' and includes the gibbons, the great apes and man today.

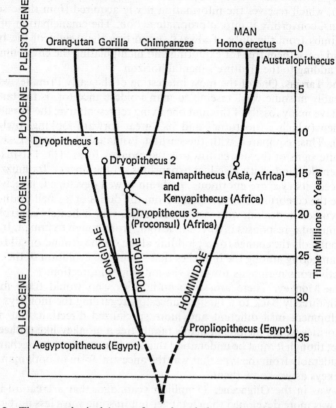

Fig. 2 The genealogical 'tree of man' and the anthropoid apes, following Pilbeam and Simons (1964–7). Much more material is needed to obtain definitive results especially from the time of 20–30 million years ago.

It is now believed by a number of investigators that this original, unspecialized, monkey-like type gave rise not to *one* hominoid line which divided into men and apes at a very late stage, but into two main streams: the *Pongidae*, leading to the great apes, and the *Hominidae* leading to man. As long ago as the Oligocene there is evidence of these two divergent types of hominoid.

It was for a long time believed that the divergence took place only 14 million years ago or thereabouts, and that a Miocene African ape, *Proconsul*, which was relatively unspecialized and had not developed the anatomical modifications for swinging in trees known as brachiation, was the common ancestor of men and apes.

More recent theories classify *Proconsul* as belonging to a most interesting and widely dispersed genus of tree-apes known as **Dryopithecus**, which was the culmination of the pongid line and which separated from the hominids 20 million years before *Proconsul*. It is thought that *Proconsul* or a similar type may have given rise to the chimpanzee and gorilla, and that another type of *Dryopithecus* may have been the ancestor of the orang-utang. The other forms of this genus all became extinct.

The hominid line never modified in a brachiating direction and never developed the powerful canine teeth found in all pongids including *Proconsul*. We know that at the same time as *Proconsul* there existed at least two distinctive hominids which are almost certainly either the immediate ancestors of **Australopithecus** (the precursor of man) or was actually the first known *Australopithecus*. These hominids are known as **Ramapithecus** and **Kenyapithecus**, the latter discovered by Leaky in 1962. *Ramapithecus* has been found in India, Africa and Europe.

Pilbeam and Simons have suggested that there may be a connexion between this hominid line and a very unspecialized little monkey-like type, **Propliopithecus**, which lived in Egypt 34 million years ago and had the pattern of teeth and jaw characteristic of the later hominids. At roughly the same time there was, also in Egypt, another type with well marked canines, **Aegyptopithecus**, which may indicate the ancestral type of the *Pongidae*.

We may now make our terminology clear. The hominoids include both the ape line—the *Pongidae*—and the line leading to man—the *Hominidae*. The *Pongidae* are represented today by the great apes—the chimpanzee, the gorilla and the orang-utang. The *Hominidae* include the fossil *Australopithecus*, fossil man, now extinct, and living man—*Homo sapiens*.

The Great Apes—Are They Human? The great apes (*Pongidae*) are not nearly as human as is sometimes supposed and as the problem-solving powers of the chimpanzee might indicate. Physically they are very different.

Their great weight has brought them to the lower branches of the trees and to the ground, and they walk rather than run on all fours, using their forelimbs as crutches, knuckles down. The feet have lost their mobility and some of their prehensility. The spine is massive and rigid, the shoulders broad, the chest barrel-shaped and the arms enormously long. Their tails have been entirely lost and their legs are short.

The heavy chewing and neck muscles are attached to remarkable bony ridges along the top of the skull. The canine teeth are well developed and the jaw pattern rather rectangular, whereas that of man is semicircular. Their brains are well developed, though far below those of *Homo erectus*.

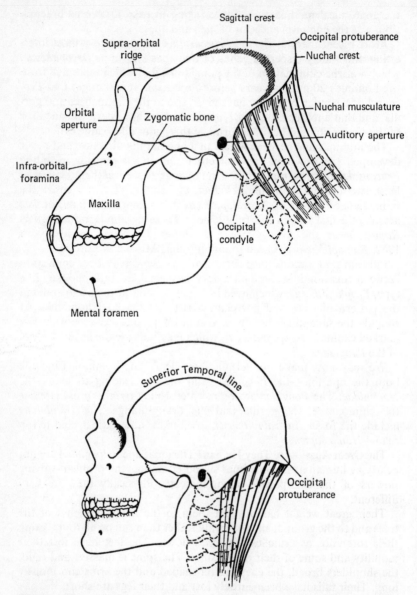

Fig. 3 The pongid type of skull (gorilla) and the hominid (man). Note massive development of neck muscles in the ape with attachment high up the back of the skull to the nuchal crest. Also in the pongid type there is less height above the orbit, while in man there is considerable height. The brain case is bigger. In man the face is vertical and there is more below the brain case than in front of it as in the ape's skull. (After Le Gros Clark.)

We thus see that a considerable degree of specialization has taken place, from which there can be no return.

No evolution of the apes in the direction of man is now possible. It is even correct to say that man is in many respects closer to the monkeys than he is to the apes, especially with regard to the generalized proportion of the hands, the development of the thumb, the leg and foot muscles, the sequence of eruption of the middle teeth, the tendency towards late obliteration of the cranial sutures, and in the absence of a curious long shelf just underneath the front of the jaw (also absent in *Proconsul*). From this it would appear that the stock from which the hominids arose was monkey-like rather than ape-like.

Descending from the Trees. At some time or other the ancestors of man descended from the trees and ran on two legs. Probably they were getting too big for high trees, so progress through the forest by the treetop pathway was impossible, or the forests were disappearing. Since they

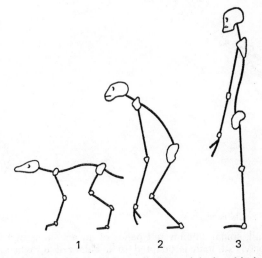

1   2   3

Fig. 4 Basic skeleton of (1) quadruped; (2) upright brachiating type; and (3) erect form, showing balance of head and proportion of limbs. Note how the head is attached to the vertebral column. In (1) it articulates *behind* the skull, in (3) *below* the skull.

could not stay indefinitely in one tree, *they must have descended in order to run from tree to tree.* Life was at stake for those who did not learn to run, as well as for those who lacked the variations in bone structure which made running possible.

Some (the baboons) seem to have descended too soon, before they had developed legs for walking. In consequence they are true quadrupeds, run on all fours and look rather like dogs. The great apes put it off for too long and were so heavy that when they did put all their weight on their feet, the bones of the feet were distorted. Man's ancestors started *before* they became too heavy, and increased their weight *after* taking to the ground.

Arm locomotion involves suspension of the body, and these creatures began to use their legs when they were holding on to branches, though the body needed support below to take most of the weight off the arms.

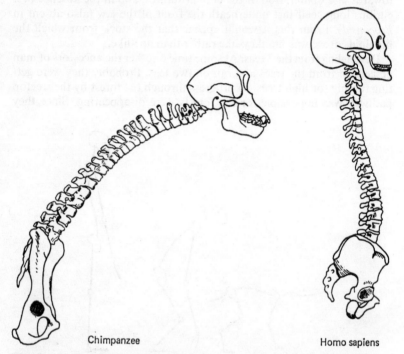

Chimpanzee   Homo sapiens

Fig. 5a   Skull, spinal column and pelvis of an ape compared with that of man. The pelvis of man is adapted to a balanced upright stance and a walking gait.

Once they were down and no longer using their arms for locomotion, they were ready to make much better use of them. Man could become a tool-user only if he achieved an upright position, could maintain his balance, and *had his arms quite free*. This development was now possible and in addition this precursor of man had developed the excellent binocular vision needed to leap successfully from branch to branch, and the strong, prehensile hands of a tree-dweller.

The evolutionary achievement of the upright posture while the brain remains small may indicate that under the treeless condition of that part of Africa this was a necessary adaptation. Any group of ape-like animals, in order to survive, must either revert to a quadrupedal habit or go to the opposite extreme and become completely bipedal. If the ape had descended from the trees after sufficient development of the legs, the latter course would have been followed. Fossil remains of such a bipedal hominid have now been found. It is known as ***Australopithecus***.

There are remarkable features about these remains: the bony ridge

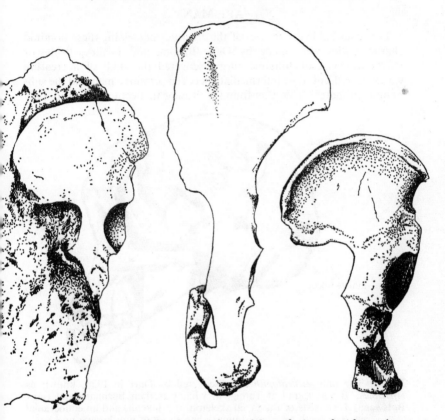

Fig. 5b The pelvic girdle, from left to right, of *Australopithecus* (embedded in rock); of an ape; of man. This marks a fundamental difference between the late hominids and the pongids.

on the skull for the attachment of neck muscles is hominid rather than ape-like. The skull is well perched on the top of the vertebral column, whereas in dogs and apes the spinal cord and vertebral column connect with the back of the skull or have moved only slightly beneath the skull. The dentition is markedly hominid—the curve of the teeth as set in the jaw being a half circle and not a rectangle; moreover the canines are much reduced. Of the greatest importance is the pelvic girdle and the thighbone. These are markedly different from those of the apes and suggest an upright posture, as does the pivoting of the skull on the vertebral column. The brain capacity is 600 c.c.; that of the gorilla is 550 c.c.

AUSTRALOPITHECUS: THE SOUTH AFRICAN APE-MAN

The remarkable discoveries of the creatures possessing these hominid characteristics were made by Dart, Broom, and Leakey. Professor Raymond Dart of Johannesburg discovered the skull of a creature which turned out to be intermediate between primitive man and the sub-human primates. This was found at Taung in Bechuanaland in 1925

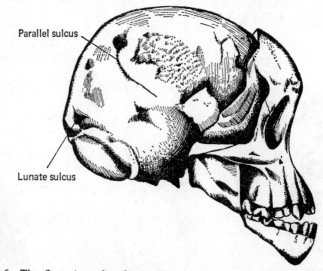

Fig. 6 The first *Australopithecus* discovered by Dart in 1925, known as *Africanus.* It was found at Taung, in what was then Bechuanaland (now Botswana). It consists of the facial skeleton of a juvenile and an endocranial cast. The teeth are more human than those of any known ape.

and has been named *Australopithecus africanus*. Further discoveries in this direction of skulls and jaws of the same species were made by Dr. Robert Broom of the Transvaal Museum, Pretoria, and by Dr. L. S. B. Leakey. It was Leakey who in 1959 found the skull and bones of a specimen very much older than any previously found. These remains were associated with crude stone implements and flakes and are classified as belonging to the same group, *Australopithecus* (or Southern Ape), in spite of considerable variation in size and other features. It is now pretty certain that they are early Pleistocene and date back possibly to a million years ago, *Australopithecus* ranged over a wide area from south of the Sahara through East Africa to South Africa under conditions closely similar to those on the veldt today.

They lived on small animals, amphibians, lizards, birds, small rodents, fresh-water fish, and vegetable food. Some types however seem to have killed antelopes and baboons. They lacked the powerful canine teeth of the *Pongidae* (Anthropoid apes) and *Dryopithecus*; they were peculiarly defenceless, depending for survival on being able to move quickly in open grasslands. In all respects they differed considerably from the apes of the great forests, who had abundant supplies of food. Faced with a difficult environment they had to improve both their bodily organism and their methods of hunting and living.

In most respects they showed a considerable difference both from the *Proconsul* type and from the chimpanzee, who evolved *parallel* with *Australopithecus*, so that it must not be supposed that the great apes were their ancestors or the ancestors of man. They had developed a bipedal stance with modified femur, pelvic girdle, and ankle bones. The vertebral column entered the skull much farther back than in the ape; and the brain case was more rounded and the frontal region raised well above the orbit. The brain had not enlarged much but the hand (with the thumb now opposed to the fingers and capable of precision grip) and the foot were well on the way to the human condition. They could now make and manipulate tools. Although the achievement was not great, the changes started a trend which could speedily show improvement and lead to the emergence of a distinctively human type. *Australopithecus*, unlike the apes which are still quadrupeds, was a biped, but the condition was not perfect and he was incapable of a striding gait; he may have walked with a kind of shuffle.

How much more do we know of *Australopithecus*? Not very much, nor may we be too speculative about matters for which little or no evidence is available. In appearance we know that he still had large jaws and was probably incapable of the complex movements of the mouth necessary for speech. Nor does the brain seem sufficiently developed for this to be possible. We can see that unlike those of the apes, the upper limbs were not specialized for arboreal life: on the contrary he possessed a mobile arm and a hand capable of manipulation. There is evidence of tool-making, but there is no evidence of making fire, and none for the existence of the family as a unit. Like the baboons, who lived in a similar environment, they probably were social in habit and moved about in troops, returning to caves in the low hills rising from the plains.

Yet it would be a complete mistake to link them closely with the baboons. The differences far outweigh the similarities. Baboons have no lasting bond between male and female; they are inbred and do not find wives in another group as primitive men do. They have no kinship groups based on marriage relationships, and later developments—

co-operation in hunting, fire-making, and food-sharing at a home base—represent a sharp break between man and the other primates.

It would appear that *Australopithecus*, which has been found only in Africa, eventually became extinct. The group of fossils which represent a later stage in human evolution and the transition to man are found in

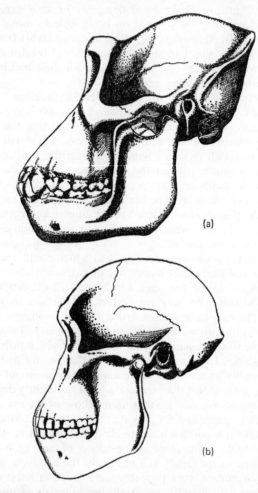

(a)

(b)

Fig. 7   Skull of a female gorilla (a) compared with that of an *Australopithecine* skull (b) from Sterkfontein. The axis of the connection with the vertebral column has moved considerably forward in the latter. The brain case is rounded and the teeth lack the well-marked canines of the ape. The jaws are still large. A detailed comparison reveals a surprising number of hominid and non-pongid features. The facial part of the skull is more below the brain case than in front of it. (After Le Gros Clark.)

the East, in Java and China, and contain two related types: the first was found by the Belgian, Dr. Dubois, in Java in 1891, and is known as **Java man**; the second was found by Teilhard de Chardin and Dr. Davidson Black at Choukoutien, near Peking, in 1928, and was called **Peking man**. Java man was subsequently named *Pithecanthropus erectus*, and Peking man was named *Sinanthropus pekinensis*. Both of them are now included under the designation *Homo erectus*—the first 'true man'.

(*Australopithecus*, if not directly ancestral to true man, was close enough to the line of descent to man to represent an evolutionary phase through which this line leading to *Homo* must have passed).

Compared with the first example of true man, **Pithecanthropus erectus** (Java man), we can at once see how far *Australopithecus* had to go. His brain was much smaller, round about 600 c.c. compared with 1000 c.c. His jaws were more massive, though teeth and dental plan were hominid. It is in fact the teeth which, with the hip girdle, long bones of the leg and ankle, show the real advance, not the jaw and brain. Le Gros Clark has shown, in his recent book *Man-Apes or Ape-Men?*, that the common ancestry of *Homo* and *Australopithecus* is evident in the initial stages of advance which persist, while not a single pongid character appears. Meanwhile, the special features of the apes had begun to appear: very short legs and long arms, broad chest and other characteristics of a bough-swinging, tree-dwelling animal (brachiation). The more primitive characters of jaw and brain case in *Australopithecus* belong to the ancestral types of both *Pongidae* and *Australopithecus*, and change much later into the human pattern found in Java man (*Homo erectus*).

Java man. The fossils found comprised a skullcap, three teeth, and a thighbone. Since then many more bones have been found, representing quite a number of individuals (see page 21).

Java man was a large primate, the size of a modern man. He walked erect, his heavily browed skull set on a powerful neck, head thrust forward. His jaw protruded and he had huge teeth. Yet he must have been much more skilful than an ape, for his pre-frontal and association areas were far larger and more complex, and all the mechanism connected with vision was perfected. Nevertheless he was not very wise, witty, or intelligent; his ideas were few and simple, and he was still the creature of impulses rather than reason.

Peking man. Definitely belonging to the same genus, Peking man was discovered in the quarries of Choukoutien, south-west of Peking. These excavations began in 1927 and continued until 1939, when they were interrupted by the Second World War. Unfortunately the most complete and remarkable series of fossils of early man ever obtained was irretrievably lost during the war, probably by the sinking of the ship in which they were being evacuated. This great loss was mitigated, however, by

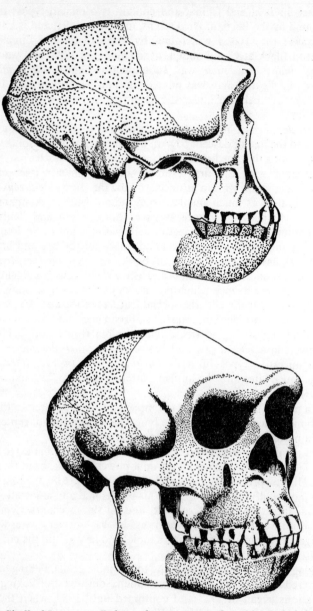

Fig. 8   Skull of Java man, *Pithecanthropus erectus*, found by Dubois in 1889. This is the first true man. The skull cap is flat and the eyebrow prominences enormous. There is no forehead, but the cranial capacity is about 1000 c.c.

the elaborate and accurate record of the find made by the anthropologist Franz Weidenreich.

Portions of the skulls of fourteen individuals, including entire brain cases, facial bones of six individuals and long bones and teeth that give us parts of almost forty more, were obtained, photographed, drawn, and carefully described.

The cranial capacities of Java man and Peking man are about 1000 c.c. —well below that of modern man, which is 1500 c.c., but much higher than that of the South African ape man (*Australopithecus*), which is about 600 c.c.

What is particularly important about Peking man is his collection of tools, which includes chopper-like cores and flakes trimmed as points and scrapers, and the remains of fires. Another matter of great interest is that all the skulls of Peking man had been opened at the base for the removal of the brains, while the limb bones had been split down their length. This suggests cannibalism, perhaps merely a matter of diet, perhaps of a ritual or ceremonial kind, with magical significance.

THE ICE AGE

It was in the Middle Pleistocene, in the second glaciation of the **Ice Age,** that this new type appeared, exhibiting a recognizable human way of life, with tools and weapons, fire, cave dwellings, and evidence of hunting larger animals on a considerable scale.

We must set this event against a time scale; and since the whole period from the earliest human fossils to the latest—the **Pleistocene**— was that in which the great ice sheets invaded Northern Europe, retreated, and then invaded again, it is the Ice Age chronology that we shall follow, though it must be remembered that there was no ice in those regions of the Far East where early man first appeared.

This age starts conveniently about a million years ago and is known as the Pleistocene. During the first glacial period, ice fields covered Scandinavia, North Germany and the Alps. This was followed by the first interglacial period, when the temperature rose again. The second and third ice ages followed, with a particularly long warm period between them during which man steadily advanced. The fourth glacial age showed considerable fluctuation in temperature and finally thawed out in the postglacial phase in which we are now. It is important to remember that each glacial and interglacial period extended over hundreds of thousands of years and that animal life was evolving right through the Pleistocene.

During the three main interglacial periods hunters using hand axes, heavy flints roughly shaped and pointed, roamed widely over northwest Europe; but during the succeeding glacial periods they seem to have been replaced in France and southern Britain by hunters using tools made from flakes struck off large flint cores. This was the period of the mammoth, primitive bears and oxen, some of the earlier horses, the sabre-toothed tiger, the mouse, and the red deer.

The largest and hottest of the interglacial periods was the second, which lasted for 200,000 years. The Alpine peaks were almost clear of snow, and much of Europe with its splendid forests and its wide, grassy plains resembled Africa (South of the Sahara) today. To this fertile area

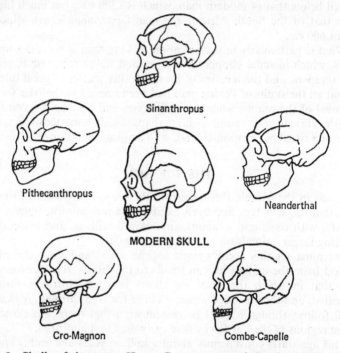

Fig. 9 Skulls of the genus *Homo*. Cro-magnon and Combe-Capelle skulls are those of the genus *Homo sapiens*. All other species are extinct.

came such a mixed assemblage of African and Asiatic animals that Europe must have resembled a huge zoo. In Asia at the peak of Pleistocene glaciation the sea level may have been 300 feet lower than it is now. (If all existing glaciers melted, the sea level would be raised another 150 feet today.)

Java man is not without companions, but what they were is a mystery, a matter for furious controversy. First, there is an enormous human tooth, six times the size of a man's; then there are two large mandibles from central Java. These may represent a more primitive type from which the *Pithecanthropus* evolved, or a parallel evolutional line which became extinct, or simply varieties of the same species.

There is a series of much better fossils from the Solo River in Java which some anthropologists regard as intermediate between *Pithecanthropus* and the much later Neanderthal man.

Other extinct types probably diverging from a *Pithecanthropus*-like ancestor have been found in Africa, notably in **Rhodesian man.** Rhodesian man has been described as an extremely rugged form of Neanderthal man, evidencing racial senility. (When a race of animals begins to develop bony excrescences, it has reached the end of its course.) The forehead is low, depressed and narrow, the eye sockets large. There is a long, projecting upper jaw and a rather small brain cavity. It probably had the thickest neck of any early man. Although it is contemporaneous with the Neanderthals, and much later than *Pithecanthropus*, a strongly held counter-opinion regards it as in no way related to or derived from Neanderthal stock, but a highly specialized offshoot of a pithecanthropoid ancestor which became extinct.

Neanderthal Man. The human type which immediately preceded *Homo sapiens* was Neanderthal man. Survivors continued to exist long into recent (that is to say, postglacial) times. They may have been the source of folk tales about ogres—great ugly, hairy monsters, lurking in forests and caves.

This type of human is found in the upper Pleistocene from about the end of the third or last interglacial period and the beginning of the fourth or last glacial period. This would give us a beginning date of about 115,000 B.C. Their last remains are dated about 25,000 B.C. The span of time during which the Neanderthal types lived was thus far greater than the period that has elapsed since the most recent specimen died.

Le Gros Clark sees a direct connexion between *Homo erectus* and Neanderthal Man, but he believes that at this point divergence took place. One line became more and more Neanderthaloid, with massive skulls and jaws, and eventually became extinct; the other line developed from the earlier basic type, which was not so specialized, and became *Homo sapiens*.

Other anthropologists see the divergence as between *Homo erectus* and both types of Neanderthal man on the one hand, and a separate group, not descended from *Homo erectus* on the other. This group first appeared with so-called Neanderthal skulls of the less long type and are really a quite separate line, the neanthropic line, which includes among very ancient fossils only **Swanscombe man** and the skull found at Fontéchevade, in the Charente district of France.

A considerable number of Neanderthal fossils have been found, including some of very early precursors of the type; and associated with this type of man is a very definite stone-implement culture, well advanced in comparison with that associated with any type of *Homo erectus*.

The earliest skulls were found in Belgium (1829) and Gibraltar (1848), and the type skeleton in the Neanderthal valley in northern Germany. These remains were at first thought to be diseased bones of modern man or even skeletons of Russian grenadiers from the European wars, but Schaffhausen of Bonn, and Huxley and Lyell in Britain, declared that they were the remains of an ancient type of man. Many more skeletons and skulls have since been discovered, notably at Le Moustier, in the Dordogne in south-western France, where they were associated with an important flint industry—the Mousterian; and at La Chapelle.

The Man from La Chapelle. This man had massive brow ridges in one solid bar and large but not ape-like teeth. The skull had a low dome but a cranial capacity of 1200 to 1600 c.c. (well in advance of *Homo erectus*); the jaw had no chin eminence. He was about five feet tall with bowed gait and half-flexed legs. He was a cave man and a hunter.

His Mousterian flint tools were chipped on one side only so that their reverse is rounded or bulbar. The typical flake has a thick base and is roughly triangular. Another type is the so-called 'side scraper', flaked on one side and then retouched. There are also a few choppers or heavy blades with thick backs and edges sharpened on both faces, producing cleaver-like tools.

The Origins of Neanderthal Man. The earliest Neanderthal types include a massive jaw, found near Heidelberg, the **Steinheim** skull, and a skull found at Swanscombe in Kent. The **Swanscombe** skull was less specialized than later and more typical skulls. This would bear out the view that the later Neanderthal type is the product of over-specialization, away from the common stem that gave rise to *Homo sapiens*. The Heidelberg jaw is early middle Pleistocene, perhaps dating back 300,000 years; the Steinheim skull belongs to the third interglacial period (150,000 B.C.), at which time the early types of rhinoceros and elephant existed. They therefore precede the true Neanderthaler by a long period of time.

There seems to have been something like a Neanderthal invasion of Europe at the end of the third interglacial period, long after their earlier precursors had somehow wandered in, and they lived on during the severe fourth glaciation under what must have been miserable conditions. Life in these forbidding times was rendered still more intolerable by the heavy rainstorms and floods of summer and the blinding snow-storms of winter. It was nearly always wet and cold and the country was often enshrouded in heavy, clammy mists.

No doubt it was these conditions which drove Neanderthal men into caves, though first they doubtless had to expel the animals that inhabited them. Had it not been for the discovery of fire they might well have perished; and no doubt fire was used not only to keep men warm but to drive savage beasts out of these refuges and keep them out.

Neanderthal man seems to have survived for several thousand years after the ice of the last glaciation began to melt. Then, at some date that may perhaps be set between 25,000 and 20,000 years ago, the Neanderthalers in central and western Europe seem to have disappeared as a distinct type. They were replaced by people of completely modern type, probably from Asia, who, with superior organization, quickly displaced their predecessors and occupied their territory. Modern man probably reached Europe between 40,000 and 50,000 years ago.

The two cultures did, however, overlap, so that Neanderthal man and

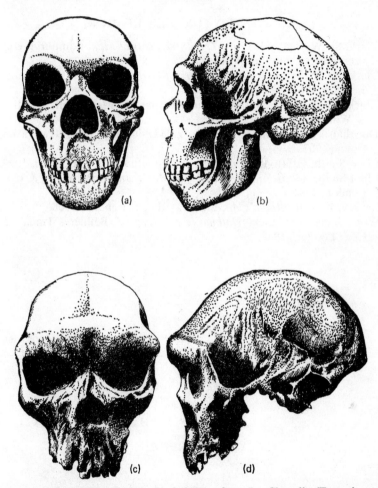

(a)   (b)

(c)   (d)

Fig. 10 Skull of (a, b) Neanderthal Man from La Chapelle (France), and (c, d) Rhodesian Man (South Africa). The teeth are hominid and though the brow-ridges are large, the cranial capacity is high. The associated limb bones are not distinguishable from those of *Homo sapiens*. This type was probably a variant, tending to a more massive skull, which became extinct.

modern man lived for a time side by side. Did they at any time inter-breed? This may be so, for near Mount Carmel in Palestine, we have found the remains of what might be called an intermediate type with likeness to both the Neanderthal and modern man; and there is also a great variety of other intermediate types here. It is possible that inter-breeding took place, but it is more probable that man changed rapidly from the Neanderthal to the modern type.

SUGGESTED FURTHER READING

Clark, Sir Wilfred E. le Gros, *The Antecedents of Man*. Edinburgh University Press: Edinburgh, 1959.

Clark, Sir Wilfred E. le Gros, *History of the Primates*. British Museum: London, 1965.

Clark, Sir Wilfred E. le Gros, *Man-Apes or Ape-Men?* Holt, Rinehart & Winston: New York, 1967.

Dobzhansky, T., *Mankind Evolving*. Yale University Press: New Haven, Conn., 1962.

Elliot-Smith, Grafton, *Human History*. Jonathon Cape: London, 1929.

Elliot-Smith, Grafton, *The Search for Man's Ancestors*. Watts & Co.: London, 1931.

Leakey, L. S. B., *Adam's Ancestors*. Methuen: London, 1968.

Wood-Jones, Frederick, *Hallmarks of Mankind*. Baillière, Tindall & Cox: London, 1948.

CHAPTER TWO

THE EMERGENCE OF TRUE MAN

TRUE MAN

The earliest true man known to us is *Homo erectus*, represented by **Java man** and **Peking man.** He lived in the second glaciation of the Ice Age, about 500,000 to 700,000 years ago. What distinguishes Java man from his predecessors and compels us to declare him without hesitation to be a man? Java man shows all the characteristics present in modern man, but in a more primitive form. He is a tool user and could make a fire. If we consider these characteristics as they appear typically they will comprise the following features:

1. *Hair:* Man is not hairless. In fact the density of hair in man is greater than in some primates; but the hairs are vestigial rather than sparsely planted. Moreover the foetus is completely hairy, which (together with other foetal characteristics) has suggested that man retains certain foetal or juvenile characters until adult age. This, as we shall see, is a matter of great evolutionary importance.

Man is entirely devoid of tactile hairs such as those found in the whiskers of cats.

2. *Man is Plantigrade.* He stands firmly and can balance himself securely. This is due principally to a remarkable development of the foot. The fifth digit is rudimentary (this is not due to wearing shoes!), the big toe springs from the anterior edge of the sole and not from a point along its inner margin, which would make it a kind of thumb; moreover it is bound tightly to the rest of the foot by the metatarsal ligament.

3. Man has *long legs* and relatively short arms. The *skeletal changes* due to his erect posture are many and include the poise of the head, the curvature of the back, the prominent buttocks and calves, and the extended position of the knees.

4. *Human teeth* are very characteristic. The horseshoe-shaped arcade, the cheek series, is bowed apart instead of forming parallel rows as it does in the apes. There are no gaps in relation to the canines, which are no larger than the others. The molars and pre-molars are also distinctive.

5. *The skull* has been greatly developed. The brain case is globular and devoid of long crests and ridges. The face is flattened, for there is no snout. Man uses his hands, not his teeth, to pick things up and sight is more important than smell. The jaws are, therefore, relatively

25

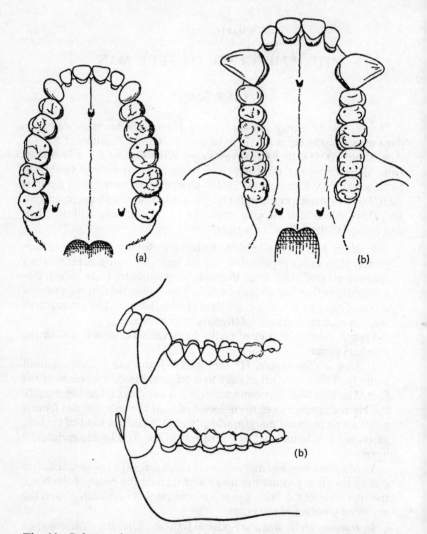

Fig. 11   Palate and upper teeth of (a) an *Australopithecine* compared with (b) a gorilla. Below is a side view of a gorilla's jaw. The typical round arcade of the hominids is found in *Propliopithecus*, *Ramapithecus*, *Kenyapithecus* and all the Australopithecines up to *Homo*, and in all species in that genus. *Proconsul* and *Dryopithecus*, along with the living *Pongidae*, all show the rectangular plan and large canines. This type is also found in *Aegyptopithecus*, a possible ancestral fossil.

weak and do not need the bony ridges to which powerful muscles are attached—hence the greater flexibility of the jaw, which contributes to the power of speech.

6. *The brain* is three times as large as that of the gorilla and contains ten times as many neurons in the cortex. The neuromotor mechanism for uttering words and using vocal symbols for things and actions is established; along with this goes the auditory mechanism to enable the spoken word to be recognized as a symbol. The association tracts are very numerous and make possible problem-solving thought vastly beyond the level reached by chimpanzees and other animals.

And so there appears that remarkable precursor of modern man—an upright, hairless, ground-living ape with a swollen head and brain, no snout, rather feeble teeth, a reduced sense of smell, excellent eyesight, remarkable dexterity, and the power of speech.

THE TRANSITION TO HUMANITY

That there is a sharp break between the truly human and the pre-human is an essential part of evolutionary theory. The bird evolves from the reptile, and there is an interesting intermediate type with feathered wings, but with a toothed mouth; but a bird is not a peculiar kind of lizard. It is a bird. And a man is a man.

He talks: that is to say, he does not merely make signals for specific occasions, he has a word for a general idea like 'walking'—for any and every kind of walking. He symbolizes. Animals do many wonderful things but there is not the slightest evidence for them symbolizing, or using general ideas. He communicates: learns, teaches, generalizes from the multitudinous array of disparate sensations and feelings. This represents a *qualitative* change, like the snapping of a stick that is being gradually bent, or the taxiing of a plane as it accelerates until it lifts and is flying.

But what is so interesting about this process is that the brain completes its development to the stage at which we can point to Java Man and cry *Homo!*, after the appearance of the hand and the bipedal condition. We now see the reaction of the development of the hand on the rest of the organism. The mastery over nature which began with the ability to manipulate widened man's horizon at every new advance. He was continually discovering new, hitherto unknown, properties of natural objects. His constructive activities helped to bring members of society closer together by multiplying cases requiring mutual support, joint activity, and by making clear the advantage of this joint activity to every individual. We can see how urgent it becomes that men shall communicate now, and every slight improvement in the undeveloped larynx and clumsy lips and tongue, resulting from a chance variation, now has a new and significant value. Physical improvement is hurried up, speech is necessary. The brain is now required to do better, and so to grow larger. This is not necessary for a happy and well-adapted ape; he does very well for himself. It *is* necessary for man, using his hands in this new way, thus creating a *selective pressure*, which puts a premium not only on manual dexterity (the hand itself has still to be improved) but on those truly human faculties of speech, foresight in planning, patience in taking

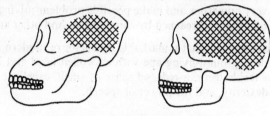

Gorilla   Sinanthropus

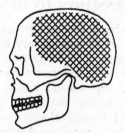

Homo Sapiens

Fig. 12 Comparative brain size in gorilla, *Homo erectus* (Java or Peking man), and modern man.

roundabout means to desirable ends, perseverance and organized co-operation.

All are dependant on nervous development. Selection is shifted to favour the most rapid growth of the fore-brain possible. So is the urgent need for communication, social organization, and moral regulation. Thus does man make himself. Our physical structure is largely the result of the earliest manufacture and use of tools, and the coming together of tool users to make the best use of them.

The Ice Age helped this process by providing exacting conditions which were ideal for the speedy and efficient evolutionary development of man, though these appalling circumstances must have seemed to him cruel in the extreme. The primitive cultural environment of tool-using ape-men increasingly supplemented the natural environment in this selective process to produce accelerated change. As Clifford Geertz says in *The Transition to Humanity*:

It appears *not* to have been merely a time of receding brow ridges and shrinking jaws, but a time in which were forged nearly all those characteristics of man's existence which are most graphically human: his thoroughly encephalated nervous system, and his capacity to create and use symbols. The fact that these distinctive features of humanity emerged together in complex interaction with one another rather than serially, is a fact of exceptional importance in the interpretation of human mentality, because it suggests that man's nervous system does not merely enable him to acquire culture, it positively demands that he do so if it is going to function at all. Rather than culture acting only to supplement, develop, and extend organically based capacities genetically prior to it, it would seem to be ingredient to these capacities themselves.

If, in seeking man's ancestry, we are looking for the *least specialized*, and are therefore rejecting both the modern monkey and the anthropoids in tracing the development from the first man, we must regard *Homo erectus* and Neanderthal not as primitive but as relatively late and highly specialized forms developing *away* from modern man. We must look for our ancestors among the less specialized forms, and these will be really primitive types.

Neoanthropic Man: *Homo Sapiens.* On this view, then, modern man takes his origin from a source quite separate from that of *Homo erectus* and the Neanderthalers, even though in the remote Pliocene they probably had a common ancestry. That source has left few representative fossils other than Swanscombe man. The opposing view regards *Homo erectus* as the true ancestor of *Homo sapiens*.

At any rate, perhaps as early as 40,000 or 50,000 B.C., modern man appeared in Europe, and his early remains are also found in parts of Asia and Africa. This was towards the end of the glacial period, during the final retreat of the ice.

The skulls and other skeletal remains show a completely modern type, utterly different from the chinless, heavy-browed Neanderthaler. The head is large and massively built, brow ridges are lacking, the forehead and skull vault are high, the face is flat and not prognathous (a person or skull with a facial profile angle of 70°–80°), a chin well developed. The cranial capacity is considerable, ranging from 1700 c.c. to 1800 c.c.— larger than the present average. The men were tall and well built, with no Neanderthal stoop.

PILTDOWN MAN

Earlier books on this period frequently devoted much space and attention to a strange find in the Pleistocene deposits of Sussex. This was the famous **Piltdown man,** discovered by Dawson in 1912.

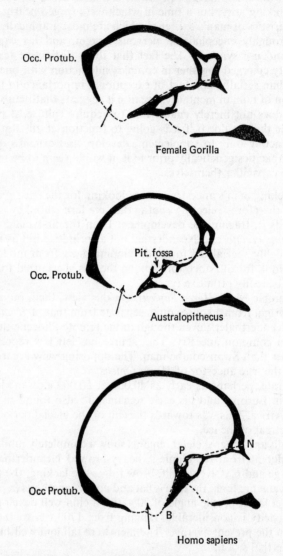

Fig. 13 Longitudinal section of the skulls of gorilla Australopithecus and modern man. This admirably shows the axis of the vertebral column as it moves from the back of the skull to a position well below central (indicated by arrow). (After Le Gros Clark.)

The skull was of a modern type, though very thick, and its date was given as early Pleistocene, which might be several hundred thousand years ago and would make it a contemporary of *Pithecanthropus*. But the most surprising thing about it was the later discovery of an apelike jaw which apparently belonged to it. So we had a modern man with an ape's jaw living at the same time as Java man. Incredible! And it was so to Weidenreich and to Miller, but not to Henry Fairfield Osborn and Hooton in the United States, and a number of able archaeologists in Britain. Then between 1945 and 1953 the whole thing was exposed by Oakley and Weiner as a complete hoax. The skull was real enough, but not more than 50,000 years old, which makes it contemporary with other neoanthropic men. The jaw is that of a *modern* chimpanzee, doctored and filed and chemically stained to make the teeth look human and the whole jaw very old. The whole thing was a brilliant fraud. The only possible explanation seemed to be that Dawson, a respected amateur archaeologist, 'planted' the chimpanzee's jaw, after doctoring it to make it look of the same period as the skull, and then took his friends with him to 'find' it.

The moral is interesting from the standpoint of scientific theory. When there are some contradictions that point to an important revision of existing theory, but others that are inconsistent with the pattern of *known facts*, it may be better to suspend judgement than to allow one's thinking to be thrown into complete confusion.

Leakey's comment before the hoax was discovered was a wise and cautious one: 'The question of whether the jaw and skull belong to the same creature is still an open one, and personally I feel that they are not.' Weidenreich was even more sceptical and declared that Piltdown man never existed and was an unreal creature of the imagination that should be erased from the list of human fossils. W. W. Howells, commenting on the fact that Piltdown man has been given a whole new genus for himself on account of his monkey's jaw, declared that 'anyone who can think of something better to do with him will be doing science a service'. Thanks to Oakley and Weiner we know just what to do with him. It remains a puzzle why Dawson should have perpetrated this gigantic fraud which puzzled scientists for 40 years.

SUGGESTED FURTHER READING

Broderick, A. H., *Early Man*. Hutchinson's Scientific and Technical Publications: New York, 1948.

Clark, Sir Wilfred E. le Gros, *The Fossil Evidence for Human Evolution*. University of Chicago Press: Chicago, 1955.

Clark, Sir Wilfred E. le Gros, *Man-Apes or Ape-Men?* Holt, Rinehart & Winston: New York, 1967.

Leakey, L. S. B., *Adam's Ancestors*. Methuen: London, 1968.

CHAPTER THREE

PREHISTORIC MAN

BRAINS AND TOOLS

That the primitive man which appeared some half-million years ago should have had within him the potentialities of civilization with all its technical achievements and rich cultures is an amazing thing, too often taken for granted. Since the whole development of man arises from what he then actually *was*, from his new human nature, it is important to investigate just what was involved in it from the very beginning.

There are three main characteristics which differentiate the man from the animal. Initially there is the power of **thought**—thinking that solves problems and therefore involves abstractions, concepts, generalizations, ideas, anticipation, and reflection. We find only the simplest beginnings of any such thing in animals, but man, from the first, schemes and plans and devises. Secondly there is **speech**—the use of language. Animals make signals to each other, uttering cries of warning and the like, but they do not use *names* for things and action; they do not converse. Thirdly there is the use of **tools**, made by himself, implements specially devised for a purpose and according to a preconceived plan. These implements are the basis of an ever-growing technique and therefore of our entire material civilization.

And now we must add a fourth characteristic—that **man lives in society.** Many animals live in groups, but only man organizes his group to make effective use of tools and weapons, to conduct planned operations in food gathering in the hunting field and, later, in the organization of agriculture.

The Tool and the Hand. Benjamin Franklin called man a tool-making animal. The emphasis is rightly on the *making*, which involves a planned modification of natural objects, based on the previous knowledge of the effect.

The tool in its turn depends on the evolution of the hand. The *organs* of the animal are its tools, and they are *permanently modified, unalterable instruments*, attached to their bodies—like the elephant's trunk or the mole's excavating forelimbs. The tools of man are separated from his body, while the human hand acts as a universal organ. By making and grasping tools, which vary for different functions, the hand–tool combination replaces the various animal organs.

There is a great difference between the undeveloped hand of the

32

anthropoid ape and the human hand that has been perfected by the labour of hundreds of thousands of years. The number and general arrangement of the bones and muscles are the same in both, but the hand of the lowest type of man can perform hundreds of operations that no ape or monkey's hand can imitate. No non-human hand has ever fashioned even the crudest stone implement.

Apart from the complex anatomy of the hand, there is its acute sense of touch, far exceeding that found in any animal. Touch is not only passive, it is active, and it is important in the acquisition of knowledge.

The hand is not the only organ of labour, *it is also the product of labour*. Only by labour, by adaptation to ever new operations, by inheritance of every useful adaptation in the development of muscles, ligaments, and bones, has the human hand attained the high degree of perfection that has enabled it to construct a watch, paint a picture, or perform on a musical instrument.

It would seem that the hand must, indeed, have played its part in the development of the brain, for the hands of the South African ape man were well developed long before his brain.

The Brain and the Hand. Since man *foresees the action of his tool*, the full use of the hand requires a considerable degree of mental development. An animal is not capable of that—even extreme emergency never makes it inventive. Visualization is required of a future use of something not existing, and this always implies conscious thought.

Thinking arises from the pressure of practical problems; it is either a comparison of various possibilities of action from which a choice has to be made, or the devising of a totally new way around a difficulty. That is to say the difficulty is not overcome by a frontal attack, but by making a detour. Men do not lift a huge stone by pushing at it; they go and get a long pole and lever it up. This new kind of behaviour is well seen in the construction of traps by primitive man.

Between the actual need originally felt and its subsequent satisfaction there comes a series of actions which only indirectly lead to the aim. In such cases there is not only a detour in *action*, but corresponding to it *a detour in thought*.

Moreover there is not one possible detour, there are many. The action can take different directions. Therefore each alternative must be present in the imagination so that a comparison and choice can be made. This weighing of one choice against the other, this choosing of alternatives, is really what is meant by both thinking and human freedom.

Men and Animals. A remarkable consequence of this human use of the tool is that, because man is an animal with interchangeable organs, he can greatly vary his reactions to arrive at a really effective one. The animal which has become capable of only *one* kind of living must perish if the reactions of which it is capable are ineffective. The rocks are full of the fossil remains of animals whose structures were specialized and limited and so proved inadequate when great environmental and climate changes occurred.

Man can equal all the specialized animals. He can burrow like a mole, cut down trees like a beaver, crush nuts like a squirrel, drive off a hostile beast like a buffalo. Whereas every animal is limited to its own habitat, man is adapted to the most varying conditions of life: he can live with axe or spade, he can fish or he can hunt, he can build or he can travel, he can cross the sea, he can construct dams and waterways.

Brains. We have already noted the immense development of the brain of modern man as compared with the brain of the higher apes or the first men. Now the difference is not merely quantitative, it is qualitative. There are *new structures*, not merely more brain cells. Thus we have, superimposed on all the mechanisms of the animal brain, more complicated mechanisms, dealing with the complexities of a richer life, which are beyond the control of the original ones. The cortex, which exercises the central regulation of all actions, consists of a dense network of about 10,000 million nerve cells and their interconnecting branches. No new neurons (nerve cells) are ever added to those with which each human being starts. *It is in the new connexions and patterns that accumulated knowledge resides.* The larger brain offers increased possibilities of reacting in various ways, a greater capacity for learning—in short, a greater intelligence.

Thought and Language. What this amounts to is the power of abstract reasoning. One aspect of this is the process of uninterrupted, intensive attention, without which problem-solving and the choice of alternatives is not possible.

Thinking is the basis of speech, and the human organism is able to speak because it possesses not only the vocal mechanisms but the cortical accompaniment. If this is missing or injured, speech is impossible.

Speech is necessary for thinking, though people often imagine that this is not so. Without language, intellect would not exist at all. Ideas and perceptions are mental constructions created on the basis of the real world of concrete things. The word is primarily the name for a *class* of objects, and is therefore outside the world of objects themselves, but it gives content and precision to our ideas and links them to objective reality.

Speech is a Product of the Community. Speech comes into existence in the community. It imparts information with regard to conditions which are of importance in the struggle for life. Communication is a preparation for action later on, but for that very reason it implies the suspension of *immediate* reaction to give opportunity for reflection, the giving of instructions, planned co-operative effort.

Speech is therefore the medium through which human co-operation is brought about. It co-ordinates and correlates the diverse activities of men for the attainment of common ends. All action is co-operation, so an organ is needed for mutual understanding, for communication, for deliberation. Speech is such an organ, and is the mightiest means for binding the community together, the most important and indispensable instrument in the common struggle for existence. It multiplies the strength of the community, because it enables the experiences of each member to become the property of the whole.

Speech and Knowledge. Speech is also the organ for verbal tradition, the treasure house of increasing knowledge. By means of speech the older generation passes on its knowledge to the younger. This cannot happen with animals, which learn but a few standard reactions and *always the same ones*. There is no accumulation of experience.

The human community is immortal, and its possession of knowledge, which is linked up with the making and the use of tools and implements of all kinds, consists of verbal descriptions and instructions. The technical apparatus could not continue to develop if knowledge and science did not develop simultaneously. Solely because this fund of knowledge is fixed, retained, and preserved by language, it can continue to increase indefinitely. Thus speech becomes the vehicle of ever-increasing human progress.

Knowledge, in fact, introduces a new dimension into inheritance. We inherit the acquired experience of both our ancestors and other races. Language renders possible an accumulation of experience, a storing up of achievements, which makes advance rapid and secure among human beings in a manner impossible among the lower animals. We might define *civilization* in general as *the sum of these contrivances which enable human beings to advance independently of heredity*.

Society and Social Consciousness. The gap between man and the other animals was at first only slight in its results, but it widened unbelievably and very quickly. It is quicker to evolve a civilization than to evolve a species. (It took 60,000,000 years to evolve the modern horse from **Eohippus,** which lived in the Eocene.) This is because of the rapid advance possible in a society in which, by speech, information can be passed *on in its accumulated form*. The experience not of *one* generation, the parents, but of countless generations, plus the latest acquisitions of the parental generation, is taught to the younger people. Thus we preserve and pass on technique, training, and the entire range of our knowledge.

A society is of course far more than this. It is an association of families in a tight group with much mutual responsibility and many strongly felt obligations. The forms of mutual aid we find in so many primitive communities are immensely developed until they become complex patterns of behaviour and elaborate institutions for trade, agriculture, fishing, and so forth. Thus in every community arise definite duties, often designed to achieve results far distant. Social rules—folkways and *mores* —arise. Morals of this sort are strictly utilitarian, but not a mere balance of immediate pains and pleasures for the individual concerned. They are, rather, socially useful and take into account the ultimate effect on social life.

Co-operation and Survival. We have been taught that competition is the law of nature and that the strongest survive in the struggle for existence, while the weakest perish. The anthropologist does not agree.

The success of the group depends upon the elimination of internal struggle and its replacement by mutual support and the care of the weaker members. Such a group has considerable *survival value*, not necessarily in competition with other groups but in the fight against Nature.

The wider these co-operative associations extend (as they do extend by fixed rules of marriage, making it obligatory to wed a person *in another group*), the more peace reigns and helpful relations strengthen the whole community.

In human evolution it is not the *man* who is eliminated. What does happen is that old *tools* are discarded as improved patterns are invented; similarly, new forms of human association replace those better fitted for more primitive ways. The human relations and labour pattern of agriculture are obviously quite different from those appropriate to hunting. Both tool and labour methods have survival value. Thus it is not the *man* who is eliminated but the antiquated *technique*.

Better tools and techniques, better organization, bring about better adaptation to the environment and especially to a changing environment. In fact the general trend of evolution is towards *greater independence of the environment*—as man builds houses, makes water supplies available, warms himself by fires, lays down roads, builds bridges. A high degree of control over Nature and independence of the environment goes with a well-organized community, with an adequate store of knowledge; this gives considerable survival value over less co-operative and less intelligent tribes.

Social Darwinism. There is nothing wrong with Darwin's conception of survival as applied to the animal world; but what has been called 'social Darwinism' is the unwarrantable carrying over of the struggle for existence into the field of human relations. This theory would attempt to explain the unique behaviour of man by the practices of the lower animals, the life of intelligence by the drive of predatory instinct.

In fact the theory of natural selection makes it a necessity that, among men, those societies should survive in which the promptings of the tribal identity have been most felt, and in which strong customs and rules of social behaviour, reflecting a morality of brotherhood, have emerged to impress themselves on the mind of young and old as the dictates of the social conscience.

The Biological Basis for Ethics. We thus see how social man is necessarily an ethical man. As Herrick says,

That social stability upon which the survival and comfort of the individual depend and that moral satisfaction upon which his equanimity, poise and stability of character depend arise from the maintenance of relations with his fellow men which are mutually advantageous.

A good man (anthropologically speaking) is one whose conduct is conducive to the enhancement of the life of his social group. Survival depends on the degree to which men can and do adjust themselves harmoniously to each other.

In particular, within the human family the father and the group as a whole look after the mother, and the child is protected for a very long infancy. This makes solicitude a habit. The community that preserves its children builds up an ethic to ensure this. Such a community is certainly more likely to survive than one which cares less for the rising generation.

Predatory behaviour arrests evolutionary progress in the direction of improved techniques and better co-operation. Carnivores are nature's discards. The human type has survived chiefly because of its co-operative nature.

Man has neither fangs, claws, nor horns, but hands and brains. With these go mutual aid. The take-all and give-nothing organisms are regressive parasites.

This points to a social ethic which does not value war as a high form of human activity. If the energies of the inhabitants of a country or continent are all employed in a struggle to defeat its enemies, for that time at least most new enterprise will cease. If all the energies of a nation are to be employed in resisting extermination, if the general relationship between peoples is to be one of mutual enmity and attack, then the prospect of an abler nation, of a race free to create, disappears.

The Principle of Progress. What distinguishes man from the animals is in the last resort his development, his progress. He is the only animal species that, from the moment he came into existence, has been continually changing in character and behaviour, and indeed becoming a different being. In the animal world one species slowly gives way to another, but there is no real history of the species. Only man has a continuous history. His history is one of constant advance which keeps on unfolding at an increasingly rapid rate. Expressed on a reduced scale of time, if a few decades were occupied in the evolution of the animal world, and a few weeks for the bodily origin of man, then civilization would have originated little more than an hour ago, and the industrial transformation of man during the last century would have taken a couple of minutes.

With the rise of the animal species *Homo sapiens*, a new principle came into the world. It introduced, instead of a slow biological development through the origin of new species, a fast development, increasing in speed, within this one persisting species.

It is the possession of tools which constitutes this new principle. Man fights the struggle for life with tools. The competition is between tools (and the methods of using them). The better tools win. The speed of man's development is equal to the speed with which new tools can be invented and made.

The body remains the same or changes so slowly as to make such change negligible. It is technical development, the history of which is written at first with hundreds and with tens of centuries, afterwards with hundreds and at last with tens of years, that counts. The biological development of the preceding millions of years is closed. Through the discovery of tools man becomes the equal in power of any animal, and through their improvement he becomes the superior in power of any animal and conquers and subdues them all. He can tame, cultivate, and even create new forms to suit his needs. Which animals and plants will exist on earth will be decided by his will. The kingdom of nature makes way for the kingdom of human technique, of culture.

Our Debt to Early Man. Material culture is a new way of adapting inner life forces to external nature, of adapting external conditions to the rule of mind. It enables the individual for the first time really or consciously to take part in evolutionary progress.

Advanced centres of culture radiate traits or influences in every direction, influences which in time raise all the recipient areas to new and high levels.

And so we find early man laying the foundations for all subsequent human life. Early man made the following contributions to human progress:

1. He explored and settled nearly all the habitable world. He located most of the places since found suitable as great centres of population. He opened trails and waterways connecting these settlements, and they still remain the avenues of commerce.

2. He identified and brought into use most of the ready-made resources—animal, vegetable, and mineral. He discovered fire, worked with metals and ores. He started agriculture and the domestication of animals. He founded the basic handicrafts and devised the basic tools.

3. He began medicine and surgery, astronomy and mathematics. The foundations of chemistry and metallurgy were involved in his early pottery making and smelting.

4. He made, as we shall see later, considerable aesthetic advances in his art, music, sculpture, dances, and ceremonies. He devised elaborate rituals to suit every critical occasion of group life. He found the sacred as an all-pervading force and established religious systems of great variety and significance to relate his life to the supernatural.

With occasional mistakes and lapses, cultural growth is continuous, undergoing change and development by gradual modification in the direction of higher specialization and greater adaptiveness towards the environment. Man makes his tools, his social organization, his culture—and his culture and technique make him. Man makes himself.

SUGGESTED FURTHER READING

McNeill, D. in *Discovery*: London, July 1966.
Osman Hill, W. C. *Man as an Animal*. Hutchinson University Library: London, 1957.
Waddington, C. H. *The Nature of Life*. Allen & Unwin: London, 1961.
Waddington, C. H. *The Ethical Animal*. Allen & Unwin: London, 1959.

PART TWO

ETHNOLOGY AND PRE-HISTORIC ARCHAEOLOGY

CHAPTER FOUR

FROM THE OLD STONE AGE TO THE DAWN OF CIVILIZATION

THE OLD STONE AGE

The first and oldest of the primitive cultures which devised and used stone implements is called the **Old Stone Age (Palaeolithic).**

In the Old Stone Age we can distinguish three cultural elements of primary importance:

1. The hand-axe industries
2. The flake industries
3. The blade industries

These three methods of making flint implements do not occur one after the other as a progressive sequence. The first two certainly go back as far as any known implements and are constantly overlapping and affecting one another. The third may go back farther than we suppose, but it does mark a new level in the making of flint tools.

Some authorities believe that the hand axe was the product of the better-brained type, while the flakes and shaped scrapers and awls were made by the Neanderthalers and other pithecanthropids, but this is by no means certain.

Cores, Flakes, and Blades. Since the two earliest types of flint implement were man's only tools and weapons for something like 250,000 years, they deserve a closer look.

Core tools were made by knocking bits off a large lump or core until the original material was reduced to one of four or five standard forms. These are the **hand axes.** They are not at all like axes as we know them, but it is too late to change the name. The hand axe is a large lump of flint, eight or nine inches long, thick, heavy, rounded at the bottom, and chipped to a point. It is usually somewhat flattened on two sides. The flakes struck off in the process of manufacture were of no consequence.

The **flake tools** were struck off lumps of flint which were then perhaps discarded; it was the flakes which mattered and they were trimmed to form a considerable variety of implements for boring, for scraping skins, and so on. Later a most ingenious procedure was evolved: by much chipping, a rounded tortoise-back flint block was prepared, and then by a skilful blow a flake was struck off with one side flat or slightly hollow and the other side rounded.

43

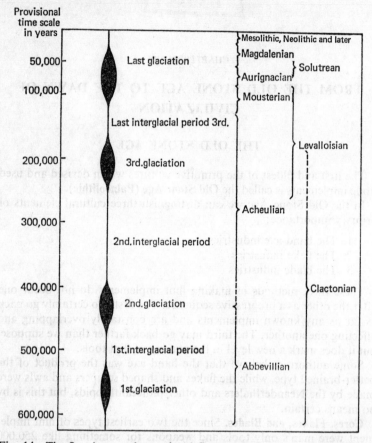

Fig. 14 The Ice Ages and associated Stone Age cultures. Acheulian and Abbevillian tools are wedge-shaped or pointed *core tools*, Clactonian and Levalloisian are *flake tools*. Mousterian tools are those of Neanderthal Man. All subsequent cultures (late Palaeolithic) are those of *Homo sapiens* and show a rapid advance in technique and in graphic art and carving, especially that of the Magdalenian culture.

The Blade Cultures. Later still, lumps of flint or glassy lava were so prepared that a whole series of long, narrow flakes, termed *blades*, could be struck off a single core. Thus the latest stone implements, the blade tools, appeared.

There is a gradual improvement in the axes and flakes, but as we move to the later Stone Age the blades virtually replace the older forms of implement, becoming increasingly refined and quite sharp. They are fitted into handles of various sorts and become very useful tools. Blades may even be fitted into curved wooden holders to form sickles.

A New World. With the last phase of the Old Stone Age we enter a new world peopled by our own species, a world limited by all the restrictions inherent in the stage of savagery, yet pregnant with all the possibilities of liberation. In the realm of tool-making we find a new

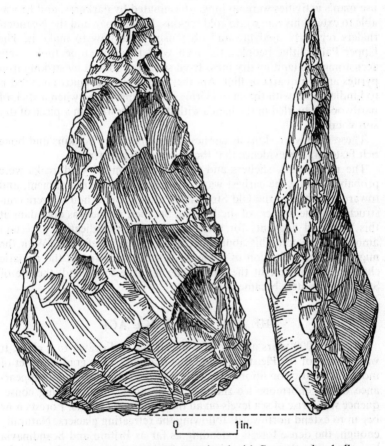

Fig. 15   Acheulian hand-axe associated with Swanscombe skull.

versatility, the use of a wider range of materials, a greater variation in technique, a more rapid evolution, new ways of making a living. Now for the first time we are conscious of men holding ideas—very complex and imaginative ideas—concerning magical practices, of which so many evidences remain in the cave paintings. We note also a remarkable aesthetic sensibility: these men are capable of a very high level of artistic creation.

Control of Environment. Yet the basis of this great advance could never have been mere spiritual enlightenment in the grinding misery of early Stone Age life. Its basis surely lies in the painfully slow discovery of better ways of controlling nature.

Learning to control fire was the greatest step forward in the direction of gaining freedom from the dominance of environment, for through its use man's activities were no longer terminated by darkness, and he was able to extend his range into cold regions. Peking man and the Neanderthalers regularly used fire and obviously knew how to make it. The Upper Palaeolithic peoples, the men with the new stone tools, were accustomed to igniting dry moss from sparks produced by striking iron pyrites against quartz or flint. Another widely-used primitive method is to kindle tinder with the smouldering powder produced when a stick of hardwood is twirled in the hands with its point resting on a piece of dry softwood.

These men wore skins as clothes. Bone and ivory bodkins and bone belt fasteners are evidence that they wore such garments.

The use of rock shelters and the construction of windbreaks were probably among the earliest ways of controlling the environment, and towards the end of the Old Stone Age, underground houses were constructed by the hunters of the Russian Steppes. Game was abundant at this time and accounts for their varied culture, indicating a certain amount of leisure. This abundance did not last indefinitely. With the migration and reduction of game herds, consequent upon the climatic changes which brought the Pleistocene Ice Age to an end, the life of Stone Age hunters became precarious.

THE END OF THE ICE AGE

About 11,000 years ago the last glacial age had drawn to a close. It was the end of the Pleistocene and was marked by the gradual onset of modern climatic conditions. The effects of the shrinkage and disappearance of the enormous ice sheets were dramatic. A disturbing consequence was a rise of sea levels on all the continental coasts. Forests now began to extend northwards following the retreating glaciers. Naturally enough, the dense forests extending as far as Britain and Scandinavia brought with them a new kind of fauna more appropriate to the changed environment. At the same time many of the ice-age animals became extinct, such as the mastodon and the mammoth. Many must have perished as a result of the successful hunting of the new and more competent modern man.

As the forests began to spread in Europe, many once fertile areas of Asia and Africa became deserts. Migration and nomadism increased. Hunting was supplemented by fishing, gathering shellfish, fowling, and sealing.

These primitive men brought with them an entirely new type of stone tool and introduced not the neolithic Stone Age, as might be supposed, but the *late* palaeolithic. Their cultural advance was very rapid. They were mighty hunters and great artists; the **cave drawings of Spain and southern France** are theirs.

There were several races and several successive migratory waves. There were also several cultures or types of stone implement. These racial types and cultures are of great importance to the archaeologist, but it would be irrelevant to our purpose to disentangle the cross threads of race and implement. It is sufficient to say that when we read of Chatelperronian, Aurignacian, Gravettian, and Magdalenian cultures, we are dealing with modern man and the late-palaeolithic Stone Age. Of course some of the older stone tools persisted, and the earlier and later palaeolithic cultures overlapped and interpenetrated. Thus the Chatelperronians had Mousterian tools, belonging to their Neanderthal cousins, as well as their own distinctive blunt-backed knives.

THE NEW STONE AGE

Between the Old Stone Age and the New Stone Age came the **mesolithic period,** extending from about 12,000 to 8000 B.C., characterized by remarkable painted pebbles and very sharp but tiny flint flakes, often set in bone and used for darts or other purposes.

The New Stone Age (Neolithic) was remarkable for its skilfully made arrowheads and for the *grinding* of axes and other implements from volcanic rocks by the use of wet sandstone. The result was a much more satisfactory tool, but it took a long time to make, especially when a hole had to be bored through the stone to take a handle.

War clubs now became differentiated from other kinds of axes which were used for working with wood. The bow and arrow became a common weapon, as countless arrowheads indicate. It was at this time that men first began to use sledges and domesticated the dog.

Eventually we get a rapid development into a *blade-tool culture*, including the use of tools to make other tools, blades in wooden handles, awls, gravers, and small saws for cutting bone. Man could now make new implements of bone, antlers, and ivory. He began to use needles and harpoons. New techniques of boring and grinding appeared and eventually he constructed a kit of woodworking tools, including planes, choppers, wedges, and chisels. A rather special type of tool is the chisel-shaped end scraper to work with an up-and-down movement.

The Mammoth Hunters. One of the most thrilling stories in the annals of archaeology is the discovery of the great camps of the Eastern Aurignacians in Czechoslovakia. Over a hundred of these have been found.

These men were great mammoth hunters. At Předmost they brought home portions of no less than a thousand of these mammoths. They fought also with the great cave bears, which stood twelve feet high on

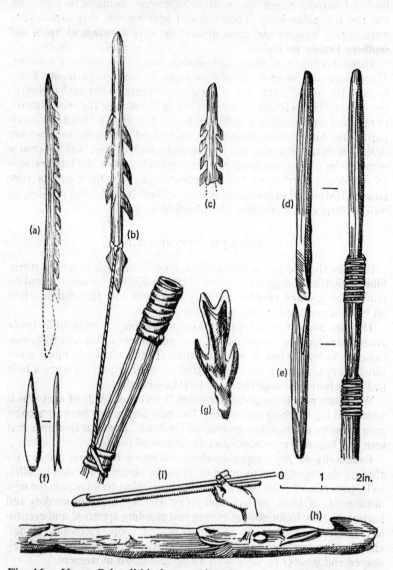

Fig. 16a   Upper Palaeolithic bone and antler weapons: (a) barbed antler point; (b) harpoon; (c) antler harpoon; (d) spear point; (e) link shaft; (f) split-base bone point; (g) forked and barbed bone implement; (h) spear thrower; (i) wooden spear-thrower. (After Broughton Smith.)

Fig. 16b   Cave art: the mammoth (Magdalenian).

their hind legs. Lions, wolves, and smaller game were also hunted, but the mammoth bones and ivory supplied the material for their implements and ornaments.

The Problems of the Fossil Record

It is often supposed that if there are evolutionary lines of development, then there must be fossil evidence for every link in the chain. This is not so, either as regards animal succession or fossil man. Most animals die and decay and leave no remains at all. It requires quite exceptional circumstances attending the death and subsequent fate of the body to ensure the survival of any remains. Shortly after death bodies must be covered by silt, or they must be deposited in caves and buried in some way. Of those that are so preserved only an insignificant fraction are ever found. It is therefore surprising that we have found so many fossil remains of primitive man.

Fossil remains became more abundant after Neanderthal man inaugurated the custom of ceremonial burial; before that only remote chance gives us any fossil evidence.

The Ancestors of Modern Man. Important consequences follow. As far as the evolution of the primates is concerned, we may expect many missing links; and if we do find a hint as to an early ancestor of man, it may not be a direct ancestor, but a somewhat similar type to a possible ancestor. As far as fossil man is concerned, we may not expect to find a complete series from remote ancestor to existing man, but many extinct lines of early men, often diverging from the progressive series leading up to modern man. If this is so we cannot say that Anthropoid apes evolved into *Homo erectus* and this ape-like form into Neanderthal man, and Neanderthal man into modern man. Some anthropologists do believe this, but the general trend of opinion is otherwise.

FROM SAVAGERY TO BARBARISM

The Origin of Agriculture. But by far the most important development of the neolithic age was the discovery of agriculture. For centuries man had remained at the level of bare subsistence, but in the mesolithic period, somewhere about 9000 or 8000 B.C., groups of people in Asia Minor began to adopt the practice of **cultivating plants** and **domesticating animals** as a source of food and raw materials.

With this agricultural revolution, especially when it occurred in the great fertile river valleys of Mesopotamia and the Nile, the era of what we call 'savagery' gave way to 'barbarism', and man moved forward to active, purposeful control and ultimate mastery of nature. At this stage we find larger settlements of a more permanent character—the first farming communities. This type of subsistence is similar to that found in the overwhelming proportion of primitive societies investigated by the anthropologist today.

The first evidence of agriculture is found among the **Natufians,** who lived in the caves of Mount Carmel in Palestine, and in the neighbourhood of Lydda. These were people with Neanderthal characteristics—and may represent an intermediate stage in the development towards Cromagnon Man (*Homo sapiens*). They had no pottery, no ground stone axes, and kept no domestic animals. They were not really neolithic. Their existence, however, was more settled than that of the earlier Stone Age communities, which was probably due to the fact that they were beginning to live on **grain,** on the seeds of certain grasses, for we find among their remains sickles made of mounted flints and polished by the continuous cutting of siliceous grasses (all grasses contain silica in varying degrees).

In this part of the Near East the wild ancestors of wheat and barley were to be found, and the Natufians, who lived by hunting and fishing, evidently reaped these grasses to supplement their primitive food gathering.

No doubt the families had at first made their way to where the grasses grew naturally, collecting their harvest there. Then later they *tended* and perhaps weeded these areas. Finally they learned to *plant* seeds near their settlements and thus transferred the grain fields to their own villages.

How this happened we do not know. Possibly women noted the growth of seeds dropped by chance, or of shoots planted without definite purpose.

Many conditions were necessary before this all-important step in human development could take place.

1. The right wild grasses had to be available.
2. The seeds or shoots had to have proper soil.
3. The primitive gatherer had to use his head. He had to put two and two together to grasp the possibility of *systematically planting a considerable area.*

Of course primitive agriculture must have been, as it still is in many parts of the world, *predatory.* The soil was worked to exhaustion, there was no crop rotation or manuring. After exhausting the area, the settlement would move on to fresh ground.

THE RIVER CULTURES OF THE ANCIENT WORLD

The first steps in such actual cultivation may be inferred from the remains of some of the earliest settlements in Europe. Here we find a definite neolithic culture, the date of which has been estimated as between 6000 and 5000 B.C., at Fayum in Lower Egypt, on the shores of an ancient lake west of the Nile. The people of this place hunted game and speared fish, but they also left straw-lined pots for wheat and barley They used the sickles we have already described and flint hoes.

The increasing lack of water in the surrounding lands forced migrating peoples to settle in the **Nile Valley** where annual floods watered the soil and renewed its fertility. At a place called Sialk, on the western rim of the deserted basin of the Iranian (Persian) plateau, was an oasis, halfway between the Caspian Sea and the Persian Gulf. Here we find seventeen successive and superimposed villages, the last of which was begun about 3000 B.C. Here, too, are the evidences of the first stages of agriculture in the earlier settlements.

We know that about this time in the Tigris–Euphrates river basin in Mesopotamia and in the great river areas of India and China other agricultural settlements sprang up and developed rapidly.

In such areas large numbers of persons were released from food production for specialized work of many kinds—for the manufacture of pottery, for weaving, basketry, hide and leather work, carpentry, boatmaking, fishing, trade and government, and religious activities.

This specialization of labour resulted in many inventions. Year-round habitations came to be more solidly constructed. Superior cutting tools were made, as we have already described, by grinding and polishing. These tools in turn made possible finer and more varied manufacture of all sorts of products. The tremendous growth in population soon made hunting inadequate, and new kinds of specialists developed **pastoralism.**

The Origin of Stock-breeding. How pastoralism (the herding of cattle) began is difficult to say. Perhaps dwindling food supplies forced animals to herd hungrily round oases, where they came into contact with human settlements. Here men had something to offer, if only the stubble of their reaped crops. Some of these animals were gradually tamed and found useful. No doubt the advantages of having half-tamed flocks around the settlement were realized, and the herds became a permanent part of the economy.

Selective breeding developed the original types of wild sheep to more useful types. Primitive sheep were hairy, like goats, with big horns—the *mouflon,* wild specimens of which may still be found in Sardinia, and the *urial,* of north-western India, relatives of which are found in the Western Isles of Scotland. By the time sheep reached Europe, breeding had produced the woolly variety—the 'golden fleece' which was subsequently exported to North Africa and Spain by the Phoenicians.

There were two kinds of primitive oxen. The long-horned *Bos primigenius* (with horns 3 ft long) which survived in Germany until the Middle Ages, and the short-horned type from Turkestan. Long-horned cattle were found quite late in Britain and the short-horned type were found in the lake villages of Switzerland and in the Celtic oxen of the late Bronze Age. The domestication of sheep may be approximately dated as 9000 B.C., of goats and pigs, about 6500 B.C., domestic cattle about 5000 B.C.

Cattle offer great advantages. The food supply is at the door and need not be hunted. Skins are as valuable as meat. They are, in fact, living larders and walking wardrobes. Later, milk and butter were found to be continuously available without killing the animals. From sheep, wool could also regularly be sheared.

Capital and Income. Even more important, the herd was continually renewed and increased by breeding so that instead of the animals being destroyed and often hunted to extinction, they formed a growing and inexhaustible supply of all that the hunted animals once supplied and much besides. This was partly because domesticated animals breed freely in captivity, and their young are cared for not only by their parents but by man.

Dividends from Nature. We thus have a striking contrast in the economic outlook of savages and the agriculturists. The former regarded animals and plants as prey to be killed and eaten, the latter treated domesticated animals as *stock*, of which only the *increase* is consumed. Whereas with the savage his quarry is of value only when it is dead and has lost its capacity to increase, with the farmer his domesticated animals and plants are carefully tended and sheltered from enemies. They are no longer victims as much as property. By breeding animals in captivity and appropriating their natural increase, man in effect *draws* *dividends* from the cycle of animal life, obtaining for himself the solar energy stored up in the vegetation consumed by his livestock.

The principal economic characteristic of farmers as opposed to food gatherers is that, where the food gatherers consume whatever foodstuffs they can wrest from wild nature, *farmers discriminate between capital and income*, consuming the increase of their fields and herds, but encroaching on their stock and seed only in direst necessity.

Transport. Wherever larger livestock species were domesticated, man acquired potential aids in transportation, and man began to control and use a kind of power other than his own muscles. Thus we reach the ox-drawn sledge and finally, near Nineveh about 3000 B.C., the wheeled cart. Later came the ox-drawn plough, symbolizing the union of stock raising and cereal cultivation—a major revolution in agriculture.

The Crafts. It took genius to discover how to spin a thread from wool, hair, or fibre for weaving into cloth; and few people realize how difficult it is to make a pot that will not crack or crumble when hardened in a fire.

The rotary motion which converts fibres into threads was in fact an empirical discovery, actually based on a molecular rearrangement within the fibres that has only been discovered in recent times. Pottery is a primitive chemical discovery, its basis being dehydrated aluminium silicate. The invention of the loom was one of the greatest triumphs of human ingenuity. Its inventors are nameless, but they made an essential contribution to the capital stock of human knowledge.

We have here the birth of empirical science and, what is uniquely human, the handing down of discoveries and techniques by word of mouth, by education—the establishing of the great *tradition* of human knowledge, depending first on speech and then on writing.

CIVILIZATION AND THE AGE OF METALS

Precisely when and where man first learned to use metals as a material for tools is unknown. But we do know that the casting of copper, as distinct from its cold hammering, first appeared in the Nile Valley in the **Gerzean period,** about 3000 B.C., and in Mesopotamia at Uruk about the same time. It was also practised in Syria.

Iron was used in Mesopotamia and Egypt in 2500 B.C. The **Bronze Age** in Greece ended about 1200 B.C., when the Mycenaean chivalry was wiped out and the iron swords of the Dorian invaders triumphed. Homer's Hellenes were men of iron, not of bronze.

Metal greatly enhanced man's mastery of stone, wood, and other substances. Its real superiority is that it is *fusible* and can be cast and moulded. Copper, when hot, melts and can be poured into a mould. On cooling, it becomes hard and will make as good an edge as stone.

The use of copper and later of iron depended on the prior art of

smelting (though copper occurs, rarely, in the metallic state and was first so found and beaten into simple implements).

Metalworking is a very complex, empirical science. It depends upon a whole series of discoveries and inventions. A temperature of 1200° C. is needed to melt copper. This requires not an ordinary fire but a blast, obtained by bellows. Furnaces, crucibles, and tongs also had to be invented and the device of the two-piece mould discovered.

Metal is also malleable. It can be hammered into different shapes; it can also be mixed with other metals to make valuable alloys like bronze, which is formed by uniting tin and copper, and is much harder than copper.

Metals, Trade, and a New World. For metallurgy to flourish where metal ores were lacking, it was necessary to maintain an extensive system of trade. Civilization implies the widening scope of trade to include substances not found locally for the manufacture of tools and objects of daily use.

This requires means of transport more adequate than the canoes and sledges of savage origin. Boats were used from early times on the Nile and the Euphrates, and a ship with a tall prow, upturned stern, and square sail is depicted on a late predynastic Egyptian pot (between 3000 and 2500 B.C.).

The transition to civilization that followed—with the appearance of town life, the temple, priest, and king; the division of labour between agricultural worker, craftsman, merchant, trader, and administrator; the appearance of the professional fighter (the soldier)—does not concern us here except as the culmination of an incredibly rapid transition, accomplishing in a few thousand years infinitely more than the men of the Old Stone Age achieved in a quarter of a million years.

Religion in the New Age. All this helped to complicate social structure and to further the integration of society, but even so, grave perils of famine, over-population, and war threatened the new urban communities so that the period of transition was one of great development in the sphere of religion. Broadly speaking the development was from domestic cult to community religion, from household shrine to public temple.

Science, whereby man acquired an understanding of causal relations between natural phenomena and so achieved confidence through knowledge rather than faith, was a later fruit of civilization, though its origins in the form of empirical knowledge goes back to the beginning of hominid history.

The World in 2000 B.C. The rapid development of Mediterranean culture did not mean that the whole world was moving forward along a parallel front. Quite the contrary. Leaving China and India out of the picture, in Africa to the south and Europe to the north man remained in stages of savagery and barbarism.

What an amazing travel book of anthropology could have been

written about 2000 B.C. by a Cretan merchant, an Egyptian official, or a Sumerian priest if he could have travelled from his civilized homeland to the wilds of northern Europe. From their well-organized countries and great towns such travellers would pass to Asia Minor or Greece, where people were becoming urbanized and were using bronze. In central Europe they would find tribes who used only copper, but were emulating their southern neighbours as well as fighting among themselves. The northern European plains held so many groups with varying cultures that it must have seemed impossible for them ever to fuse into nations. Late Danubian, modernized mesolithic tribes, battle-axe warriors, men of the older neolithic cultures, western neolithic folk from Switzerland, megalithic mariners, and mixtures of all these fought and traded with each other, learned from and married each other; but all would have seemed barbarous to educated visitors from the ancient civilizations. Still farther north they would encounter only hunters and fishermen ignorant of farming and, in most cases, even of pottery making. These people would seem as different from them as the Eskimos are from the modern scientists who study them. This is a picture of our world in the second millennium before Christ.

SUGGESTED FURTHER READING

Boas, Franz, *The Mind of Primitive Man*. Collier–Macmillan: New York, 1965.

Burkitt, M. C., *The Old Stone Age*. Bowes: London, 1963.

Childe, V. G., *The Dawn of European Civilisation*. Routledge & Kegan Paul: London, 1957.

Childe, V. G., *Man Makes Himself*. Watts & Co.: London, 1936.

Childe, V. G., *What Happened in History*. Penguin Books: London, 1942.

Clark, Grahame, *The Stone Age Hunters*. Thames & Hudson: London, 1967.

Clark, Grahame and Piggott, S., *Prehistoric Societies*. Hutchinson: London, 1965.

Elliot-Smith, Grafton, *Essays on the Evolution of Man*. Oxford University Press: London, 1927.

Hawkes, G. F. C., *The Prehistoric Foundation of Europe*. Methuen: London, 1940.

Oakley, K. P., *Man the Tool Maker*. British Museum: London, 1950.

CHAPTER FIVE

THE RACES OF MAN

In this chapter we are concerned with such matters as migration, interbreeding, and overlap. It should be noted at the outset that man has been constantly migrating and interbreeding since the advent of human history. Mobility and interbreeding have produced in part the phenomenon known as overlap, and have resulted in a condition which we must understand before going further—namely, the condition that mankind is composed of hybrid races, so that there are no 'pure' races of man.

WHAT IS RACE?

Once we understand that there are no 'pure' races, we can define the term race, for our purposes, as follows: **a race is a major grouping of interrelated people possessing a distinctive combination of physical traits which are the result of inheritance.**

This definition is based on the biological principle that general anatomical resemblances imply relationship. Numerous similarities of face and form indicate common ancestry and are the product of continuous inbreeding.

ORIGINAL RACES

Although today we tend to divide man into three major races—the Caucasoid, the Negroid, and the Mongoloid—and several minor ones, **these are not the original races of man nor are they the final or ultimate races.**

If the races of man as we know them today are not the original races, then where are the original races? If they are not the ultimate races, then what will the ultimate races be like?

To answer the second question first, we should say that the ultimate races of man will be a product of ever continuous evolution and that nobody can, at the present time, answer this question. As for the first question, we shall have to return to the very beginning of man's life on earth.

It is known that modern man evolved through the successive and parallel species of primitive man until the appearance of *Homo sapiens*.

It is believed that modern man made his appearance in Europe about 50,000 years ago, probably coming from Asia. There were several races and several migratory waves. It is these migratory waves which are important in the development of hybrid or secondary races.

Where the Races of Man Came from. The evidence strongly suggests that the world was first peopled by a generalized protohuman form. Each division of mankind would thus have had its ancestors in the common stock of the Pleistocene period, and differentiation would have taken place after migration into different regions. Some, but not all, of the differences which arose would be due to climatic surroundings.

As to man's cradleland there have been many theories, but the weight of evidence is in favour of the Indo-Malayan area. How then did every part of the globe come to be inhabited by men? This problem has been met by geology, which proves that the earth's surface has undergone great changes since man's appearance and that large areas of land, long since submerged, once existed, making a complete land communication from India and Malaysia.

Thus the ancestors of man were free to move in all directions over the Eastern Hemisphere. The Western Hemisphere was almost certainly connected with Europe and Asia in Tertiary times by a land mass, the existence of which is evidenced by a submarine bank stretching from Scotland through The Faroes and Iceland to Greenland, and on the other side by continuous land at what is now the Bering Straits.

ORIGIN OF RACE

All the racial characteristics we shall be discussing originated at some moment in the past as what the geneticist calls a **mutation**—that is to say a change in the gene structure of the reproductive cell that influences bodily development. Such heritable changes take place regularly, though not frequently. A good example is the loss of pigment in the skin resulting in the **albino type,** which we find in human beings and also in white mice and white rabbits. Mutation occurs suddenly and is inherited. An area where such mutations and variations occur is known as an 'area of characterization'.

Under very early, premigratory human conditions populations could be completely isolated for so long that the various mutations would establish themselves among virtually all the inhabitants. There would thus arise a racial type.

How Race Originated. Before the close of palaeolithic times all the primary divisions of man were specialized in their several habitats by the selective influence of their surroundings and by chance variations in relatively isolated populations. It is important to understand how these differences occurred.

Four factors are responsible for racial differentiation. They are:

1. Gene mutation
2. Natural selection
3. Genetic drift
4. Population mixture

1. **Gene Mutation.** *This is a change in the gene structure of the reproductive cell that influences bodily development.*

Such changes are heritable and take place regularly, though not very frequently.

2. **Natural Selection.** *Genes which produce variations that have survival value* in a particular environment will rapidly establish themselves. Thus *albinism* offers no advantage and is rare; but heavy skin pigmentation is advantageous in the tropics and quickly spreads.

3. **Genetic Drift.** If a migrant group by chance bears *characters unlike those of the larger group* from which it separates, then in the course of time, especially if further splitting occurs, a population would emerge which was different from the ancestral population. The American Indian has almost certainly lost some of the traits of his Mongoloid ancestors in this way.

4. **Population Mixture.** The coming together of racially distinct populations followed by inter-breeding will give rise to a new race or racial group. Most existing racial groups are of this type.

Migration and New Races. Few, if any, of the original 'areas of characterization' exist today. What has happened is that the original races migrated and mixed with others, and the hybrid race then settled long enough in one place to create an entirely new 'area of characterization'.

Practically all existing races are *new* races in this sense. The process has been repeated again and again, bringing new races such as the Polynesians, American Indians, and most of the original European races into existence.

There is, however, so much migration today, as there has been for so many centuries, that it is increasingly difficult to find easily distinguishable types, except where populations have been isolated for centuries. Such a condition can be found only in remote and isolated areas of the world.

So we can see that the combination of migration, interbreeding, and isolation has broken down the basic racial types which originally inhabited the earth and will continue to do so. Therefore as time goes on, the present characteristics will be less descriptive of the races currently inhabiting the earth; this is why the number of variant subgroups is so numerous and why there are so many mixed groups all over the world.

This is particularly true in Europe and America, where there is not even sufficient time to allow the interbreeding types to establish a recognizable new race. Such a process would take centuries and require isolation for that period. Neither condition is fulfilled today and, therefore, it is useless to look for distinct races among Europeans and Americans.

HYBRID RACES

As the original races migrated from one area to another, they interbred with the inhabitants, who may or may not have been an original race. The product of this interbreeding was a hybrid race. The hybrid race remained in isolation within a particular area for a period of time, probably several centuries, and then moved on to another area. Here the hybrid race formed another hybrid race by interbreeding with the inhabitants of the area into which it had moved. If we multiply this process many times, we will understand something of the evolution of the present-day races and those of the future.

It is the hybrid races now living on earth that we shall study in the remaining pages of this chapter. As we study them, we must bear in mind that they are not the original races of man and that they are not the ultimate races of man.

PHYSICAL TYPES

All human beings belong to a single species. Within this species we find many varieties, but all can interbreed. When we say that all men belong to the same species, we are really indicating that the different races of man have more common characteristics than they have differentiating characteristics. For example, the mating of the most diverse types of man results in men who are also fertile. All men have the power of speech with which to express ideas and all have conventional habits and customs in contrast with the instinctive behaviour of other living creatures.

Let us now consider some of the physical differences that differentiate men. About these it must at once be said that they are more *superficial* than they are *fundamental*. Whatever significance has come to be attached to them is far more because they have become group badges than by reason of any *intrinsic* differences which may be associated with a particular type.

This is not to say that a particular group may not come to possess certain habits, customs, and mental attitudes. They may and do. But these attitudes are neither caused by nor dependent upon the physical features of the group. It is social tradition, conditioning, education, and culture which have produced them.

This view receives strong support from the science of genetics. There is no clear connection between skin colour or hair texture and intelligence or basic instincts. In other words, these obvious physical differences are relatively unimportant in themselves, no matter how significant they may be socially or politically.

Skin Colour. A simple and somewhat persistent division of man by skin colour divides man into the white, yellow, red, brown, and black races. For convenience of classification most anthropologists reduce and simplify the varieties to three basic skin colours: white skin, yellow skin, and black skin.

These types of skin colour are usually, but not always, associated with the division of mankind into the Caucasoid (white), Mongoloid (yellow), and Negroid (black) races. An entire absence of pigment cells occurs as a somewhat rare mutation among all races (and among animals) and is known as albinism. There are pure-white Negroes.

These distinctions arise as a matter of pure chance and are due to the appearance of a heritable change in the gene pattern. When such a mutation produced a darker skin, it proved advantageous as a protection against the ultraviolet rays of sunlight. The heavy concentrations of these pigment cells in most equatorial populations is thus a product of **natural selection;** pigmentation has therefore established itself in hot climates because it has **survival value.**

Skin colour is not, however, as useful as might be supposed in classifying races because *the range in each group is very large* and some Caucasoids are darker than some Negroids. Furthermore there are some types which are black in skin but not otherwise Negroid—the Australian aborigines, for example—while certain light-coloured tribes cannot be classed as Caucasoid. (For a detailed explanation of the science of genetics consult *Biology Made Simple*.)

Overlap. It is of great importance that we understand the basic principle of overlap in this connection. Quite simply it implies that although there may be a larger number of blue-eyed people in one area than in another, for example, this does not mean that all the blue-eyed people are in the first area and that there are no blue-eyed people anywhere else.

The Swedes are generally regarded as Nordic—that is to say a considerable portion of them will be tall, fair-haired, blue-eyed—but among Swedish army recruits only 11 per cent possessed *all* the Nordic traits and only 29 per cent were tall, fair-haired, and blue-eyed. On the other hand there is a good proportion of Nordic types in other European countries.

This indicates that whatever characteristics we adopt to clasify races, great numbers of individuals cannot be assigned to any of these groups on the basis of skin colour or eye colour or whatever features are selected as a basis of classification.

Eye Colour and Form. All non-Caucasoid populations have a dark-brown or black iris. Only the Caucasoids have eyes ranging from light blue to brown. But many Asiatics have in addition a fold of skin covering the inner angle of the eye (the epicanthic fold) that gives the eyes the appearance of being slightly slanted. (They are perfectly level, as a matter of fact.) This is a good example of a physical trait with no conceivable correlation with individual or group psychology.

OTHER BODILY CHARACTERISTICS

Hair form is very distinctive. In general, Negroes have frizzy hair, Mongoloids have straight, lank hair, and the Caucasoids have wavy hair.

You have probably heard of long-headed and broad-headed people. This characteristic is measured by the **cephalic index,** which is the ratio of breadth to length seen from the top. Narrow- or long-headed people have a cephalic index of below 75 and are called **dolichocephalic;** broad-headed people have a cephalic index of over 80 and are called **brachycephalic.** The intermediate group (cephalic index between 75 and 80) is known as **mesocephalic.**

The cephalic index is not a very useful criterion, since dolichocephalic, brachycephalic, and mesocephalic people are found in all the major divisions of mankind. The cephalic index may be of limited use in characterizing certain smaller populations or groups within a fairly large area.

Finally we may mention **stature, nose shape, lips, ears,** and **body hair.** None of these is very important, but it is interesting to note that many of the traits that some people associate with primitiveness, such as thick lips, are in point of fact among the least ape-like of human characteristics. Apes have *thin* lips. Negroes are, in fact, the least ape-like or simian-like in six traits, and the Caucasoids are the least ape-like in only three traits. The attempt to associate Negroid traits with primitiveness is both unscientific and ridiculous, plainly contrary to the observable facts.

Blood Groups. There are four types of blood: A, B, AB, and O (and many subdivisions of these which are not, for us, basically important). These blood groups provide emphatic confirmation of the unity of mankind. It is an erroneous conception that blood is the factor that distinguishes one race from another and that it is mingled in cross-breeding. In the first place, blood is so similar that transfusions can take place between compatible blood groups in different races and lives can be saved, providing the type taken from the donor is compatible with that of the recipient.

Nor in cross-breeding is the blood mingled. In fact blood is of absolutely no significance in marriage apart from the Rhesus (Rh) factor, which can affect any couple within any single race as well as couples in mixed marriages. All human groups have the same basic assortment of hereditary characters, for the most part, but *in different proportions*; and this holds true for blood groups, all of which are found in every race but, as might be expected, in different proportions.

In the Caucasoid and Mongoloid races we find an almost equal correlation of blood types. For example, on a proportionate basis there are about as many people in each race who have blood type O. The same can be said about the other three major blood types. This is true even though the two races differ in other bodily characteristics.

The majority of American Indians belong to the O-type blood group. Going across Europe in an easterly direction from England to Russia, we find an increase in the number of people who have B-type blood. The Negro group in the United States generally tends to have the same proportion of people with O-type blood as the rest of the population. Fewer American Negroes have A-type than B-type blood. But as our previous discussion of *overlap* indicates, an enormous number of eastern Europeans and Negroes have *exactly the same blood* as many western Caucasoids.

There is one extremely important consequence that follows from the inheritance of blood groups: it provides completely convincing evidence of certain important racial admixtures. Thus the theory of the common ancestry of American Indians, Asiatics, Pacific Islanders, and Australians is supported by the fact that they all possess a distinctive element in their blood.

In general the proportions of blood groups in the different peoples of the world tend to divide the world's population into *five* major races— the **Caucasoid, Negroid, Mongoloid, American Indian,** and **Australoid.** The American Indian is closely linked to the Mongoloid race, but evidence from blood types indicates the emergence at some past time of a separate racial group.

CLASSIFICATION OF RACE BY INHERITED PHYSICAL FEATURES

We have previously defined race as a major grouping of interrelated people possessing a distinctive combination of physical traits that are the result of inheritance. We concluded that many similarities of face and form tend to indicate that such a people have a common ancestry. This leads to the general hypothesis that if a population is closely inbred for many generations, all the people will have common ancestors and be very much alike.

When we proceed to classify men on this basis, we find that there are three major races: **Caucasoid, Mongoloid,** and **Negroid,** and a few minor races such as the **Australoids,** the **American Indians,** and the **South African Bushman** (though these minor groups may once have been widely distributed over the world).

It is extremely important to remember that no useful purpose can be served by trying to fit every known group into one of the three major races or the better-known minor races. All that we can accomplish by this classification is the realization that there are, in point of fact, three large groups with recognizable physical types. Above all, these types do *not* represent three of the original races of man—on the contrary these races have themselves emerged; others have also emerged and declined, and others may still be in the process of formation.

PHYSICAL CHARACTERISTICS OF THE THREE MAJOR RACES

Trait	Caucasoid	Mongoloid	Negroid
Skin colour	Pale to gold or dark brown	Yellowish to yellow-brown	Brown to brown-black
Head form	Long to broad	Broad	Long
Hair	Blond to brown Straight to wavy Often much body hair	Brown to black Coarse, straight Little body hair	Brown-black Frizzy Little body hair
Eyes	Light blue to brown	Brown to dark brown Epicanthic fold	Brown to brown-black

THE CAUCASOIDS

The Caucasoids comprise about 1,000 million people who display variable skin colour, from the lightest 'white' to dark brown. Their hair form is variable, but never woolly, and body hair is often thick. Their lips tend to be thin. The head is neither predominantly broad nor long.

The Caucasoid race falls into three subdivisions: the **Nordic**, the **Mediterranean**, and the **Alpine**.

The **Nordic** group in northern Europe is composed of people who are frequently tall, blond, and narrow-headed. The members of this group are found in Scandinavia, the Baltic, some parts of Germany, in France, and Britain.

Members of the **Mediterranean** group are found in southern France. The people in this subdivision are lighter in body build, dark, and narrow-headed. Included in the Mediterranean group are the Egyptians, the Semites (including the Bedouins of Arabia), most Persians, and many Afghans. The Welsh probably belong to this subdivision of the Caucasoid race. Apart from the groups mentioned, we find this subdivision in Spain, Italy, and among the Berbers of North Africa. Some members of this subdivision can be found in India and Indonesia.

The **Alpine** group extends from the Mediterranean to Asia. The members of this group are broad-headed and have broad faces with sharp, square jaws. Their skin is olive and their hair is brown. The **Alpines** are concentrated in the eastern, central, and southern parts of Europe and in Asia Minor.

The people of India are hybrids, combining the traits of the early inhabitants, the dark Caucasoids, and the later immigrant Caucasoids of a Mediterranean type.

To achieve genuine scientific descriptive classification we would have to break these groupings down into a large number of subgroups and allow for much overlapping and many doubtful cases.

THE MONGOLOIDS

The Mongoloids form the most populous of the present-day races. They display variable skin colour, but the average is a yellowish light-brown.

Mongoloids fall into three main groups:

(*a*) The natives of eastern Siberia, the Eskimos and similar far-northern tribes, and the American Indian (when not classified as a separate race).

(*b*) The inhabitants of Japan, Korea, China, and the adjacent districts.

(*c*) The Indonesian Malays, who inherit certain characteristics from short-statured aborigines and Mediterranean Caucasoids.

There are many admixtures with Caucasoids and, in the Pacific Islands, with Negro strains and Mediterranean types.

THE NEGROIDS

The Negroid group is made up of the 100 million people who inhabit Africa south of the Sahara, and the Melanesians of the South Pacific. It has contributed to the hybrid types found elsewhere in the Pacific, where Negroes have mixed with Mongoloids, Caucasoids, and other lesser strains.

This oversimplified classification leaves out the Central African Pygmies, the Bushmen, and the Australoids. It gives, however, some idea of the main groupings of human beings into roughly similar physical types. Yet great numbers of individuals cannot be assigned to any of these groups, and few of the traits selected for any one main group are lacking in individuals of other groups. It is the *preponderance* of this or that type that makes for distinguishing characteristics.

We might conclude our discussion of the races of man—past, present, and future—by quoting from an old hymn which states: 'The blood of noble races commingled flows in thine' and we shall not be far from the truth.

Of greater importance than our mixed ancestry is the relative stability and unifying power of the social tradition. It is this that makes nations—not eye colour, pigmentation, or the cephalic index.

(*Suggested Further Reading*, see page 72.)

CHAPTER SIX

RACE AND CULTURE

Three important questions arise from the study of racial differences:

1. What is the effect of hybridization? Is it harmful or beneficial?
2. Are there superior races?
3. How do we account for backward races?

MISCEGENATION

Miscegenation means the simple act of interbreeding between different races. As we have seen, it has always taken place, it is still going on, and all existing races are its product. What are its consequences?

It is useless to argue that it must have ill consequences, for it is universal in human history and at no time has it arrested or changed the course of civilization.

Biologically or medically there is no shadow of evidence for any unfortunate consequences either physically or psychologically. Occasionally there does seem to be a period of hybrid vigour, as when the first generation of Pitcairn Islanders were physically taller and stronger than their parents; but normally there is little evidence for this.

Of course the consequences of the migration or conquest which led to racial intermixture have sometimes been good and sometimes bad, but this has nothing to do with 'blood' and is entirely due to the social and historical conditions at the time.

Conquest has always been a common cause of racial admixture, the victors intermarrying with the conquered. This is well seen in the armies of occupation after recent wars. Not only are the effects free from any unfortunate physical results, but historically the result has been racial improvement, caused by greater variety and perhaps a stimulating psychological impulse. History indeed shows that mixed races have flourished and progressed even in those extreme cases where intermixture has been across the colour line, as, for example, in the continuous intermarriage of Caucasoid Arabs with Negroids in Africa. Moslems have never frowned on such unions.

In Hawaii, in the West Indies, and in South America racial interbreeding is common, usually carries no social stigma, and raises no problems.

Yet elsewhere the half-caste can be a problem, notably in India and the United States. But the reason is recognized by all anthropologists to be social rather than genetic. If such unions are frowned upon or are taboo, the children may be maladjusted and the parents may suffer social ostracism. This is because both races may object and social disapproval result. In places where there is no disapproval we find no association between emotional difficulties and mixed heritage.

No physical problem arises, such as when we cross horses and asses. Regardless of external racial differences, every human being has the same kind of hereditary mechanism and can produce a perfectly normal family with any other member of the opposite sex of the species *Homo sapiens*.

Racial amalgamation is in full swing all over the world, and even the American Negro population contains so many genes from Caucasoid and Indian stock, now disseminated through the entire race, that there is a marked difference between its members and Africans. This mixed blood of the American Negro results in what is called *family variability* —that is to say, striking differences in the members of the same family. This is not the case in populations with a genuinely common ancestry, such as the Eskimos, who are all very much alike. Family variability is a sure sign of a heterogeneous ancestry. It is found in both black and white populations in the United States.

A close marriage group is not always racial. In India it is a matter of caste, and in many countries it is a question of class or religion. Conventions of mating can thus set the limits within which the hereditary mechanisms operate and so give rise to inbreeding and even the emergence, as a result, of a recognizable type.

The American anthropologist Herskovits has drawn our attention to a curious ideological phenomenon—the emergence of racial *words* with no biological meaning. These refer to groups that exist by *definition only* and correspond to no ascertainable physical type, as for example 'coloured' in South Africa and 'Negro' in the United States. In both cases any suspected admixture of Negroid blood is sufficient to classify someone with full Caucasoid racial characters as being in the Negroid race, which is completely absurd.

ARE THERE SUPERIOR RACES?

A familiar modern doctrine is the racism that holds that a particular group is basically superior to others.

There is, however, no evidence whatever for the correlation of superior mental aptitudes with racial types.

This question may be considered on the basis of *brain size* or on the basis of *intelligence testing*.

Brain Size. It is true that the average weight of the brain in proportion to total body weight is smaller among Negroids, Australoids, and Pygmies than among Mongoloids and Caucasoids, and also that the Mongoloid brain is smaller than the Caucasoid. But in the first place, the *overlapping* is so great that almost *any individual brain might belong to any race.* Secondly, we must draw a sharp distinction between the differences in brain size that occur between apes and men, or between *Pithecanthropus* and *Homo sapiens,* or between a normal man and a microcephalic idiot, and the relatively unimportant differences that exist between normal people in any population (which are quite considerable, but not correlated with any ascertainable difference in intelligence)—for instance, the differences in brain size between men and women and between different races. These are so small as to be of no consequence at all. Pygmy brains are not less efficient, but are simply smaller in proportion to the slight body build.

Intelligence Testing. As is generally realized today, intelligence testing gives suggestive but often quite unreliable results. This is because of the difficulty of separating innate intelligence from the effects of social training. It is also unsatisfactory to employ tests suitable for one community to a community with different habits and attitudes. In spite of this the tests are not without their value.

What do they show? And what do they prove?

Since much work has been done on this subject in the United States, let us consider the results of subjecting American Negroes and Caucasoids to such tests. Tests comparing White and Negro intelligence in the United States showed that Negroes scored one point below Caucasoids on the Stanford–Binet IQ test; other tests have confirmed this. But it is also true that Southern Negroes have a lower IQ than Northern Negroes. Could the explanation of *both* results be dependent on social environment and education rather than on racial factors? The following test results throw an interesting light on this problem:

1. Testing Southern Whites against Northern Negroes, the Whites show a lower score than the Negroes.

2. The test scores of Northern Negro children are much higher than those of Southern Negro children.

3. Testing Negro and White boys both in North and South, it was found that the Negro scores were below the White in Nashville, equal to the White in New York, and slightly above the White in Los Angeles.

4. The average score of all the recent immigrants to the North was no higher than that of the Negro boys who remained in the South.

5. But the lowest intelligence quotient in the North was that of the newest arrivals, and the I.Q. went steadily up with the length of residence.

6. Nor were the scores of the new arrivals inferior to the scores of those who had arrived in earlier years; on the contrary they were slightly higher.

What conclusions can we draw from these results?

The first results suggest that it is as Southerners that the IQ both of Whites and Negroes is low. This was borne out by the higher IQ of Negro boys where the education was superior. Nor was this, as some suggested, due to the cleverer Negroes moving North.

The general result was that *whenever the environmental advantages became similar, the 'inferiority' of the Negro tended to disappear.* But the environmental advantages of the Negro in the United States never equalled those of the Whites of the same economic level, hence the lower IQ for Negroes as a whole, compared with Whites.

Whenever such tests are made, we can never know to what extent the results are influenced by training. As a test of racial superiority, they are thoroughly unreliable.

Intelligence Tests and Anthropology. Anthropologists have come to use these tests with great caution for the following reasons:

1. Some native groups will not attempt to solve a problem individually, because they are accustomed to helping one another and arriving at a co-operative result.

2. It may be contrary to custom to give rapid oral responses, or it may be contrary to habit to give any answer which is less than certain.

3. The group may be quite uninterested in the questions, or think them foolish, or have hostile feelings towards the tester.

Thus a test whose content and method of scoring were developed by the carriers of one cultural heritage appears to be valueless for any determination of the native ability of groups who have other cultures.

Intelligence Testing and Overlap. Intelligence tests as applied to populations are misleading for another reason. Once again *there is a considerable overlap*. The differences in intelligence between races become insignificant beside the differences between individuals. Even if any particular race showed an advantage over another, it would mean very little if anything. For a population or race is composed of individuals and *is not a unit*. A considerable proportion of the less gifted race would nonetheless be more intelligent than very many of the more gifted race.

In general we may conclude that 'race' easily becomes an inadequate explanation for differences, the real reasons for which may be traced to causes in the physical or social environments or historical circumstances. John Stuart Mill expressed this well when he said, 'Of all vulgar modes of escaping from the consideration of the effect of social and moral influences on the human mind, the most vulgar is that of attributing diversities of conduct and character to inherent natural differences.'

'BACKWARD' RACES

Can the technological backwardness of some areas of the world be regarded as evidence of racial inferiority?

If this backwardness is not due to racial inferiority, to what is it attributable? The reason appears to be the location of the wild grasses which were the precursors of wheat and barley in Europe, and of maize, which came to form so important an article of diet in America, as well as the proximity of fertile river valleys in these localities. Wheat was discovered and exploited only in the Fertile Crescent of Asia Minor. It was here that the peoples who learned how to make use of these grains acquired food surpluses which released considerable numbers for specialized skills and crafts and developed commerce and trade.

Distant populations cut off by deserts, tropical forests, or oceans developed in this way only much later.

The very general belief among those for centuries responsible for colonial enterprise in Africa, and equally for American negroes, is that Africa has had no culture historically, and is the home of 'savages'. We are now beginning to discover evidences of the lost civilizations of Africa. Archaeology has found remarkable ruins of great buildings. The great kingdom of Ashanti, Dahomey, and Yoruba we now realize were highly organized communities.

In Egypt a strong Asian influence was impressed upon a basically African culture. By 2000 B.C. Egypt had influenced the Nile region as far as the third and fourth cataracts, and here the Cushite civilization appeared in 1000 B.C. and continued until A.D. 300. A second centre of culture in this region was Meroe, an iron-producing area of importance. This iron culture reached Ashanti, Dahomey, the Yoruba States, and Ghana.

From 100 B.C. until A.D. 300 the region of West Africa which had received this Sudric influence was covered by a culture known for its pottery, its terracotta ware and its iron industry. The Meroitic Divine Kingship was grafted on to these cultures to produce the State of Ghana which flourished until over-run by the Moslems in A.D. 900.

But from 4000 B.C. the growing desert conditions in the Sahara were cutting off the Mediterranean coast of Africa from everything to the south of the desert. Africa and Asia moved apart. The routes still open were the caravan routes and the Nile valley. A most powerful destructive force both in the east and south of the Sahara was the overthrow of the developing civilizations by the Arabs. It was only after the long period of isolation which followed that Africa was to be re-discovered. Even so, there was a good deal of commerce between Eastern Africa and Asia across the Indian Ocean during the period when Europe was cut off from the East.

The civilizations of Egypt, Mesopotamia, Greece, and China did not develop in isolation. They received important contributions from surrounding peoples with whom they came in contact. Wars of conquest and trade relations led to a mixing of races and transference of technological and agricultural experience.

When these civilizations declined, it was not due to racial degeneration but to economic and political causes. Historical and geographical conditions and circumstances, not genes, are therefore the immediate determinants of a people's cultural achievements.

Why does cultural achievement rise and fall in the same race?

The same people may exhibit astounding cultural energy at one period of their history and be almost wholly devoid of it at another. Peoples who have been culturally quiescent for centuries suddenly advance without any change in racial composition.

When Mediterranean culture was flourishing under the Greeks and Romans, Gaul and Britain were living in savagery, and Cicero said of the Britons, 'Do not obtain your slaves from the Britons, for the Britons are so stupid and so dull that they are not fit to be slaves.'

The centres of culture did not shift to northern Europe until after the Renaissance. During the Dark Ages, the Maya Indians of Central America showed greater cultural achievements than the Europeans. At the same time there was a great Arabian civilization extending from Baghdad and Alexandria through North Africa to Spain. Medicine, mathematics, and philosophy flourished here and the Arabs became the tutors of backward Europe. Their opinion of the barbarians of the north was a poor one: 'Their temper is slow and their humours raw; their hair is long and their complexion pale. The sharpness of their wit, the perspicacity of their intelligence is nil; ignorance and indolence are dominant among them as well as crudeness and lack of judgement.' Yet today it is the Arab communities that are backward, largely ignorant, and poverty-stricken.

Changes in Europe, which meant not only general cultural advance but the transformation of the Germanic tribes into industrialists was not due to changes in racial composition. The England of Elizabeth and Shakespeare changed in one man's lifetime to the England of Cromwell, and then again to the England of the eighteenth and nineteenth centuries. We can trace the causes in political and social conditions, but not in any change of racial composition. Whatever list of striking achievements can be drawn up, none of these can be attributed to the 'blood' of any people.

No connexion has been found between the biological constitution of the peoples and the level of their past or present culture; nor is there any hereditary or other biological reason for supposing that because White civilization is leading today, it will necessarily be leading tomorrow.

CULTURAL DIFFERENCES

The United Nations Educational, Scientific, and Cultural Organization (Unesco) has very well summed up the position of contemporary anthropology on cultural differences.

The scientific material available to us at present does not justify the conclusion that inherited genetic differences are a major factor in producing the differences between the cultures and cultural achievement of different peoples or groups. It does indicate on the contrary, that a major factor in explaining such differences is the cultural experience which each group has undergone.

Available scientific knowledge provides no basis for believing that the groups of mankind differ in their innate capacity for intellectual and emotional development.

Vast social changes have occurred that have not been connected in any way with changes in racial type. Historical and sociological studies thus support the view that genetic differences are of little significance in determining the social and cultural differences between different groups of men.

(*Statement on the 'Nature of Race and Race Differences'*
prepared by Unesco, 1952.)

People find it difficult to understand that genetics has nothing to say about the attitudes, endowments, capabilities, and inherent tendencies of different groups of human beings as we can certainly *describe* them today. It has always been assumed that different groups had, permanently, innately, certain well-marked types of character, intelligence, initiative, laziness, emotionalism, dourness, or whatever. People explained all history in terms of racial characteristics. Yet strangely enough in a much shorter time than genetical variation (which proceeds very slowly) could effect the transformation, the magnificent Greeks turned into a feckless, inefficient mob, and the stern, efficient organizers of the Roman Empire turned into nineteenth-century Italians, for whom very few people had respect. Meanwhile in the far north the bloodthirsty pirates of the Scandinavian and Danish peninsulas turned into incredibly sturdy pig farmers. Genetical variation? Rubbish! Twentieth-century science has recognized that its predecessors were mistaken. The twentieth-century man-in-the-street has not quite caught up.

The Plasticity of Human Behaviour. We see, then, that on the basis of the racial inheritance which they possess, and without marked change in this, men can pass through the most radical social changes. Man's inherited traits are not specific and do not lay down his whole way of life. Human nature is infinitely malleable or plastic in its expressions, and no one can estimate its full potential.

Man reacts to his environment and, instead of allowing himself to be moulded by it in his bodily form over millions of years, he himself modifies it by his tools and by co-operative effort. The methods he adopts and the social organization that comes into existence as the one appropriate to a particular level of technique shape directly and indirectly the whole social pattern with all the varied aspects of its culture.

This affects in turn every individual in that society, so that the cultural pattern of man is not determined by his genes but by the society he creates and lives in. Any normal human being, if given the necessary opportunity, can therefore learn the way of life of any people existing on earth today.

Every large human group contains the entire range of human capability, whether in intellectual, scientific, or artistic capacity. How it uses that endowment is a matter of history and social organization, not biology.

Man has not evolved as a species since his ancestors left their rudimentary tools in the caves of the Quaternary age, some 50,000 years ago. The enormous difference is the work of civilization, that is to say of culture, gradually accumulated and transmitted by social tradition, of culture basically modified from pattern to pattern in different ages and climes. If it were possible to bring a newborn child of the Stone Age into our own time and to bring him up like one of our children, he would become exactly like us, equally capable of discussing existentialism and Picasso.

What new patterns of society and of human nature lie before us we do not know. The bodily pattern changes so slowly as to be negligible, but the social changes which lie before us are still boundless in potential.

SUGGESTED FURTHER READING

Benedict, Ruth, *Race and Racism*. Routledge & Kegan Paul: London, 1942.

Dobzansky, T., *Heredity and the Nature of Man*. Allen & Unwin: London, 1965.

Linton, Ralph, *The Study of Man*. Owen: London, 1965.

Shapiro, H. L., *Man, Culture and Society*. Oxford University Press: London, 1954.

Shapiro, H. L., *Migration and Environment*. Oxford University Press: London, 1939.

'The Race Concept' in *The Race Question in Modern Science*. UNESCO: Paris, 1951.

PART THREE

EARLY SOCIETY AND ITS ORGANIZATION

CHAPTER SEVEN

PATTERNS OF SOCIETY

Wherever we find a community—however primitive, however complex—we find more than an association of individuals, each pursuing his own life and possessing his own ideas; we find a social pattern, a coherent body of customs and ideas, an integrated unity or system in which each element has a definite function in relation to the whole.

But what determines the pattern? It is, says Radcliffe-Brown, 'the *necessary conditions of existence* of the social organism'. To this the social institutions must correspond. In turn the necessary conditions of existence, at any stage of social development, depend on the geographical situation and the level of technology. This is true from the Stone Age to modern industrialism.

Basic to every form of social organization is the method of obtaining those items essential for human survival. In other words, how do the people of a particular society produce their food, clothing, tools, and other items that they need in order to live as human beings?

These 'necessary conditions of existence' shape the relationship of men to each other. Men carry on a struggle against nature and utilize nature to produce the necessities of life not in isolation from each other, not as separate individuals, but in common, in groups, in societies.

But at different stages of development people make use of different modes of production and therefore lead different kinds of life. Correspondingly the whole social pattern, including religion, morals, customs, and ideas, differs from age to age. Whatever is man's manner of life, such is his manner of behaviour and of thought.

Within such a system we must ask of any custom, or magical practice, or marriage rule, or taboo, what contribution it makes to the total social life, and to the functioning of the total social system. The system will then be found to regulate the relationship of all the individuals in that society; it will provide such adaptation to the physical environment as to make possible an ordered social life; it is, in short, *a method of survival*.

The Web of Custom. Anthropology no longer merely records and compares interesting customs, *it compares total patterns*, the web of thought and action. It is this web rather than any elaborate system of government that holds primitive societies together. Its bonds are *internal*—the habits of thought, of obligation, and of custom shape attitudes and behaviour.

This interior force is as real and authoritative as the external environment. The two together constitute the very nature of man in any particular society. This sum total of customs, rules, beliefs, marriage systems, and so on is called the *culture* of that society.

Culture maintains and enhances life.
It builds up and strengthens the group and helps it to satisfy its needs.

Culture, then, is the integrated system of learned behaviour patterns characteristic of the members of a society. It constitutes the way of life of any given social group. It is also a social heritage, transmitted from generation to generation and instilled into the minds of the young not only by education and initiation, but by the long, unconscious conditioning whereby each individual becomes the person he ultimately is. It thus becomes a form of *social heredity*.

Such an interpretation of the structure of the social organism is called 'functionalism'. It is thus described by Radcliffe-Brown:

> The function of culture as a whole is to unite the individual human beings into more or less stable social structures, i.e. stable systems of groups determining and regulating the relations of those individuals to one another, and providing such external adaptation to the physical environment, and such internal adaptation between the component individuals or groups as to make possible an ordered social life. That assumption, I believe to be a sort of primary postulate of any objective and scientific study of human society.

> (*The Present Position of Anthropological Studies.* Presidential Address to the British Association, Section H, 1931.)

It must be realized that such a pattern of society is an *evolved* harmonious whole. It survives and flourishes because it successfully maintains solidarity among its members, and to attain this, *all* the institutions interacting within that society and constituting it contribute to that solidarity. The people concerned in such a society do not, of course, *see* the model constructed to explain it to the Western student of anthropology. The analysis into a pattern of institutional relationships is one thing, the actual working of the system is not realized to be 'a system' at all by the people within it. It is just the usual way things get done. The scheme as worked out by the *functionalist* would be quite unintelligible to them, for they would not be interested in considering the kind of questions with which the anthropologist is concerned,

The Three Aspects of a Culture. Every culture, from that of a simple, food-gathering community like the Eskimos to our own, has three fundamental aspects: the **technological,** the **sociological,** and the **ideological.**

The Technological. This aspect of culture is concerned with tools, materials, techniques, and, in our day, machines. The tool is basic. The bronze axe is not only a superior instrument to the stone axe, it carries with it a more complex economic and social structure.

Therefore we shall consider, as part of the technological basis, the types of culture dependent upon such tools and techniques as the digging stick and spear, the hoe and garden, the herd of cattle, the ox-drawn plough.

The Sociological. This aspect of culture involves the relationships into which men enter, especially in work and in the family. These will always involve some form of co-operation, and may be basically free from exploitation, as among very primitive tribes, or may reflect some form of conflict, domination and subordination as in more advanced societies.

The Ideological. This aspect of culture comprises beliefs, rituals, magical practices, art, ethics, religious practices, and myths. In developed civilizations it includes the philosophies and legal systems of the society. Changes in technology and social organization will bring forth changes in the ideas, beliefs, in fact the whole spiritual life of man, but such ideas will always react back on the social organization. It is a reciprocal process.

PRIMITIVE SOCIAL AND ECONOMIC SYSTEMS

There are great varieties of primitive cultures, but they fall into four basic types. The most fundamental division is between those which produce no *surplus* or a very small surplus, living from hand to mouth—a bare subsistence economy—and *those with a reasonable or large surplus*. Only with the latter shall we find permanent settlement and complex social organization. *Surplus* determines many things:

1. The density of **population.**
2. The degree of **specialization.**
3. The forms of **ownership,** exchange, and inheritance.
4. The amount of **leisure** available for arts, crafts, and ceremonies.

Simple Food-gathering Systems. We find this level of attainment among the Australians, the Eskimos, the South African Bushmen, the Shoshones, the African Pygmies, the Veddas of Ceylon, and some South American Indians. There is no future for any of these groups—they must either perish or be absorbed into higher forms of civilization. These groups are of special interest because they give some indication of the mode of life that our most primitive ancestors lived.

Some of these groups fish, some gather wild plants; all engage in hunting. Some cattle-herding tribes which practise no agriculture do not rise above a subsistence economy.

Strategic Areas. Such communities stake out and roam over fishing areas, hunting districts, and wild-plant collecting sites. These territories are not owned by individuals, families, or tribes, but the particular group knows them, exploits them, and moves over them.

Social Organization. First we have a certain *division of labour as between men and women*. Among the Australians the women dig for roots and witchetty grubs, the men hunt kangaroos. Then we find *work parties*. A squad or group of men sets off to hunt or fish.

Population groups, of course, are small, the self-sufficient unit consisting of 40–80 persons. The entire community makes seasonal moves for the sake of food.

Distribution is generally shared. There are no significant surplus products and no inequalities in ownership of wealth.

MORE ADVANCED HUNTING AND FOOD-GATHERING SYSTEMS

These were probably widespread in prehistoric times, and were most recently found in the lower coastal river and tidewater villages of North American Indians—from northwestern California to Alaska.

There is now a surplus and the headman or chief organizes the tribal activities and work parties and receives a larger share of the product. Class distinctions now emerge between the rich and the poor. Once we reach this level, we find that there are even slaves who do the menial work, such as carvers, canoe-makers, and basket-makers. There is also some trading.

Populations are much larger. Self-sufficient village communities contain about 50 persons, and market villages of many hundreds appear.

War and Work. Predatory activities now appear. Distant villages are raided for slaves and booty. This is possible once there is a surplus to fight for.

At this stage the warrior caste emerges—the hunter–fighters, who tend to despise routine labour in favour of exploits which testify to personal prowess. Scalps, trophies, and booty are evidence of this and are more worthy than goods obtained by labour.

There may even come a time when indignity is imputed to hard work, which therefore becomes irksome. A radical distinction develops between work, which is ignoble, and non-productive activities such as raiding and fighting.

In so far as slaves or women can be compelled to do the work, the warriors can free themselves from productive labour to employ themselves in more dignified and meritorious ways.

The Potlatch. In some Indian communities, status and importance were determined by the amount of conspicuous waste which chiefs and aspirants to social honour could demonstrate. This is seen today among the Kwakiutl Indians of British Columbia.

The *potlatch* is a great and expensive feast requiring the accumulation of considerable wealth and bringing great glory to those who give it. The aim is *rivalry*, a contest to see who can give the biggest feast. Honour comes from *giving away*, even from *destroying* wealth. The gifts include paddles, mats, dishes, canoes, blankets, and engraved copper shields. During the feast thousands of valuable blankets may be burned, canoes broken, and copper shields smashed.

Rivalry between chiefs and clans finds its strongest expression in the destruction of property. A chief will burn blankets or break a copper shield, thus indicating his disregard of the amount of property destroyed and showing that his mind is stronger, his power greater, than that of his rival. If the latter is not able to destroy an equal amount of property without much delay, his name is 'broken'. He is vanquished by his rival and his influence with his tribe is lost, while the name of the other chief gains correspondingly in renown.

(Boas, *The Social Organizations of the Kwakiutl Indians.*)

AGRICULTURE WITH A SMALL SURPLUS

This form of economy is found everywhere in the Pacific Islands, in the north-eastern portions of North America, along the upper Missouri, in Arizona and New Mexico, and in Brazil. It is also found in Africa. Probably a few million persons all over the world lived in such economic systems 300 years ago.

Population groups are larger than such groups would be in advanced food-gathering societies. Villages contain hundreds of persons. The basic type of agriculture is the garden, which can be run by a family, with communal help to clear the ground to get it started and for harvests. Work parties fish, hunt, or collect wild plants.

Strategic Resources. The gardens are worked, if not owned, by families. But control and assignment remains with the community. Produce is kept by individual producers and shared only in time of community need.

Surplus. There is now enough surplus to permit a certain amount of leisure from subsistence work; individuals are released for specialized work or crafts such as pottery, weaving, carving, or for ceremonial activities. Surplus may also be given away or bartered from community to community. The existence of this surplus does not yet result in imimportant inequalities of ownership, hereditary nobles, or taxation.

ADVANCED AGRICULTURAL AND PASTORAL SYSTEMS

Most of the living peoples studied by anthropologists organize their production by these methods.

The villages are not only more populated but are grouped in larger areas, welded together by trade and for defence. Hence the appearance of the tribe—a cluster of economically interdependent village communities sharing a common territory, language, and culture. Specialization may now exist between villages. Intercommunity barter becomes important.

Production. This is not only agricultural but pastoral—that is to say, cattle- and sheep-owning communities now appear and, in the north, reindeer-owning groups. Strategic resources are privately owned and may include land, herds, and slaves. Production is by individuals, and sometimes by slaves owned by the rich. There is definite production for market needs, and villages begin to specialize.

THE SOCIAL CONSEQUENCES OF
DEVELOPING AGRICULTURE

Before the discovery of agriculture the land was just there, open to all. Groups were widely dispersed and but seldom came into contact; they wandered from place to place gathering what they could find and hunting. Certain groups may have come to be associated with the food-gathering area frequented by them, and the same would be true of pastoral peoples—the scarcer the water and grazing, the more likely would be claims to certain areas at certain times of the year. Even at this level people would combine for certain purposes. The more arduous the conditions, the more necessary is economic co-operation and mutual support. Men are united firstly in carrying out the same tasks as hunters, fishermen and cultivators, and in a general way everybody does much the same things. Later come forms of specialization of individuals or groups, but all being dependent on the others. One group will do the hoeing, another will build a house; of this latter group some will collect poles, others will thatch, and others again will do the building. This results in the recognition of reciprocal obligations and rights, which must be maintained for the safety and existence of all. It is only very much later that this solidarity gives way to something like *business contracts*, people engaging in a certain job under an arrangement which promises a certain definite recompense in kind.

At this stage, over any considerable tract of country we shall recognize different subsistence areas. In Africa, for example, there are the grain farmers occupying the grain belt, there are areas cultivated mainly for roots (yams, manioc, taro, and sweet potatoes), and there is the banana (plantain) belt. Large areas are entirely devoted to cattle herders, these people living on milk mixed with blood to secure a sufficient protein content. Most native Africans, except those in the big towns, are farmers. Normally they are pretty well fed until problems arise—erosion, exhaustion of the soil, war, or young men going off to the Johannesburg mines. In the past much of the best land was appropriated by white settlers.

THE OWNERSHIP OF LAND

We are accustomed to parcelling land into plots and selling it, or establishing personal ownership in some way. But Africans have never divided up their territory into freeholds; they see it in terms of social relationships between groups. Thus a group known as a lineage (i.e. descended from a single known ancestor), will be associated with a certain area of land; an associated lineage (one having an ancestor in common with the first) will use another area, and so on until all the associated lineages work over an area of say 200 miles across.

This may be called a genealogical map, and it moves about the surface of the land in response to the needs of the farmers. The association of any family with a particular plot is of brief duration. It is under its control while it is cultivated but no longer. The map is seen in terms of social relationships, and the land is an aspect of the group. Nobody *owns* the land, but every member has a right to farm sufficient to support his family. These rights are inalienable. It belongs to him as a member of the lineage and as long as he remains so.

(Bohannan, *African Outline*.)

Even where it is no longer necessary to pass on to fresh ground when the area under cultivation is exhausted (the slash and burn procedure), rights in land are vested in groups rather than individuals. A religious factor now appears, since the spirits of ancestors have an effective joint interest in the land with their living descendants. We may therefore find shrines dedicated both to these ancestors and to the earth itself.

When the first European settlers arrived in Africa they were totally ignorant of these facts, but proceeded to stake out claims to tribal land, persuading illiterate native chiefs to sign appropriate deeds. The chiefs understood this only to be a concession for temporary cultivation; the idea of outright sale would have been impossible for them.

Where kingship exists, a modified form of feudalism may appear. Land held by grant from the king (even though the king does not *own* the land he administers in the name of the community) is in exchange for services; even so, the holding of such a right never amounts to ownership. Beattie, who is an authority on the Kingdom of Bungoro in East Africa, says that with regard to such a piece of land, the king, the local chief, the family or lineage cultivating it, and the man actually digging it, all have rights. No one can say in such circumstances: who owns this land?

In such communities when the agricultural way of life is well established, a more settled way of life appears than was possible in food-gathering and hunting communities like the Pygmies, the Bushmen, and the Australian aborigines who still pursue this primitive way of life. We now find a greater population density, a certain stability about the settlements, and wider scale political units than the family or clan. In some fertile areas urban districts may grow up, and where a sizeable surplus appears so does an entirely new phenomenon, leisure—a leisure class, or groups of people able to expand their activities well beyond subsistence cultivation.

WEALTH AND TRADE

Inequality. With the larger surplus, economic inequality appears. Distribution is now for the first time unequal, and a class of nobles or rich farmers and chiefs appears. Money now plays a part in the economy and can be accumulated as wealth, which, unlike food, does not decay.

Serf-like or slave-like labour, or a large class of poor persons, appears. The rich are also supported by retainers and the proceeds of taxation. They exercise authority by the aid of armed retainers.

Wealth. With the increase of wealth and the appearance of economic inequality, marked distinction in dress appears, and in some societies sumptuary laws state what you may or may not wear, according to rank.

Wealth buys women, and polygamy really implies inequality, since clearly there is no community in which the population contains three or four women for each man. Women are important because they do the work and produce children to build up the political, military, and economic power of the man or of his class. Wealth confers prestige, privileges, the right to sing songs, perform dances, boast publicly, and insult others.

Trade. Trade begins with barter or gift exchange. Island villages in New Guinea trade with each other or with offshore islands. Each item has its recognized equivalent. Every coast native has a kinsman in some offshore village. It is only with these that he makes exchanges. There is no bargaining, but hints are dropped as to what is expected in return for what is received.

Pottery, say, is taken by canoes to some neighbouring village which does not specialize in this art. The pots are then presented. The potters remain for two or three days and on the last evening receive quantities of taro or sago. Persons not related to the visitors do not take part in the negotiations.

The **market** eventually becomes the principal medium for the distribution of economic goods, affording a channel through which the products of farmers, artisans, and craftsmen flow to the ultimate consumer while the producers get what they need in return. The market is also a centre for social activities.

In Dahomey (West Africa) as many as 10,000 people pass through a town market-place on some days. Those who sell sit on the ground on mats or on low stools, the vendors of a given commodity grouped together with their wares spread about them. There is a constant hub-bub of conversation and much loud argument as bargaining proceeds.

Among the goods bought and sold are mats, pottery, native cloth, live animals, foodstuffs, cooked and uncooked, hoes, axes, knives, cala-bashes, and in addition to these native products there are now many articles of European manufacture.

OWNERSHIP AND PROPERTY

Primitive society seldom shows any indication of our Western Euro-pean and American concept of absolute personal ownership. Very few things, with the exception of weapons, tools, houses, etc., are possessed personally and unconditionally. Livestock is very seldom owned by individuals, but by the lineage or tribe. All such rights are conditional, and it takes considerable patient investigation on the spot to find out exactly what these conditions are.

With the appearance of settlements and some degree of specialization of crops, by more efficiency in agriculture and a surplus, there comes the possibility of many members of the community being set free to develop the crafts. Then the opportunity for trading appears, and also a method which seems strange to us—the distribution of the surplus *by giving it away*. Hence the *potlatch*, which we have already mentioned primarily as a way of obtaining prestige, also a good deal of feasting, gift-giving, and institutional exchanges. What is particularly strange, from our point of view, is that our type of business deal is not the basic pattern. It is not at all the principle of 'every man for himself' and 'the buyer beware' (*caveat emptor*). Personal economic advantage is not the main thing; social ends must also be served. The maintenance of good rela-tions is of the first importance, even where institutionalized exchange has its economic importance. What is really at issue is the relationship between people.

This is admirably displayed in the socio-economic exchanges of certain islanders in the Western Pacific called the *kula*, which was the subject of an epoch-making study by Malinowski.

The *kula* is a ceremonial exchange of objects of no commercial value in a circle of islands (including the Trobriands) where Malinowski carried out his investigations.[1] The object of these exchanges is not primarily economic, though this is a valuable consequence. The *kula* is

[1] A full account, based on Malinowski's own records, will be found in Field Study No. III, on page 91 of this book.

associated with many other social activities, of a ceremonial or *expressive* kind. The exchanges and the gifts are symbols of fellowship and mutual interdependence. Participation in the *kula* is also an indication of social status, and to possess many partners (in other islands to which the gifts are taken and from which other gifts are received) is to enhance one's social standing in the community. Secondly, the *kula* involves such other activities as canoe-making, and these in turn entail important cycles of economic and magical activity. Third, although *kula* valuables themselves are not traded, there is trading on *kula* expeditions, and Malinowski notes the contrast between the bargaining and haggling that takes place when ordinary goods are bartered and exchanged, and the formal ceremony of the *kula* exchanges. Fourth, the possession of a *kula* partner or partners in a foreign country provides protection from the dangers which are to be expected there from both the human and the spirit inhabitants. This leads to the final point, stressed by Marcel Mauss in his celebrated *Essai sur le don*, that the *kula* is a means to social integration; it brings people into institutionalized relationship with other people, and so, in some sense, makes them members of one society.

Malinowski insists that this is not to be explained in terms of our economic principles at all. 'Economic man' is an absurdity. Nobody is activated by motive of economic self-interest. There are always other, more highly regarded, values involved, and above all, such exchanges are the means of establishing and maintaining good social relations, mutual advantage, and peace between neighbouring communities.

Professor Raymond Firth[1] has developed this conception on the basis of his own field-work in Tikopia. Discussing the concept of *value* he points out that this for primitive peoples is not what it means for our economists. It does not mean, however, that 'primitive' means irrational, or childish, or even that it is of less significance than the conceptual patterns of Western economic life, which have been known to get into conditions of imbalance—'poverty in plenty', trade crises, overproduction—unknown to people working with a rather different view of *value*. Men in primitive societies are not, for instance, entirely concerned with *earning* a living in terms of cash. If they have economic sufficiency they see no reason why they should not enjoy themselves, or exercise 'the right to be lazy'. This infuriates white people, who in West Africa, used to impose taxes on the natives so that they would *have to work* in order to pay them.

All this is very clearly shown when we look for the thing called 'money' and discover that it doesn't exist. (An exception must be made for the Banks Islands which does use strips of shell-discs in fathom lengths as a kind of primitive money.) We value goods by having a standard substance (which theoretically is gold) in terms of which we

[1] Firth, *Elements of Social Organization*.

value other things. This allows us to state a *price* for everything, on the basis of which economic exchange takes place. Now primitive societies have no such measurement of value. There is not even any widespread system of directly matching one object of exchange or service against another by constant daily exchanges. A man makes a gift to another and may get a return through a set of other gifts and services spread over a considerable time; and some of them may come from one of the relatives. There is an idea of some equivalence. But it is not expressed in any precise terms.

A great deal of primitive exchange takes the form of present and counter-present, and it took Professor Firth a long time to understand it and *himself practice it*, as he had to, if he was to live in any kind of real relationship with his Tikopians. They would bring him some fish, as a gift. He would at once go to his store and produce a pocket-knife, or a spoon, and give it as a gift in return. If he did not, the man would turn up some days later and *ask* for something that he wanted, as a gift. At first Firth was a bit hurt at this idea of never giving a present without expecting an equivalent in return; but as he got used to it, he saw that really it worked very well indeed, and made for good feeling and mutual advantage.

In some cases there is, in addition to this form of exchange, a process of barter by haggling, which is sharply distinguished from it, and is regarded with suspicion and some distaste. Firth, in 'Orientation in Economic Life', in *The Institution of Primitive Society*, sums it up rather well:

> The technological skills and productive capacities of primitive societies extract from their economic relations rich and varied satisfactions. They make their economic relations do social work. . . . There is not necessarily any attempt to get an exact equation between amounts of labour contributed and what is received. . . . The concept of rationality (in exchange) is not absent but must be understood to include immaterial as well as material advantage. Between the economic interest of 'the market', 'which knows nothing of honour' as Max Weber says, and the interests of the social order where honour rules, there is often contrast and even conflict. Man may seek his individual gain in primitive as in civilized society. But unless there are external pressures (from Western economic interests) which tend to break up the form of the society and disturb its values, the interests of the social order tend to win.

SOCIETY AND THE DOMESTICATION OF ANIMALS

When man's relation to the animals passes over from hunting and destroying to herding and breeding, as it does in the last and most successful phase of primitive economy, a new factor is introduced into social life. These domesticated animals breed freely in captivity and are readily tamed. As a consequence they become adapted, physically and in disposition and conditioned behaviour, to human existence. The dog, indeed, becomes the 'friend' of man; the horse becomes almost part of his personality. The term 'chivalry' stands for the horsed nobleman. The Arab, the nomad Mongol, the horsed invaders of Genghis Khan are what they are because of their horses. In agriculture the ox and, later, the horse, play indispensable roles. The introduction of the war chariot, drawn by horses, marks as great a revolution in war as the tank.

Wherever the large livestock species were added to his resources, man acquired further aids to transport, vital sources of food, materials for tent covers, cord, and leather containers.

The *reindeer* supports itself, where dogs have to be fed. The reindeer is invaluable for transport and adds milk and flesh to the larder.

The *camel* can travel at four miles an hour for weeks, keeping a steady pace for eight or ten hours a day. It finds its own food and can go without water for a long time. It also provides milk, and its hair is used for cordage and for tents.

Whole tribes of pastoral nomads have practically abandoned agriculture. They live on mutton, beef, horseflesh, milk, and cheese, depending almost entirely on their flocks and herds.

They need *large* flocks, because they have no other means of subsistence; therefore, the nomad must have abundant grazing grounds. This requires a migratory existence. Thus his whole psychology and social habit is conditioned by his pastoral life.

Of great historical interest is the appearance of conflict with the sedentary farmer, and in consequence the incursions into more settled agricultural areas by the raiding and predatory nomad.

A capricious irrationality checks the full and most economical exploitation of domestic beasts. This takes many forms and shows the enormous importance of custom in determining mental attitudes and values. The Chinese have kept cattle for thousands of years, but they have never milked cows or any other animal. Many sheep breeders never made woollen textiles. Eggs are loathed by some tribes. Fowl may be kept not for laying or for eating but for auguries. (See Field Study No. VIII, *Witchcraft, Oracles, and Magic among the Azande.*) In Turkestan people live on mare's milk; Europeans never use it. Some African tribes use butter only as a cosmetic. The Egyptians make no use of swine. Many cattle breeders don't eat meat, accumulating their herds for sheer acquisitiveness. Mutton is taboo for the sheep-raising Baganda of East Africa.

THE EVOLUTION OF CULTURE

The Function of Culture. Culture is the mechanism whose function it is to make life secure and continuous for human beings. It is based on a particular way of obtaining and utilizing energy, and its success depends largely on the efficiency of the method.

Other factors remaining constant, culture evolves as the amount of energy harnessed *per capita* per year is increased, or as the efficiency of the instrumental means of putting the energy to work is increased.

(Leslie A. White, *The Science of Culture*.)

Culture and Energy. As the discovery of new modes of subsistence and sources of energy increase the efficiency of culture, the whole pattern changes and new principles and laws come into existence.

The degree of cultural development is therefore to be measured in terms of needed goods and services produced per unit of human labour, by the amount of food produced, the efficiency of shelter, transport, and control over disease.

The amount of energy available at the food-gathering stage is very small, amounting over the whole population to about one-twentieth horse-power *per capita*.

Such a system, depending for its energy on man-power alone, cannot develop very far. Fire, water, and wind were utilized as sources of power to a very limited and insignificant extent during the first hundreds of thousands of years in which culture existed.

Energy from Plants and Animals. Plants, however, are a source of energy, for their starches and sugars contain the energy of the sunlight by means of which they were built up. At first this energy was only available in wild plants, but the yield of plant food in energy was greatly increased by the discovery of agriculture. Cultivation, fertilization, and irrigation, of course, increased the yield. All the great civilizations of antiquity were brought into being by the cultivation of cereals.

With the domestication of animals, the muscular power of oxen and horses became available, and, with the discovery of sails, the wind became available. Windmills, however, were a very late invention.

The Fuel Revolution. These sources of energy set the limit to the achievements of society down to the Middle Ages. Culture was able to surge forward once again, as it had done when the greater river-valley civilizations, based on agriculture, came into existence, only when entirely new forms of energy were tapped in the form of **coal, oil,** and **gas.** From these sources arose the 'fuel revolution' of modern times, which is still in progress and is likely to receive a great new impetus from the harnessing of atomic energy.

FIELD STUDIES

A great deal of information that anthropologists have gathered about primitive cultures dating back thousands of years has come from field studies of civilizations living at varying cultural levels. These field studies are the backbone of anthropological knowledge and are important in understanding the culture of other societies as well as our own.

FIELD STUDY NO. I—THE ESKIMOS

A simple, food-gathering, hunting community, little removed from Stone Age man, but receiving the impact of modern civilization.

The Eskimos inhabit the northern shores of Canada, Alaska, Greenland, and Russia. They are seldom found far inland, but recent studies have been made of one rapidly declining inland tribe.

The word Eskimo means '*eaters of raw flesh*', as indeed they are. They are engaged solely in hunting and fishing, getting most of what they eat from the sea. No cultivation of plants is possible. They live, therefore, on seals, whales, polar bears, and reindeer. They use animal oil for their lamps, which are used for cooking, heating, and light.

As a people they are skilful in their limited crafts, intelligent, lawabiding, friendly and hospitable. The custom of lending wives to visitors is fairly general.

They possess an extensive folklore and their religion appears to be a vague animism with belief in good and evil spirits. An important type of medicine man is the *shaman*. They have no system of government.

Their health is precarious. Tuberculosis and starvation take a heavy toll.

The Eskimo language is complex, as are many primitive tongues. Their daily vocabulary exceeds 10,000 words—four times that of the average English-speaking person.

Living in a very specialized habitat, they have developed extraordinary adaptation to its requirements. Their dome-shaped snow houses—the igloos—are models of effective engineering technique, using the only material available. The use of walrus ivory for sled runners, or even for eye shields to protect against sun glare, is ingenious and effective.

It is interesting that Siberian tribes, such as the Chukchi, live quite differently, although their surroundings are much the same. The Siberian tribes inhabit tents or shelters made of skins. They are herders of reindeer rather than hunters. Yet their method of survival is as effective as that of the Eskimos.

The People of the Deer. Against this background let us look at one *inland* tribe of Eskimos about which Farley Mowat has made a special investigation. They are 'the people of the deer', who traditionally hunted the great herds of caribou which migrated across northern Canada each year. Upon this animal they were completely dependent. This tribe, while recognizably Eskimo, lived exclusively by hunting, with bow and copper-tipped arrow, and with the spear. They never used the harpoon or killed seals. They lived in leaky tents and igloos (often of stone rather than snow). They dressed in two suits of flexible caribou skin and used the dog sleigh. They were peaceful, not only among themselves, but between tribes. There appears to be no evidence of innate aggressiveness.

This tribe was once composed of 1,000 people, but has now been reduced to about 20. This is mainly because of its dependence on *one source of food* in a barren land. The herds of caribou were recklessly slaughtered when the tribe switched from the bow to the rifle. The tribe then abandoned this form of hunting and shot silver foxes which they brought in to trading stations. Under declining economic conditions these stations were closed and the tribe found itself in a desperate situation. Its men had lost their skill with the bow and no longer had money with which to buy ammunition. The caribou grew scarcer and the tribe starved or succumbed to disease. A small fishing industry was set up for the survivors but failed. Thus a tribe which could have maintained itself with the bow has drifted practically into extinction.

The Greenland Eskimos. In contrast we may note what Denmark has done for the Greenland Eskimo. Here shrimp and cod fisheries have been established and canneries set up. There is some mining of cryolite, lead, and zinc. Present plans call for the establishment of reindeer farms, fox farms, and mink farms. The native crafts have been organized and now produce model kayaks and sledges from walrus tusks, paper knives, ash trays, sealskin bags, belts and shoes and various kinds of beadwork. There is organized export of all these things and of furs, blubber, eider down, and sperm oil. In exchange the Eskimos can buy a variety of goods imported from Denmark and sold at certain stores.

Several small hospitals have been set up, but there is still much tuberculosis.

The country now has all the main institutions of a modern democracy and sends two representatives to the Lower House of the Danish Parliament.

Housing is very bad, but is improving somewhat. Living conditions are inferior and sanitary conditions bad. The language is now written and printed and books are available in small quantities.

The Samoyedes of Northern Siberia. The Royal Institute of Anthropology (London) has recently published information concerning a somewhat different development in northern Siberia. Here reindeer breeding has been developed on a large scale among tribes almost identical racially with the Eskimos. A society for this purpose, composed of twenty families with a herd of 3000 reindeer, was founded in 1930. A settled base has been set up near the routes of the grazing and migrating herds and near fishable rivers. The herds are still moved south in the winter and back again in the spring, but those not engaged in this task, instead of wandering back and forth, nomad fashion, with the herds, fish and breed cows and fur-bearing animals. Here the beginning of a modern, civilized community is in process of formation.

There are now five times as many reindeer. Education and health have made advances. The economy has now definitely emerged above the subsistence level. The arctic is coming to life.

FIELD STUDY NO. II—THE SHOSHONES

A tribe of American Indians of a rather backward cultural level, showing many primitive characteristics.

The Shoshones are descended from lowly hunters and food-gatherers living in the western deserts of North America. Some 600 years ago one section of these Indians moved into Central Mexico and founded the **Aztec** culture. The next migrant group were the **Comanches** of the south-western plains, who became robbers and fighters. Finally the **Shoshones** were left; they remained in the desert and advanced very little. They therefore preserve something of the primitive culture from which the three tribes were derived.

This demonstrates how little ancestry has to do with culture—these three totally different peoples were racially similar and were of a common origin.

The Great Basin Shoshones were called the **Diggers** because they moved from place to place seeking roots, seeds, and nuts, of which they gathered a hundred different species. In this they resembled the Australian aborigines. The roots were extracted with a simple digging stick, probably the simplest wooden implement known. Seeds, of which those of the sunflower were the most liked, were collected with the aid of a woven basket. Insects were also eaten, just as the Australians eat the witchetty grub. Among the Shoshones grasshoppers were a popular article of food; they were driven inward by a large circle of men, women, and children until they all fell into a pit in the middle. They were then roasted and eaten. Ants were also a favoured delicacy and small rodents were trapped and eaten. Fear of starvation constantly haunted them, as it does the more primitive Eskimos. All this, of course, refers to a not-too-distant past still remembered by Shoshone Indians.

These people were semi-nomads and each group required a considerable area from which to obtain nourishment; nevertheless a given band kept to its own territory, with which it was intimately familiar and where some stores of food might be concealed. They did not, however, own the land in any way. Even the roving groups did not claim ownership of the land they wandered over.

Again, like the Australians, they constructed a simple windbreak for shelter in the summer. Their highest attainment in housing was a bee-hive-shaped grass hut. Australians wear practically nothing, but keep themselves warm, even when on trek, by carrying firesticks. The Shoshones, living in a more temperate climate, wore rabbit-skin robes.

Government was very simple. As among the Australian aborigines, it was the elders who provided leadership; the chief was the only leading one among them.

Few pure food-gathering communities still exist. We may mention the African Bushmen, Negritos with Mongoloid eye form and skin colour, a race that has been in South Africa for at least 15,000 years. They have left some of the most remarkable rock paintings in the world.

FIELD STUDY NO. III—THE TROBRIAND ISLANDERS

Malinowski's classic study of the Trobriand social system (*Argonauts of the Western Pacific*) admirably illustrates the importance of a total *pattern* or design for living based on a system of economic activity appropriate to a simple agricultural community. This study reveals the profound difference that exists between the Trobrianders and ourselves both as to institutions and ideas. We seem to live in two contrasting worlds.

The Trobriand Islands. The Trobriand Islands are about 120 miles north of Eastern New Guinea. They are flat, fertile, and densely populated. The natives live by agriculture and fishing and eat the fruit of certain trees. They are expert sailors and they have developed a remarkable system of trading with neighbouring islands.

The Kula. The islanders and the inhabitants of some neighbouring islands form a kind of league for the exchange of certain ceremonial objects, long necklaces with red shells and bracelets with white shells. In the system of exchange, the *kula*, the necklaces pass from island to island one way round the circuit, and the bracelets pass the other way round.

The objects have no practical value, only a ritual and prestige value. A man gets great renown by receiving, possessing, and then passing on these articles. He always has a special partner on each island whom he visits, and the exchanges take place with formality and without haggling. When the ritual exchange is over, ordinary commercial exchange begins with plenty of bargaining.

Overseas Trading. To carry out these exchanges, the chiefs of the villages organize large trading expeditions. This means the preparation of canoes, the knowledge of magical spells, the accumulation of food, and so on. The spells have myths accounting for their origin.

The partners have heavy responsibilities in that they must act as hosts, patrons, and allies to one another in a land of danger and insecurity, and this creates social ties and establishes a system of friendly relations between neighbouring islands.

The articles vary in size and value. They are carried from one island to another in large fleets of canoes. The exchanges are made publicly and with great ceremony. Both they and the expeditions are accompanied by the performance of much ritual and many magical rites.

The *kula* exchange therefore provides the incentive for many of their other activities and helps to unify them into an ordered whole.

Kula as a Social Pattern. In one way or another the whole economic and social life is determined by and woven into this curious system of trading. The whole thing forms a system because each activity is dependent on the others, and the function of each is the part it plays in the total set of activities which have a direct or indirect bearing on the exchange of the ritual objects of the *kula*.

A number of important social and ethical principles are implied in this social pattern.

1. The principle of *reciprocity*, according to which it is the duty of a partner to make a return gift of equal value in due course.

2. The principle of *credit* and commercial integrity involved in the transaction.

3. The principle of *interdependence*, by which almost every aspect of life, from religion to economics, from canoe building to agriculture, from magic to social rank, intertwines and receives mutual support.

4. The principle of *prestige*. This depends not so much on the exclusive ownership of wealth as on possessing and being in the position *to give away* valuable objects. The higher the person's status the greater the obligation to give generously and with good grace. Generosity thus becomes the highest value in their moral code.

Kinship and Magic. Malinowski's study also covers both the system of magic and religion and the kinship system of the islanders. It must not be thought that these are something isolated from and independent of the *kula* system; on the contrary they are closely bound up with it at every point. One's family position involves many social obligations and duties in the way of work and economic organization, and certain responsibilities in the exchange system, while magic and religion play their essential part at every stage of social and economic life. To these two topics we shall return in subsequent chapters.

SUGGESTED FURTHER READING

Benedict, Ruth, *Patterns of Culture*. Routledge & Kegan Paul: London, 1934.

Bohannan, P., *African Outline*. Penguin Books: London, 1966.

Evans-Pritchard, E. E., *Social Anthropology*. Cohen & West: London, 1951.

Firth, Raymond, *Elements of Social Organisation*. Watts & Co.: London, 1951.

Forde, C. D., *Habitat, Economy and Society*. Methuen: London, 1930.

Gluckman, Max, *Institutions of Primitive Society*. Oxford University Press: London, 1963.

Kluckhohn, C., *Mirror for Man*. Harrap: London, 1950.

Lowie, R. H., *Social Organisation*. Routledge & Kegan Paul: London, 1942.

Malinowski, B., *Argonauts of the Western Pacific*. Routledge & Kegan Paul: London, 1960.

Radcliffe-Brown, A. R., *Structure and Function in Primitive Society*. Cohen & West: London, 1925.

CHAPTER EIGHT

MARRIAGE, KINSHIP AND THE CLAN

THE FAMILY

The basis of every human society, from the most primitive to the most complicated, is the family. There is no form of society known to us in which this is not the case.

There is no evidence of primitive promiscuity or group marriage. Freud's theory of the primeval horde in which the old male had all the wives until he was killed by his sons does not tally with any form of society known to anthropological research. On the contrary the family, consisting of at least parents and children, is a universal social unit, the one social phenomenon we are justified in calling 'natural'.

But the family can take many forms, and not all of these forms are identical with the family as we know it.

The Conjugal Family. We are perfectly familiar with this type of family unit. It consists of a man and woman and their children.

It serves a number of important social functions:

1. The co-operative division of labour between man and woman.
2. The protection and nurture of the young over a considerable period.
3. The primary education of the children in social habits, customs, and basic knowledge.

As we shall see, the conjugal family may extend its limits so that more than one woman feels a direct responsibility for the child, and more than one man can fill the role of the father. Where this is so the actual parents still maintain their special relationship and responsibilities.

It was no doubt the discovery of the extended family which led some anthropologists to speak of group marriage and primitive promiscuity. This was simply due to lack of understanding.

The conjugal family has certain limitations:

1. It is not a permanent affair, for it lasts for slightly more than one generation. It is a discontinuous social unit.
2. It can break up, owing to marital disagreement.

The extended family and certain special forms of the primitive family provide safeguards against these dangers.

Polygyny. This type of system also produces a conjugal family, but there is more than one wife. (This is generally but inaccurately called **polygamy.**) It is a rare form, since most people must be monogamously married because the sexes are roughly equal in number. Therefore it exists only where a wealthy minority can obtain wives when other poorer men are deprived. Sometimes it reflects the inferiority of women in a particular society and indicates that wives may be purchased. But where there is a good deal of inter-tribal fighting there will be fewer men than women and polygyny corrects the imbalance.

A man with many wives can present a richer and better-equipped household to the world. A man who has many wives has great prestige.

Women do not object to their husbands' taking on additional wives. The women of the Kikuyu informed a visiting anthropologist that they never married anyone they did not want to, and that they liked their husbands to have as many wives as possible. In fact the poverty-stricken condition of the 'rich' white man with respect to wives aroused considerable interest. Polygyny is approved by African women for these reasons:

(*a*) It implies a superior social position.
(*b*) It means easier domestic chores, since the work is shared.
(*c*) If one wife is indisposed, the husband can find a substitute.
(*d*) If one is ill or dies, there are others to carry on.

The relation between co-wives is usually friendly, but competition for the husband's attention is possible. To meet this difficulty the wives may be graded; competition is thus lessened because it then occurs only between those who consider their rights equal. Sometimes wives have separate huts and domestic utensils. A wise husband will try to be impartial among his wives, but the potential instability of the system is generally recognized.

Polyandry. Is the reverse situation ever found—one wife and several husbands? Very rarely, but it has been found in Tibet and among the Todas, who live in the Nilgri hills of India. Here all the brothers marry the same woman. This is due to a shortage of women as a consequence of female infanticide. All the brothers live together and share their wife without friction or jealousy.

Wife Hospitality. It is a widespread primitive practice (as, for example, among the Eskimos) for men to share their wives with other men on special occasions, such as the visit of an over-night guest. This has been explained as a necessary pledge that a guest is a friend and not an enemy.

The Kinship Group. The bond of kinship extends to a great range of relatives so that a whole group of related persons is recognized as an entity. This is the extended family. In our society an extended family is bilateral, which means it includes relatives of both the husband and the wife. In primitive society the extended family usually includes the relatives of either the husband or the wife, not of both.

Moreover in any primitive family group of this kind, all the men of a certain status are classified as 'fathers' and all the women as 'mothers'. This system provides substitutes for the real father if he is unable to function, extends the range of responsibility, and thus gives greater security to everybody, especially to the children. Kinship is the rod on which one leans throughout life. No one can be relativeless while the community itself exists.

In some communities everyone with whom the individual comes into contact is a relative. Moreover everyone knows his own status and the status of everyone he meets. This sets precise standards of behaviour—the degree of respect, the duties owed, and so on. If you do not know exactly who a man is (a 'brother', an 'uncle', or a 'father') you do not know how to treat him, and all intercourse is impossible.

The kinship system offers a great bond of unity and has considerable survival value among primitive people. The kinship system of the primitive community is not based on a competitive, individualistic society. Survival in the struggle for existence is not dependent on greater ferocity, but is based on co-operation and mutual support. The kinship group, unlike the single family, is continuous; it stretches back into the past and goes on into the future. The extended-family system gives greater security than the ordinary conjugal family.

The very complex pattern which the anthropologist disentangles, abstracts, and turns into a sort of algebraic problem, bears no relation to what is in the minds of the people concerned. They do not so much think of the actual relationship in terms of a genealogical tree showing whose second cousin twice removed someone happens to be. It is conceived wholly in terms of rights and duties. Uncles and aunts are persons with specific responsibilities. What is indicated is not a physical kinship, but a pattern defining a person's behaviour towards different people and their behaviour and responsibilities to him.

Why people fill a certain role may be shown in a kinship table, but how this pattern is presented may be in the form of a myth. The real explanation, which is entirely functional and social, settles the questions of who obeys, who are friends, whom you marry, from whom you inherit, and who tells you what to do and whom you may tell what to do. All duties are related to kinship, so are all questions of authority, subordination of economic exchanges, and in fact the whole way of life.

Joint Families. A rather different form of extended family is found where all the brothers with their wives and children continue to live with the father, either in the same house or in a cluster of adjoining houses. Often the earnings of all the brothers are turned over to the father.

There may also be a kinship group consisting of a woman, her brothers, and her offspring. In some cases the house, the stored corn, and other such property belong to the women of the household, the grandmother and her sisters, her daughters, and their daughters. Husbands may come and go, but the women stick together. It is their brothers who are united with the household in all important affairs. This system also gives greater permanence and security than the ordinary conjugal family.

The Unilateral Family Group. Of very great importance is the kinship group that is organized through the male line back for several generations—**the patrilineal family,** or through the female line—**the matrilineal family.**

This system excludes from the family many of those who would belong to our type of *bilateral* family. For example: in a matrilineal family the husband and wives of the grandmother's children (the mothers and fathers) are not full members of the family, because in such a society the members of a family are not related to their brothers- and sisters-in-law. A man's sister's children are closely related to him, but his brother's children are not closely related to him.

All this may seem very complicated to us, but to the members of such a family everything is obvious, logical, and simple. We, for our part, would confuse certain primitive tribes because, for instance, it is not clear whether by 'grandfather' we mean our father's father or our mother's father. This leads to what is called *the classificatory principle, which puts people into certain family categories*—often ignoring actual blood relationship. Thus in a matrilineal family all a man's mother's sisters are 'mothers' and all their children are his sisters and brothers (*not* his cousins). This man traces his descent through his mother and her mother and so on, not through his father, nor through his parents, as we do.

The Matrilocal Family. Now it may well happen that the married couple live with the wife's group. All the husbands of the women in such a family either visit their wives periodically or come and live with the matrilineal family. The women do not leave their families and go and live with their husbands. In such communities the daughter is greatly valued. She will always remain with the family and will not be lost at marriage, whereas the boys will go to live with the families of their wives. A daughter is complete fulfilment to the mother. She is her mother's constant companion in joy and sorrow, additional hands and feet for an overburdened body, security in old age, contributor of children to her clan.

In some matrilineal families the mother rules, but most anthropologists do not believe that true matriarchy exists. Supported by her brothers, the mother manages her children without the father, for he is but a stranger from outside, just as her brothers are strangers to the women with whom they go forth to consort. Among the Zunis the power of divorce remains with the woman. If she doesn't like her husband, she puts his belongings outside the door and thus indicates that he is no longer welcome.

The Patrilocal Family. The tracing of descent through the male line exclusively gives us the **patrilineal** family, and this may be also **patrilocal,** the women coming and living with their husbands' families.

Lineage and Clan. A **lineage** is a kinship group descended from a known ancestor so that the whole sequence of ancestors for five or six generations is known. That relationship, as we have seen, may be traced exclusively through either the female or the male line.

A **clan** is a much larger kinship group, in which all actual lineal relationship with the ancestors is lost, but all the members are *supposed* to be descended from one man. There were many examples of this among the tribes of biblical Israel and among the ancient Greeks.

There will usually be a rich mythology recounting the origin of the clan and relating the exploits of its mighty ancestors.

The Care of Children. As we have already pointed out, the extension of the category 'father' and 'mother' to many other than the actual parents results in the sharing of responsibility and the strengthening of security. Thus a man's sister, mother, father, brother, and his wife's brother, mother, father, and sister, not to mention several others, consider themselves responsible in some measure for the welfare of his children. This applies even though the children of one line may not be the concern of the other line; there may not be a strong affection between sisters and their children.

When children are thus protected and educated by a large circle of relatives, and when they are equally at home in a variety of homes or even villages, the biological family of man, wife, and children ceases to be the kind of institution it is in our society.

This arrangement also reduces the necessity for the permanence of the biological family. This is particularly the case in a matrilineal family, because a group of sisters living together have stronger bonds of affection for each other's children than would a miscellaneous assortment of wives assembled with a patrilineal family.

Of particular significance in a great many primitive societies is the relationship of *the mother's brother* to her children and to the matrilineal family. Where the family is matrilineal, it is this man who is the head of the family. This is because the husband's real house is that of his mother. In the dwelling of his wife and children he has no status except the position he may enjoy as a result of long residence and the personal regard in which he may be held. The mother's brother is responsible for the children and it is he who exercises authority over them; he controls the family finances and speaks for the family.

Exogamy. In a primitive society one cannot marry whom one likes. One cannot marry anyone in one's own group. Marriage must be out of the group, hence the term 'exogamy'. In other words there is a segment of the community from which no mate can be sought and a remaining portion from which the mate must be obtained. Lineages and clans are almost always exogamous.

This serves a double purpose. In the first place it prevents the complications of sexual relations within a close association such as the family and the extended family. But in the second place it establishes friendly relations with groups which might otherwise be regarded with hostility. It establishes co-operative relations with the group to which so many members of the family have gone as brides and husbands. This makes for mutual aid in hunting, in food gathering, and in defence. The alternative to marrying out is to be starved out or killed. The practice of outgroup marriages thus allies two separate social units, strengthens the position of each, and adds to their ability to cope with the external forces that confront them.

Marriage may thus be regarded as a method of *exchange* between separate groups of men. One group receives a wife, the other obtains a bride-price in exchange. As Lévi-Strauss describes it, it becomes 'a mechanism which "pumps" women out of their consanguineous families to redistribute them in affinal groups'.

Incest. Exogamy means that all marriage within the group is regarded with the same horror as we would regard the mating of father and daughter. Incest is the term applied to any such prohibited union. It is essential to an understanding of this question to realize that prohibition extends to those cousins who are held to be within the family, even though they may be several degrees distant and biologically hardly related at all. For instance, it is almost universally held that a man may not marry the daughter of his mother's sister, who is a *parallel cousin*, for she is a 'sister', or any second or third cousin only distantly related through his great grandmother; but he may marry the daughter of his mother's brother, who is a *cross cousin*. (An exception to this is the Bedouin, who practise preferential parallel cousin marriage, known as **endogamy.**)

Much has been said about instinctive repugnance to incestuous unions, and Freud in particular has based his theory of the Oedipus complex upon this, making it the source of very powerful taboos. This view receives no support from anthropology for the following reasons:

1. It is not an instinctive repugnance, nor is the inclination so to mate a perverted instinct. It arises out of propinquity and opportunity. It is condemned for *social* and not for biological reasons. It would tend to disrupt the family from within through sexual jealousy and rivalry. Moreover it keeps the bonds of union within one small group, instead of forging bonds with outside groups, thus expanding society.

2. There is no evidence for biological ill effects from close interbreeding (except in rare cases where negative or recessive genes are involved—that is, where both partners suffer from a constitutional

defect which may be passed on to their offspring). The available evidence shows that in the overwhelming majority of cases there are no unfortunate results to incestuous mating. Would savages, in this case, be likely to find any correlation? It should also be noted that incest is just as strongly prohibited where paternity is not recognized as where it is.

3. Intermarriage between very close relatives is not only allowed but considered desirable among many peoples today, notably within Indian castes. In Western civilization social classes are prone to exhibit similar tendencies without recourse to explicitly prescribed rules. Its roots are in the desire to retain the exclusive and distinctive qualities of self-regarding in-groups.

Incest is regarded by all primitive people as a worse crime than murder. It pollutes the tribe and this happens whether it was intentional or not as in the well-known Oedipus legend. But the reason is not that it is instinctively repugnant; it is purely a practical question of preventing the disruption of the family.

Preferential Mating. We have already mentioned the prohibition of marriage with *parallel cousins* (the daughter of a man's mother's sister or father's brother), and the correctness of marriage with a *cross cousin* (the daughter of his mother's brother or his father's sister). Thus a man may marry his mother's brothers' daughter, who is his niece, and this is regarded as quite proper. The result is to create what would appear to us to be a queer state of affairs, for his mother's brother is not his wife's father, and his wife's mother is his father's sister.

So narrow is the circle of inter-marriages that many relatives are found fulfilling what to us would appear to be more than one kinship role. There are other preferred or required marriages, for example:

(*a*) **The Levirate.** After the death of her husband a woman may be required to marry his brother. This has the useful effect of maintaining the link between two kin groups that was established through the original marriage.

(*b*) **The Sororate.** Here a sister is substituted for the deceased wife.

The Classificatory Relationship System. This complex system which is unlike anything in Western culture is necessary for the organized cohesion of the tribe and inter-tribal relations. All relatives are classed in categories which follow strictly logical patterns, but the attitudes to one another are unfamiliar to us. Thus, though a child knows perfectly well who his mother is, his mother's sister will fulfil the functions of a second mother. In the same way his mother's sisters' children will be called by the same term as his own brothers and sisters, and treated as though they were. The mother has many distant 'sisters' (whom we would call cousins), whom the child also calls 'mother'. In the same way the child has many additional fathers (in name and function) other than his real father, including all his father's brothers and cousins.

But these close relations on the father's side are not in the same category as those on the mother's side, and the child's attitude to each group of close relatives is different.

Thus there are not only two different types of cousin (cross cousins and parallel cousins), but two different types of uncle and aunt. The mother's brother is in quite a different relation to the child from that of the father's brother, who is a kind of 'father' and not an uncle at all; this particular uncle may well have more responsibilities for the child than his actual father.

Marriage. It might be supposed that we all know what marriage signifies and that our account of the family might well begin with this assumption. It should now be plain that marriage among primitive people is not what it is to the romantic novelist. Love is not the basis of marriage, though it may well follow marriage. No society could afford to depend on such a fickle and ephemeral sentiment as the basis of an important institution.

Marriage and the family are society's first and most fundamental way of making provision for its economic needs. Sex is by no means the most significant fact about it. In fact its physiological significance may not be known. Marriage, to the anthropologist, is an institution based on economic organization, concerned with division of labour, care of women in pregnancy and while nursing, and the protection and education of children.

Marriage as a Relationship. Marriage is a group affair—the individual has little choice—and affection is not one of the values expected from it. Indeed affection and comradeship are provided by separate institutions and associations.

The husband reserves his friendship for his male companions and his affection for his sisters and other members of his father's family. The wife bestows her affection on her children and her brothers and her companionship on her female friends. She continues to worship the spiritual beings associated with her father's family; it is to her brothers and her other near kin that she turns for advice in perplexity and flees for help and protection if she finds life too difficult.

Marriage is basically a secular rather than a religious affair, as it has come to be in our society. It is a matter of reciprocal obligations between two clans. It is a contract validated by economic exchanges and mutual services. It may, however, be accompanied by magico-religious ceremonies. Among the Bantu people, sacrifices are made to ancestral gods with a prayer offered for the prosperity and future welfare of the bride.

In primitive marriage ceremonies nothing is said about mutual affection or regard. The woman has done her duty by her husband if she cultivates his fields, cooks his food, and rears his children. He has done his duty by her if he supplies her with a hut, cattle, and other necessities.

The marriage relationship is closely bound up with the division of labour; men do one kind of work, women another. Men also do the heavier work of hunting, fishing and building; women are immobilized for considerable periods by child-bearing and the care of infants. In the event the different roles become traditionally and firmly established.

The question of *status* depends on whether the family is matrilineal or patrilineal. In a matrilineal society although the husband rules, the woman's brothers hold paternal authority. Women often play a leading part in retail trade, and among the Ibo of Nigeria they have their own societies, manage their own affairs and own property.

Relations with the 'In-Laws'. These are regarded as strangers with whom special relations of politeness and obligation (providing one with a useful wife) are necessary. There will be a strict etiquette to prescribe correct behaviour which will require a man to treat his wife's father with deference but never with intimacy. In a patrilineal society he will avoid all contact with his wife's mother and will never speak to her directly, or, in some cases, even mention her name!

Bride Price. If a woman is lost to her clan, the husband's clan must pay compensation or 'bride-price'. This is not a purchase in any sense— the woman is not being sold in the marriage market—it means that women have a value both to the family or clan they leave and to that to which they go.

The bride's family has lost a working member and a potential child-bearer and must be compensated for this loss. The kinsman of the bride-groom all contribute to the bride-price and the kinsmen of the bride all share it. This becomes security for the bridegroom's good behaviour, for if he maltreats his wife she may leave him and the bride-price will not be re-paid. But if she behaves badly, she goes back and it will be re-paid.

The payment emphasizes the fact that marriage does not concern the marrying pair alone. Marriage is an alliance between two kin groups in which the couple concerned is merely the most conspicuous link. The man marries not only his bride but all her relatives as well.

Bride-price also cements the links in the web of kinship, allaying disputes and hostility and imposing a check on the disruptive tendencies of intergroup conflict. The provision of the price, whether in money or cattle or other commodities, is made by a number of the bride's relatives and benefits as many persons on the other side. It involves a number of kinsmen in a network of economic obligations and experiences.

It also helps to consolidate marriage, for having received the bride-price, her relatives do not want to see her return for they would then have to return the bride-price. So divorce is a rare thing in societies where the bride-price is an essential feature of the marriage contract, as it is in three tribes out of four.

(*Recent studies by Leach show that this theory does not cover all cases of bride price.*)

Premarital Relations. In primitive societies premarital relations among the younger, unmarried persons are sanctioned, and in some cases are general, though regulated. This must be related to the sharp divisions between marriage as an economic institution and sexual gratification.

Premarital intercourse is therefore not taken too seriously and among adolescents is an aspect of courting experience, or simply a matter of indifference.

Age of Marriage. Primitive people marry young. An unmarried person as old as seventeen or eighteen is likely to be a person in some manner inadequate. The lowlier the economy the more necessary it is that every-one be married, so as to function most effectively in productive work. The young begin to participate in general adult activities at an early age, learning the techniques of hunting and fishing or women's work; they are therefore soon ready for marriage. Widows and widowers remarry promptly. There are no bachelors or spinsters, but rather there is a place in the community for everyone.

This reflects, as we have already seen, a far less romantic conception of marriage than that which popular art and literature encourage amongst us. But the emotional responses of people who live under entirely different conditions cannot be judged by the measuring rod of the emotional responses that are engendered by our own heritage of values and conditions of living. Our customs have made our values and emotional responses seem right and natural, but the customs of other peoples make their values and emotions seem just as right and natural to them.

FIELD STUDY NO. IV—FAMILY AND COMMUNITY IN SOUTHERN IRELAND

This pre-war study of a rural community in southern Ireland shows how the form of the society and the lives of its members must be related to the background of the relations of blood and marriage exhibited by these peasant people.

Southern Ireland is a Catholic country, largely agricultural and poorly developed industrially. The population has been steadily declin-ing for many years, largely because of emigration, but also because of too few marriages and too late marriages. In 1841 the population was 6,500,000; in 1941 it was 3,000,000. This decline has taken place while other nations, many of comparable size and also mainly agricultural, have made great advances both in population and in economic pros-perity.

It should be stated that some of the Catholic clergy are well aware of the situation, deplore it, and are making strenuous efforts by educational and social organizations to improve it. The facts and figures given below have been compiled and published by a group of distinguished Irish priests and writers (Father John O'Brien, *The Vanishing Irish*, 1948).

The average rate of emigration from 1946 onwards was 24,000 a year. If emigration were to cease, the decline in population would cease, but the population would increase only if normal marriage relations came about. The marriage system that is peculiar to Ireland is partly a reflection of agricultural poverty and partly a reason for Ireland's social decay.

A priest writes: 'A ride through the Irish countryside is a melancholy experience today. Everywhere the discerning traveller sees signs of abandonment, decay and incipient death creeping like paralysis over what was once a great and populous nation.'

The situation is revealed in the following statistics:

80% of males between 25 and 30 are unmarried;
62% of males between 30 and 35 are unmarried;
50% of males between 35 and 40 are unmarried.

This is a larger proportion of unmarried persons of all ages than in any other country.

The marriage rate is far below that of all other European countries.

Why do so few Irish marry? The reason is to be found partly in the economic situation and partly in the system of marriage and inheritance, but these forces interact.

Economic. 75 per cent of the young people in rural Ireland are unable to settle down because of economic conditions. Agricultural poverty is the real deterrent. Ireland has more reclaimable wasteland than all of Central Europe combined.

Father Edmund Murphy alleges that Irish farmers produced 250,000 acres of grain in 1952 with only 50 per cent of their land in tillage, and that twice as many acres could have been worked if more time and labour had been spent on the idle acreage.

(*The following study based on field work by Arensberg and Kimball was made in 1937. Since then considerable economic development has taken place as a result of German investment in industry. The conditions described continued until well after 1948.*)

Marriage and Inheritance. The chief custom in the way of normal marriage is the one by which the parents retain the ownership and administration of their little farms even until they are in their seventies and eighties. Meanwhile the son who is to succeed his father is prevented from introducing a new mistress into the house. He cannot marry. He usually abandons prospects of marriage until his parents retire or die.

The parents still retain the exclusive right of admitting or rejecting the proposed daughter-in-law. She must be their choice, not his, and before she can be accepted she must be endowed with certain qualifications, not least of which is a handsome dowry.

Relations of Kindred. The farm always passes to the selected son and to *one* son only. Brothers, until the selection of the inheritor, occupy the same status and work together; usually there is strong solidarity. All but one renounce their rights in the interests of the identification of the family group with the land they work. The inheritor stays at home as successor to land and chattels. The family property—house, stock, and land—descend to him intact. The rest of the family must usually leave home. As the phrase goes, 'They must travel'.

Family Transition at Marriage. The long-postponed marriage of the inheriting son, when it comes, brings a complete change in the life of the whole family group. It involves transfer of economic control and land ownership, change of family ties, advance in family and community status, and entrance into adult procreative sex life.

The old couple retires to a very special chamber, built on one side of the house, called the 'West Room'. It may be the only room in the house other than the general living room and the loft. The good furniture and the family photographs and religious pictures are placed here. The pathways of the 'little people' (fairies) always pass by the West Room.

Until this day the father rules his family and his sons. At market the father bargains. The father collects the pay his son may have earned outside the village, even though 'the boy', as he is still called, may be fifty years of age. 'You can be a boy here forever, as long as the old fellow is still alive,' a countryman remarked.

Match-making. The arrangement of the marriage is in the hands of a match-maker who is not a member of the family. He will find a suitable girl bringing in a dowry which will recommend her to the old man. He must then persuade the girl's father that the farm of which his daughter will become the mistress is worth the money. On an appointed day he will come and inspect it. The old man will furbish it up and maybe borrow some stock and implements, and even sacks of potatoes to put in his barn, in order to make a good impression.

If the father of the girl is satisfied—and very often he is not—the match-maker and the two fathers go to the country town to meet a lawyer and draw up a settlement. This is a legal document stating just what has been decided, how much dowry the girl is to bring, what the farm contains and consists of, and, above all, a stipulation to the effect that the retiring father and mother will continue to live on the farm and get food.

In this transaction there is no 'bride-price'. The girl's father loses both daughter and dowry. When the marriage has taken place, no special relationship is established between the two fathers-in-law and mothers-in-law.

Love and Courtship. What about romantic love? Love enters the situation only to complicate it. A runaway match upsets the whole pattern—the interplay of dowry, land, portions for children, and all the other transactions.

The attitude toward sex is bound up with this type of family and succession. It is the interest of the family-farm economy that matters and nothing else. Thus the trouble with a girl who goes wrong is that she cannot easily be married off to a substantial farmer. Nevertheless, matches have been broken off because of the reluctance of a matched pair to unite.

Courtship, therefore, must always be understood in terms of the dominant pattern of the farm and family. The rules proper to such a system are identified with the whole code of morality of the community. There is little use in attacking the system of dowries and arranged marriages or in stressing the well-known fact that a country couple very frequently obtain their first view of each other before the altar rails. The following exchange between father and son after the wedding aptly sums up the situation.

Son: 'You didn't tell me she was lame.'

Father: 'Go along with you; sure it's not for racing that you want her.'

SUGGESTED FURTHER READING

Evans-Pritchard, E. E., *The Nuer*. Oxford University Press: London, 1940.

Firth, Raymond, *We, the Tikopia*. Allen & Unwin: London, 1964.

Mair, L., *Studies in Applied Anthropology*. University of London Press: London, 1957.

Malinowski, B., *Sexual Life of Savages*. Halcyon House: New York, 1929.

Mead, Margaret, *Coming of Age in Samoa*. William Morrow & Co.: New York, 1928. Penguin Books: London, 1944.

Mead, Margaret, *Growing Up in New Guinea*. William Morrow & Co.: New York, 1930. Penguin Books: London, 1943.

Mead, Margaret, *Sex and Temperament in Three Primitive Societies*. William Morrow & Co.: New York, 1935.

Radcliffe-Brown, A. R., and Forde, Daryll, *African System of Kinship and Marriage*. Oxford University Press: London, 1950.

Rivers, W. H. R., *Kinships and Social Organization*. Constable & Co.: London, 1914.

Schapera, I., *Married Life in an African Tribe*. Oxford University Press: London, 1966.

Westermarck, E. A., *The History of Human Marriage*. The Macmillan Co.: New York, 1894.

CHAPTER NINE

CLASSES, CASTES AND CLUBS

Besides the organization of primitive people into tribes, lineages, and clans there are many other associations of considerable importance often cutting across these more basic kinship systems. These are:

1. Age groups and sex distinctions
2. Clubs
3. Secret societies

Then in some societies, all those above a subsistence economy, we have the emergence of **class.**

Finally, in some societies only, we have the **caste** system, which may be of great social significance.

AGE GROUPS AND INITIATION

As we have already pointed out, there is a definite status or rank, with corresponding rights and duties, for everybody from childhood upward in primitive societies.

The transition from boyhood to manhood is marked by elaborate **rites of initiation.** When these fall into disuse, as is happening in many parts of East and South Africa, the rising generation is not taught the tribal traditions, nor does it have much respect for the rules of social living. The result may be social disintegration and a growing lack of respect for authority.

In Africa age groups are of great importance. Each group may include all persons who were born from four to seven years apart. The male members of an age-grade constitute almost a club. They dress alike and, in East Africa, enter the army together. They marry at about the same time.

The Kikuyu, before the almost complete disintegration of the tribe under the impact of white settlement on the more fertile areas, and the agricultural decline which followed, exemplified age groups very well. The successive steps were as follows:

1. The *young boy* had the length of his hair fixed, was not permitted to eat certain joints of meat, and could not have an initiated boy as his friend.

2. The *initiated boy* considered himself an accepted fighter, dancer, and eater. He was now a full member of the tribe and could inherit

property. Now he began to think seriously of marriage and building a hut. He had definite responsibilities and could be punished if he did not fulfil them.

3. The *married man* had still further duties and rights, and by his marriage he linked two families. At the birth of his first child he was allowed to take part in certain ceremonies.

4. The *Elder*. When his child was initiated, the father became an assistant elder and gave one sacrificial sheep for the ceremonial feast at which the new elders were sworn in. After some years, and following the sacrifice of several sheep and goats, he became a member of the court of elders, and could take part in the administration of justice. Finally, in advanced maturity he wore the brass earrings of a dignified elder and, among other privileges, decided the dates of important feasts and initiation ceremonies.

Initiation Ceremonies. These, for both boys and girls, separately, were once of immense importance. They not only effected, psychologically, a sharp break with childhood, but they very strongly impressed on the youths and maidens the sanctity of tradition and the authority of the elders.

The boy initiate was taught how to bear pain; and the ordeals to which he had to submit—the knocking out of a tooth, a long and dangerous vigil in the jungle, circumcision—really inculcated a seriousness and dignity that made him virtually a new person.

He was now impressed with the fact that he must work hard on his plot or garden, obey those older than himself, help the enfeebled, and be loyal to the chief.

Finally he received full sex instruction and became acquainted with rules of married life and those governing his relations with his wife's family.

CLUBS

These are men's associations, often of warriors who learn special songs and dances and feast together. They function as mutual-help groups or, sometimes, as a kind of special police during such events as a buffalo hunt.

In Africa, among the more warlike tribes, men join a *regiment*, which cuts across all lineage groups and age groups.

Secret Societies. In Africa we find certain secret societies of ill fame such as the 'Leopards'. They pretend to be leopards and waylay unwary people and kill them, probably for certain sacrificial rites. The members wear leopardskin cloaks and have wooden models of leopard paws with which they can make imprints to leave the impression that real leopards have done these deeds. With claw-like knives they mutilate and lacerate the flesh of their victims.

The slayings all follow a pattern. There is a scream in the night from a native hut. Fierce growls are heard. In the morning the body of a native is found some distance from his hut, slashed and clawed.

These clubs, too, may act for the mutual aid of their members. They may counterbalance the power of the king and keep tyranny in check. They may also protect their members against the world at large, collect debts, and punish transgressions against the brotherhood.

They are dangerous, however, because there is no check on the temptation to use their power in their own interests.

Among the **Pueblo Indians** special dances and rituals are the responsibility of secret fraternities and are carried out for the benefit of all the people. Their object may be curing or rain making.

Clubhouses in New Guinea. The widespread existence of these associations indicates that they answer a fundamental need of social man. The most striking example is perhaps the club and its clubhouse as we find it in New Guinea.

Membership in these clubs is in part by descent and in part by choice. Descent may determine that one joins the club of one's mother's brother. Even if a person joins two clubs—and that is possible—one of them demands a member's major loyalty. Women may never enter a clubhouse.

The house itself is a vast and impressive structure, often with a high-arched roof, built on poles on a platform. Some clubs are exclusively for young men, and they spend most of their spare time and all their nights there.

The club is not purely recreational. It provides a work group for certain types of organized labour like house building or canoe construction. While not providing the important craftsmen for these jobs, the club may make itself responsible for supplying meals for the workers, or take over the task of sawing and planing the wallboards of the house, or thatching. Some clubs will, for example, make fishing their special activity and may own a reef net and a canoe.

Marriage is a club matter. The young people must accept the mate approved by the elders of the group. After a general discussion to investigate the virtues and views of possible candidates and their families, the final choice is made. Having settled on a girl, the club will then find another girl to hand over in exchange as a wife for the bride's brother.

Club Feasts. One of the most important activities of clubs is to *help in the great feasts*, particularly those in which several villages join. This may require weeks of collecting yams, pigs, taro, and other food. High office is the reward of great generosity and the provision of mighty feasts. But the leader has even more responsibilities than the provision of the feast itself—it is his job to renew and refurnish the clubhouse. Only a small minority wish to hold office. The privilege involves status only; the responsibility entails much expense and hard work.

When such a leader is going to give a feast, he drops hints that a squaring of accounts would be welcome. Then all those who owe him anything proceed to bring contributions to the feast. Kinsmen pay up first, and then other debtors. Those under no such obligation will, however, make offerings so as to pile up assets for future use. Distant kinsmen will be paid for pigs at the full market price. The average villager will provide from one to four pigs, a ton or two of taro, a few hundredweight of sago.

SOCIAL CLASSES

Social classes appear only when the simple food-gathering economy has given way to one involving agriculture, which provides a substantial surplus.

Differences of class must be distinguished from differences based on skill, prowess, achievement in hunting, or even wealth. Such societies may be equalitarian in a socio-economic sense, in spite of these differences, if there is undisputed access to all the means of subsistence or group ownership of productive resources—such as, among the Eskimos, caribou herds and sealing areas.

On the Pacific north-west coast of America, in spite of agricultural backwardness, real class inequality appeared because of the surpluses attained on the shellfish beaches and by fishing. There was a class of hereditary wealthy persons and a class of poor persons. The former secured an unequal share of all the major products.

Here, too, we find clear evidence of class distinction in the existence of slavery. In the early nineteenth century slaves numbered from 10 to 30 per cent of the total population. They were, in effect, a depressed caste whose function it was to produce food for their masters by hunting and fishing. They were also required to do the menial work in the village. There were also distinctions within the master class, but these did not deprive the less worthy of their rights or involve any form of exploitation. The differences were in degree rather than in kind.

Civilization and Class. While there were slaves in every early society that produced abundance, the appearance of the slave state required the highly organized state which we find in the great river-valley civilizations, made rich by agriculture and powerful by war.

The increase of production in all branches—cattle raising, agriculture, domestic handicrafts—gave human labour the power and the capacity to produce a larger product than was necessary for its bare maintenance. At the same time it increased the daily amount of work to be done by each member of the community. It was now desirable to bring in new labour forces. With the increase in the productivity of labour, and therefore of wealth, and the extension of the field of production, the first great *social* division of labour was bound to bring slavery in its train.

Thus we reach the first great cleavage of society into masters and slaves.

At this stage the second great division of labour took place: *handicraft became separate from agriculture*. The continuous increase of production and, simultaneously, of the productivity of labour heightened the value and power of labour. Slavery, which during the preceding period had been still in its beginnings and sporadic, now became an essential constituent part of the social system; slaves no longer helped with production—they were driven to work in the fields and the workshops. And now, with the separation of handicrafts and agriculture, the exchange of commodities in commerce appeared.

The denser population necessitated closer consolidation both for internal and external action. The tribes confederated and the nation emerged under the control of the military leader, who became a permanent head of the state. In its early stages this form of society became a sort of military democracy, with an assembly of the people and a council of elders, but organization for war soon became a regular function of national life, and as emergency followed emergency, the military leaders gained in power. As booty increased their wealth, the separation of the leaders and people became economic as well as military. Finally the distinction became political and the monarchy emerged.

War. Their neighbours' wealth excites the greed of peoples who already see in the acquisition of wealth one of the main aims of life. They think it easier and in fact more honourable to get riches by pillage than by work. War, formerly waged only in revenge for injuries or to extend territory that had grown too small, is now waged for plunder and becomes a regular industry.

The organization of tribes for the free ordering of their own affairs is thus transformed into something very different—an organization for the plundering and oppression of their neighbours; and correspondingly its organs change from instruments of the will of the people into independent organs for the domination and oppression of the people. This process follows, however, not only from the emergence of predatory militarism, but from the prevailing greed for riches, from the transformation of the unity of interests which once prevailed into an antagonism of interests, and from the influence of slavery in making working for a living seem fit only for slaves and more dishonourable than pillage.

SLAVERY

War thus helped bring about a major discovery: that *man as well as animals can be domesticated*. Instead of killing a defeated enemy, he might be enslaved; in return for his life he could be made to work. In any case by early historic times slavery was a foundation of ancient industry and a potent instrument in the expansion of wealth. Bound captives, doomed to servitude, are depicted in some of the old figured documents (seals) from Mesopotamia. Thus arose the great slave states of the eastern Mediterranean.

These slave societies we find in the great river-valley civilizations of the Euphrates and Tigris (Babylon and Assyria), Egypt, the Indus, and China. Greece and Rome subsequently also became slave societies. The slave populations largely consisted of prisoners of war, and whole communities of conquered countries were thus reduced to slavery. In the possession of Rome at the most flourishing period of slave ownership there were some 13-14 million slaves. It was, of course, slave labour in Egypt which was used to construct the pyramids.

The fertile river valleys were developed and exploited in this way and, on the basis of this improved method of production, a class of rulers, organizers, administrators, clerks, accountants, traders, ecclesiastics, craftsmen and nobles was maintained. This was an advance, economically and culturally, made at the expense of the exploited millions, who were without rights, unprivileged, and regarded in classical times as without souls.

African slavery was of a different kind. It was domestic and not a class of servile workers. European slavery on the other hand, from the days of the Romans, was economic and industrial. But in more recent times, the West African kingships readily joined forces with traders from Europe to supply slaves for the plantations of America.

Original African domestic slavery was something entirely different, as Bohannan explains in his *African Outline*. When war captives were turned into slaves this

> meant giving them a special (and humble) status in which they could be carefully watched at the same time that they were given security and position. The word 'slave' in this sense refers to people who are attached to domestic groups by non-kinship links of a sort that contains elements of servility. Many slaves could occupy high positions within households . . . a slave was, thus, a kind of kinsman—with different rights from other kinsmen, different positions in the family and household from other kinsmen, but nevertheless a kind of kinsman. . . . Such slaves did work—often at the hardest work—but they married, brought their families into the social group, and formed a thorough-going part of the extended household.

CLASS AMONG THE AZTECS

The remarkable Aztec civilization developed from a simple classless society prior to A.D. 1300 into a highly organized state in the fourteenth century.

Aztec society consisted of royalty, nobles, common freemen, a propertyless class of workers, and slaves:

The *king* was elected from the royal lineage by the great council of lords.

The *lords* formed a nominally non-hereditary order of merit with various grades for military achievements, service to the state, or religious devotion. They wore the beautiful and elaborate costumes depicted in Aztec art. In fact they became an hereditary aristocracy.

The *free commoner* enjoyed the right to cultivate a plot of garden land and to have a small house. He could become a craftsman and had security and continuous employment, but he was obliged to render military service.

The *common people* were aliens whose goods and lands had been expropriated, and Aztecs who had failed to fulfil their clan obligations. They did the coolie work and performed menial tasks.

The *slaves* were those who were in debt, criminals, alien children taken as tribute, or people who sold themselves.

This is similar to the great slave states of the lands east of the Mediterranean. But the Mediterranean states lasted much longer and became more stratified and rigid.

SEX DISTINCTION

Until the last period of the Old Stone Age, each sex had its assigned special occupations and skills and there was no more than a sexual division of labour. The men hunted and fished, while women were assigned any productive work that could be done by persons who lacked much freedom of movement for long periods.

Men owned no productive property of a kind denied to women. Nor were women servile drudges. They merely did another kind of work that was of equal value to the community. Villages were run democratically.

The increase in productivity which followed large-scale agriculture also affected the relationship of the sexes. All the surplus which the acquisition of the necessities of life now yielded fell to the men; the women shared in its enjoyment, but had no part in its ownership. The same cause which had ensured women their previous supremacy in the house—that their activity was confined to domestic labour—now ensured man's supremacy in the house. The domestic labour of women, which had previously produced such necessities as pottery and woven cloth, no longer counted beside the acquisition of the necessities by the men; the men were everything, the women an unimportant extra. Specialized crafts were now producing what had previously been made in each separate home.

It is plain that when the advanced food-gathering societies began to produce considerable surpluses, the status of men rose and that of women fell. With the rise of *organized government* and the power to secure the proceeds of taxation, men attained a definite economic superiority. Money and money values now became supreme and women were overtly purchased in marriage. Slaves were purchased, too, and every form of human property, slaves and women alike, became a kind of marketable commodity.

The status of women fell to its lowest level in the classical Mediterranean civilizations of Egypt and Mesopotamia and also in India and China.

Chattel slavery in Europe disappeared only with the fall of the Roman Empire. In the Middle Ages the status of women began to improve.

CASTE

Caste is the freezing of social classes by means of endogamy, i.e., marrying within the group instead of without—the reverse of the almost universal practice of primitive society, i.e. exogamy.

Status is thus a matter of heredity. It is a device by which a dominant group attempts to perpetuate and guarantee for itself and its descendants a special and favoured position in life.

India offers the most striking example of caste.

The three great divisions are:

The **Brahmins**—the priests, scholars, and teachers.
The **Kshatriyas**—the warriors and princes.
The **Vaisyas**—the agriculturalists and merchants.

All these higher castes represent the Aryan invaders of India, who kept themselves distinct from the older and darker-skinned Dravidian population whom they conquered. The latter they designated **Sudras,** or serfs. There may be as many as fourteen Sudra castes, including vegetable and rice growers, carpenters, iron-workers, water-bearers, potters, shepherds, and so on. A man's trade is strictly limited by his caste.

Beneath the Sudras are some eight grades of outcastes (the so-called 'untouchables') including washermen, leather-workers, and cesspool cleaners.

Castes do not intermarry. They practise every kind of strict avoidance of contact with one another; in consequence each caste becomes a kind of sub-society with its own sub-culture; circumstances which give the caste a strong solidarity. Thus the caste not only has its own special objects of worship, but its members exclusively eat together, and, of course, exclusively intermarry. A solidity is thus given to these groups which has no counterpart in the Western world.

The caste system is, of course, strongly opposed by Indians who espouse democratic ideas.

SUGGESTED FURTHER READING

Hutton, J. H., *Caste in India*. Cambridge University Press: London, 1963.

Junod, H. A., *The Life of a South African Tribe*. Macmillan: London, 1927.

Kuper, Hilda, *An African Aristocracy; Rank among the Swazi*. Oxford University Press: London, 1947.

Lowie, R. H., *Primitive Society*. (Chapters 10 and 11.) Routledge & Kegan Paul: London, 1921.

CHAPTER TEN

LAW IN PRIMITIVE COMMUNITIES

What is Law? When we think of law, we picture the Law Court, the judge, the barristers, solicitors, the jury, impressive-looking law books, and the entire trappings of a modern legal system.

But when we turn to some simple, primitive authority, we find nothing like that. Are they then without law? Is law something which appears much later in the history of man?

Let us turn to a community still at the food-gathering stage and see what germs of legality we may find.

Eskimo Law. In these small communities there is no lineage, no clan, no club, and no government. Each group has a leader, but he is no more than first among equals. He leads but he does not govern.

There can be no theft among the Eskimos, for there is nothing to steal. Weapons are freely borrowed. However, prestige rivalry among men may be strong, and much glory can be won by taking another man's wife. This is naturally the cause of disputes. But there is no judge, no court, and no law. What happens? The injured party challenges his rival, and this results either in murder or some kind of contest, such as one in which the two opponents abuse and insult one another in turn in songs composed for the occasion. The tribe enjoys this and applauds each contribution. The person who gets the most applause wins. Thus the case is settled without reference to the rights and wrongs of it, and the dispute is laid to rest.

There are also cases in which sorcery is suspected or a shaman (medicine man) is accused of manifesting greed and violence and using witchcraft for his own ends. Then, by common consent, a few men are empowered to kill the offender.

New Guinea Law. Let us take another case, this time in a simple agricultural and fishing village in New Guinea, which anthropologists have recently studied thoroughly. Once again there is a headman who is responsible for the whole village and who preserves harmony between the different club groups and arranges all important undertakings. He keeps in very close touch with the elders and never makes an important decision without consulting them.

Suppose one man has a serious complaint against another man? In such cases, all over the world, the initial step is an attempt to secure private justice. The injured party sets off, supported by his kinsmen, to

116

exact punishment of the wrongdoer or get compensation. He may be able to achieve this, but if it appears likely that a brawl will develop, *the headman intervenes* and the matter may be brought before the village assembly. Here, after long debate, public opinion and the counsel of the elders will make their influence felt, and a decision is reached. Very seldom is any dispute unresolved—that is to say, there is finally a settlement satisfactory to both parties.

Serious crimes are rare. In the twenty years before the coming of the white man there were only ten cases of adultery in this New Guinea village.

Accusations of sorcery are not uncommon, but they are almost always aimed at other villages. It is seldom that any member of the local community is suspected. The integrity of ordinary citizens who fulfil their obligations with care is seldom doubted. Villagers who are living together in amity attribute misfortunes to strangers. Someone from within is blamed only when he has aroused enmity by continual bad behaviour.

Australian Law. Here again the only crimes are wounding, homicide, and adultery. When an enraged man wants to take justice into his own hands, the elders intervene. Their aim is to prevent further trouble. The anger of the injured man or his friends has to be dealt with, so has the fear of the offender and the desire of the group for peace and unity. How can limits to the disorder be set? One way is for the offender to submit himself to the throwing of spears by his opponent, it being agreed that as soon as the offender is struck, the affair is over.

Or when the wife of a man has run away with another man, the assembly intervenes and a long discussion ensues. Then the offender will stand up and call out to the man whose wife he has taken: 'I took your woman—come and growl.' The injured man then throws spears and boomerangs at him and the offender guards himself with his shield, but does not retaliate. After a time the onlookers will say: 'Enough, leave him' and restrain the man who is seeking vengeance. This man, after cutting his wife with a flint knife, will shout, 'You keep her altogether. I throw away,' and in this way she is abandoned to the wife snatcher.

How the Law Works. Now we can see what is happening. The important thing is to prevent the extension of the quarrel and to limit the disorder. The elders intervene to make peace. There are no courts, no counsel, no legal code, and even no trial; but public opinion makes itself felt, and public wrong is condemned. Precedent is clearly in the minds of all, but so is the necessity of taking new factors into account—of enlarging precedent where it is necessary. Either the complainant is given scope to exact a moderate vengeance as the agent of public opinion or, in extreme cases, a man may be put to death by some appointed persons.

As a rule the punishment is seldom more than strong general

disapproval and a certain degree of ostracism. This, however, is almost unbearable in such a community and it is certainly a powerful deterrent. When a man is an habitual wrongdoer his neighbours shun him, and members of his community boycott his family. His own clan may then decide to expel him. In this primitive society a man without a clan is a man without citizenship. His family may not avenge his death nor claim damages in his behalf.

When community life and moral integration are well developed, the prospect of such condemnation appears as a grave sanction. It is seldom resorted to.

LAW IN PRIMITIVE SOCIETIES

We now have something to go on if we want to trace law back to its earliest origins. The first thing that becomes clear is that with us the state alone has the right to use force in correcting wrongs, and the state is distinct from the constituent elements which make up society. We may see then that *primitive societies are stateless*. But they are not without authoritative means of redressing wrongs and, if necessary, exercising force to do so.

The problems and grievances with which law, of whatever kind, has to deal concern the assertion of individual interests which conflict with the general interest, the conflict of the sectional interests of a single clan, or other small group, with the interests of all the clans considered as a whole, or conflicting claims of individuals. What we require is first of all a *public opinion* rather than a code of rules which expresses not the sectional interests of individuals or minor groups but the common interests which link them together.

If we visit such a community we shall soon discover the instrument of such a public opinion in the council of elders, usually meeting under a shady tree and ready to hear complaints from any source. Each council is led by someone who has won the respect of everyone owing to his experience, common sense, and age. None of these elders is appointed by any higher authority. They are not appointed, but they reach their position by common consent. They both lead and recognize public opinion and the common good.

They usually know most of the facts and are aware of antecedent facts known only to the oldest members of the community. After a long consultation a verdict emerges from the council which seeks to satisfy all parties, and the aim in relation to any particular grievance is not the *punishment* of the offender, but *indemnification* of the injured party.

It is important to note that unlike many of our Western court cases there are no *criminal* proceedings on behalf of the whole community (with the rare exception of the community boycott previously mentioned). These cases are really *civil* actions, grievances of individuals or perhaps homesteads seeking redress. Murder however falls outside the law and could demand an equivalent killing; but since this might lead to a serious breach of the peace, the elders intervene to persuade the kinsmen of the murdered man to accept compensation. So usually it is the individual or a sectional group which has suffered wrong and not the community as a whole.

The question arises of how far it is possible to go in the effort to find a consensus of the widest possible range. One can indeed secure the assertion of tribal good as against the interests of groups within the tribe. Even so it is remarkable that there is no *political* institution like the state to approve and enforce that right in these primitive, stateless societies.

The principle that operates there is always to get the elders of quarrelling factions to try to sort things out, and they will invite as arbitrator a neutral elder of recognized authority. If, after the hearing, the weight of opinion is going against one of the parties and he refuses to give way, he may then be asked to take an oath affirming his innocence, perhaps on the skull of a dead man. He will be unwilling to do this if he is guilty, nor will his kinsmen support him, because this involves a curse which might have disastrous consequences on them all.

It is important to see that there is no *court*, and no *authority*, neither is there a codified body of law. Law enforced from rules by special people would appear tyrannous. Settlement is not even by precedent as with us, but by lengthy discussion from which emerges a consensus of opinion. The task is to *avoid* an open breach between households or lineages, bearing in mind that once a man has suffered injury, all his immediate kinsmen will support him, and all the kinsmen of the defendant will support *him*. To make the peace it is therefore necessary to secure the intervention of an elder from the wider group of which *both lineages* are members.

One unfortunate result of not understanding this procedure followed the arrival of the British and their administrators in Africa. With Western law and political authorities in mind they looked for African state officials who maintained order and, of course, *did not find them*. They then settled on certain persons they took for chiefs and forced authority and responsibility upon them. Neither those so appointed nor the community had the faintest comprehension of this procedure; nor did such chiefs in any sense represent what corresponded to the Western idea of magistrates.

Evans-Pritchard found among the Nuer of the Sudan certain people called *leopard-chiefs* (who wore leopard skins), but they were not chiefs at all; they were arbitrators called upon to sort out grievances and secure redress. For an administrator to mistake them for chiefs with governmental responsibilities and authority would be a serious mistake.

THE BLOOD FEUD

Feuds are not tolerated because, owing to exogamy, a man who intends to injure another group is bound to have relatives in it; especially the children of his sister, for whom he has an almost paternal responsibility. The danger that a man may involve his kin in unwanted hostilities may restrain him from killing a man in the opposing group, perhaps in revenge for someone killed (perhaps accidentally) in his own. If he does not himself refrain, institutionalized action will restore the *status quo*. In every such case the aim is never punishment but to restore the *status quo*. The result will be that the feud is settled by compensation, and among the Nuer it will be the leopard-chief who settles the matter in consultation with both parties.

This distinguishes a blood feud from a raid or from war. It *aims* at a settlement—'an eye for an eye', which allows all to cry 'quits'. Another death will do that, theoretically but is likely to lead to reprisals. The compensation achieves 'quits' and the matter goes no further. (A vendetta is not a feud, which is between different groups; it is within a society in which there are no acceptable means for final settlement.)

THE DEVELOPMENT OF LAW

As the state begins to appear in Africa the whole situation changes. More authority rests on special persons, and rules, even if not codified, are recognized. These rules ensure that standards of justice will be maintained, and, what is even more important, there are agents for enforcing the law in the last resort. We may now define law, when the minimal type of state has appeared, as **a social standard maintained by the sanction of force by an agent acting with the authority of the community,** even though the executor of justice may be the complainant himself.

Again let us note that there is a difference between public wrong and private wrong, between *criminal* and *civil* cases. Many cases are complaints of injustice, but others are forms of behaviour which are contrary to social peace.

Here again are the fundamental issues of all law.

Primitive Law. As agriculture develops, wealth increases and slavery and war make their appearance. The chief becomes important and takes a definite and conspicuous part in discussing the guilt of the offender and arranging action against him. The aim is still to check the spread of disorder, but the method is not exposure to spears this time; it is peaceful persuasion.

There emerges **the peacemaker**—perhaps an elder in whom all have confidence, or perhaps the chief himself. But the peacemaker has no code of rules to go by, and we cannot call him an arbitrator or judge.

His procedure will be an extension of the older method of the headman: he will hear both sides, and this will often take many hours or even days; then he will strive to arrive at some decision which both parties will accept. A very powerful force is the gradual exposure of the real facts in such a way as to arrive at a considered opinion which represents the general will of the tribe.

As wealth and class divisions increase, the rights attributed to families and individuals become more specific and concrete. Ownership now becomes important and the subject of dispute. Serious offences against order, especially murders, are rare. In most cases of murder **blood money**—payment in compensation for life—provides the necessary satisfaction. Theft is rare. Among the Trobrianders, famous for their remarkable *kula* trading system (see p. 91), shame would fall upon anyone stealing vegetables, since it is vital to the self-respect of a native that he should be a good gardener and have plenty of food from his own plot.

As for criminal offences, there is still witchcraft, and there is also the breaking of the complicated marriage laws, as, for example, the marrying of a parallel cousin instead of a cross cousin, which is regarded as incest (except among the Bedouin).

Public opinion will also, in a small community, perform something like the fact-finding function of the courts, since it knows all the circumstances in the case fairly well. Thus it is seldom necessary to resort to formal methods of adjudication.

Punishment is not important and only very occasionally, when the offender becomes a general nuisance, will he be punished by violent means at the hands of an agent of the chief or of one or more persons who have the consent of the rest.

Law among the Trobrianders. In these islands there are no courts and no notion of law, but the chiefs are men of great authority and the community works by certain implicit rules.

In *Crime and Custom* Malinowski says:

> There must be in all societies a class of rules too practical to be backed up by religious sanctions, too burdensome to be left to mere goodwill, too personally vital to individuals to be enforced by any abstract agency. This is the domain of legal rules.

Malinowski then mentions *the rule of reciprocity* and several other principles of social conduct. We also know of the prescribed marriage rules in this community and some rules of descent and inheritance.

But there is as yet no code of laws and no properly constituted court of law.

The Rule of the Elders. The council of elders does not hold office from a higher authority. The elders are not appointed but emerge as leaders. The mainspring of their power rests on their capacity to dominate public opinion. They are effective because they are intimately acquainted with the litigants and they know the background against which claim and counterclaim are pitted against each other. One of their real tasks, and it is essentially the foundation of law, is to give expression to a public opinion reflecting not the sectional interests of groups but the common values which link them together. They will, therefore, often be called upon to preach in word and action the pre-eminence of tribal values over sectional values. This happens before any common political organization has arisen.

Law among the Cattle Keepers. In advanced communities of this kind (but not in less advanced ones like that of the roaming Masai) there begins to emerge a code of law, at any rate as far as a list of fines is concerned. The fines do not always go to a wronged individual. The chief himself may collect the payments for homicide and other serious wrongs—that is, payment is made to the community, in the figure of the chief.

The punishment for theft is not only a fine but a payment based on the rule of multiple restitution—that is to say, payment of an amount which is a multiple of the value of the thing stolen. Here is a code of civil sanction of the Akamba of Kitui in Africa. It is, of course, unwritten. Writing is unknown.

Homicide:	of a man	14 cows 1 bull
	of a woman	7 cows 1 bull
	of a child	6 cows 1 bull

(The bull goes to the tribunal as a court fee)

Injuries:	loss of a finger	1 cow 1 bull
	loss of leg or arm	7 cows 1 bull
	loss of an ear	5 goats
	loss of a tooth	1 goat
	rape	1 large bull
	bride-price	3 cows 2 bulls

Definite courts now appear. Laws relate mainly to civil wrongs. There is a new type of wrong—namely, trespass of land. There are well-defined rules as to marriage, inheritance, and property.

Law is now in full force and is unmistakable. Men are perfectly familiar with courts and actions in the courts. They find them fascinating and are familiar with judgements. But they do not think about law in the abstract—they only speak of 'custom'. They have no word for 'law'.

A Primitive Court in Session. Among the Akamba a court hearing takes much the same general form as in a Western court. The chief and members of his council of elders sit in public. The proceedings are usually protracted, and the spectators listen in silence as a rule. But since their interest is warm, the murmured expressions of opinion that do occur will have a certain effect on the mind and judgement of the court, which is always anxious that its decision should meet with the approval of public opinion.

The accused answers the complaint and is cross-examined. The witnesses are heard. The trial is based on evidence presented by both sides. But sometimes the charge is based on a matter on which, in the nature of things, there would be no evidence except the plaintiff's—a charge of witchcraft or a claim for compensation for adultery. How then is the court to decide the matter?

Where there is no evidence (except the defendant's) on which a case can be decided, methods of divination are used to ascertain the guilt or innocence of the defendant. In practice this occurs almost always when the charge is witchcraft.

The chief listens in silence and at the end passes judgement. The relationship between him and the elders who sit with him is the same as in tribal government. They are his advisers and their views influence him. If they all agreed he would not usually decide against their opinion.

A Bantu Court in Session. Africa is one of the homes of advanced legal institutions. Perhaps the most famous of these institutions are the courts still found among the Bantu states of the southern third of the continent. Here the local or provincial chief is one of a number of judges on a large and inclusive bench. The bench includes representatives of all the important social groups of the community, whether they are seen as territorial segments and communities, kinship units such as clans, or age-sets. The judges form a regular and pronounced hierarchy, and are seated in a row or an arc. The provincial chief sits in the middle; at his immediate right is the second most senior person (however seniority might be computed locally) and at his left the third most senior. To his right, but farther removed, the fourth most senior, and so on, right and left, until the whole court is deployed more or less in a row.

There are, then, certain areas in which the litigants are to stand, or more often, sit on the ground. There are assigned places for witnesses, for the nobility, for the followers and backers of the litigants, and for the community as an audience. These court sessions are often held out of doors, but there might be a building for them—colonial governments preferred them inside so that regular schedules, based on clock and calendar time, could be maintained even in the face of hostile weather.

There is also a known, and demanded, decorum and order of proceedings. The plaintiff (to use a roughly parallel English term) makes his plea—usually without counsel—and is allowed to finish his whole complaint, so long as he speaks well and to the point. The defendant (another translation that does not fit precisely) then makes a reply and tells his version of the story. Witnesses are called—including what we would call expert witnesses and character witnesses. Then, after the principals have each told their side of the dispute, and after witnesses have been heard, the most junior member of the bench, down at the far end, pronounces sentence. His statement probably includes moral lectures concerning the proper kind of behaviour that should have been carried out in the situation, and he may even cite precedent. His judgement would be followed by that of the man at the other end of the line, his immediate senior, who might disagree, and who adds new views and new opinions. The third most junior man follows, and so on until they arrive at the middle where the head chief pronounces the final sentence. He has heard everything that the representatives of the community have to say. He has a chance to weigh the evidence, the judgements and the opinions of his junior judges. His word on the decision becomes final.

Ordeal and Oath. Ordeals are found in all primitive forms of legal action and continue well into the Christian era in Europe.

Ordeal by poison is known in many parts of Africa. In Ashanti the defendant in a trial may drink a poison brew. If he vomits, he is innocent. If he does not vomit, he dies. And that is proof enough.

The medicine man commonly conducts the ordeal, for its administration by an expert lends an impressiveness to its use and this is of the highest importance to its usefulness. The ordeal is not applied to a witness.

The oath, among primitive and superstitious people, can be a very serious thing. The form used implies that some supernatural judgement will follow perjury.

The oath may run as follows: 'May this spear kill me if I do not tell the truth,' or, 'May I die like a beaten goat,' or, 'I swear by my sister's garment,' or, 'by the dead'.

Among the Nguni (a Bantu African tribe) in addition to ordeal by poison we have ordeal by hot water and ordeal by hot iron. These ordeals remained in use in England and France for many centuries after the introduction of Christianity. Oaths are not used by the Nguni.

In Christian times the secular court might adjourn for the defendant to swear his innocence in church with his hand on the altar. In such cases the oath administered by the priest took the place of the ordeal administered by the medicine man. There also arose rules providing that the defendant must swear his innocence with a fixed number of swearers who took the oath with him.

The Function of Law. We may now sum up the functions of law as we find it operating among primitive peoples:

1. It asserts what activities are permitted and what are ruled out. This is necessary for the integration and normal functioning of any group.

2. It seeks to tame naked force and maintain order. It sanctions and, where necessary, appoints the agent of the physical force necessary to achieve social ends.

3. It disposes of such disputes as are brought to the notice of the authorities and seem likely to cause a breach of the peace. **Its aim is always to restore harmony.**

4. It may redefine customs and rules in relation to changed conditions or exceptional circumstances.

It is obvious that as the efficiency of production increases and the culture becomes more complex, a greater divergence of interests is possible. Conflicts of interest grow and the need for legal methods to settle and control these antagonisms begins to be felt.

It is only with the emergence of literate civilizations that a written code appears, notably that of Hammurabi and the Hebrew code in Exodus. But this takes us beyond the province of anthropology.

SUGGESTED FURTHER READING

Diamond, A. S., *The Evolution of Law and Order*. Watts & Co.: London, 1951.

Gluckman, Max, *The Judicial Process Among the Barotse*. Manchester University Press: Manchester, 1955.

Hobley, C. W., *Ethnology of A-Kamba and other East African Tribes*. Cambridge University Press: London, 1910.

Hogbin, I., *Law and Order in Polynesia*. Christopher: London, 1934.

Malinowski, B., *Crime and Custom in Savage Society*. Routledge & Kegan Paul: London, 1926.

Radcliffe-Brown, A. R., 'Primitive Law' in *The Encyclopedia of the Social Sciences*. Collier–Macmillan: New York, 1937.

CHAPTER ELEVEN

GOVERNMENT

WHY GOVERNMENT?

Some people suppose that man can live ideally without government in a state of blissful anarchy, in which each person is granted his rights by his fellows and there is no governing or being governed. According to this view, all government is usurpation, depriving man of his rights and liberties and, by impressing iniquitous laws (in the interests of few rather than of all) actually creating the crimes it then proceeds to suppress by the organs of the state.

This, however, is not the case. Every form of human society, even the smallest, requires some form of government. It is true, however, that the more wealthy and complex societies provide themselves with governments which, while maintaining order and social solidarity, maintain a privileged group and subordinate the majority to this group, as among the Aztecs.

Government is necessary because men live in society and act corporately —nor can they do otherwise. If each were to go his own way, it is likely that only confusion and chaos would result.

Decisions have to be made as to the collective goal and the means of achieving it, and as to the co-ordination of behaviour in order that this policy can be put into effect.

In a healthy society, even if leadership is focused in a chief, social interaction plays its part in coming to such decisions, producing mutual modification in the acts of the participants. *The collective action of the group tends to be different from the action of the individual members of the group taken separately.*

GOVERNMENT AT THE FOOD-GATHERING STAGE

Can Eskimos and Australian aborigines be said to have any form of government at all?

They do indeed possess a form of government which is **democratic** and gives special authority to **elders** and a **headman,** these things being not contradictory but complementary. The people of a basically democratic and equalitarian small autonomous community, such as an

Australian encampment, are likely to follow those who are most experienced. All simple food-gathering societies are guided by older people. The basic feature of government in such societies is government by majority rule, or common consent.

At tribal gatherings of Australian aborigines the older and more important among them seem naturally to associate together as an informal, but at the same time all-powerful, council, whose orders are implicitly obeyed. The fact that any individual is the headman of his local group gives him, in itself, no claim to membership in these councils. If, however, he has shown that he can be trusted, and his knowledge of tribal matters is acknowledged, then some day the older men will invite him to come and consult with them. After being invited several times, he will gradually take his place as a recognized member of the inner council of the tribe, his influence increasing as he grows older. Even in the modern world very similar institutions may yet be found in rural communities (see *Field Study* No. V, p. 135).

Neither these societies nor simple agricultural communities have chiefs in the sense of autocratic functionaries. Powerful, self-perpetuating or hereditary leaders who are not subject to a majority decision of the people are conspicuously absent. But leaders are found usually from among the older people, because in a democratic group whose insecurities are many, the older people are likely to be more experienced and safer to follow.

It is the Eskimo view that a skilful man with willpower and authority unconsciously subordinates his neighbours, so that it is he who makes dispositions when important decisions are to be made. The influence of age is reduced to an essentially psychological question of mental superiority. When a number of families are gathered in a group, there is often an elderly man who is tacitly looked upon as the leader—*he who thinks for the others.* His advice is always taken, but voluntarily; he has no legal authority at all and cannot be called a chief in the ordinary sense.

Chieftans. Complexity of social life sharpens the need for leadership and the delegation of responsibility. When we meet the tribe we also meet the chieftain, who is more than a headman, because both his authority and his social distinction are greater.

Among North American Indians we find both *war chiefs*, who are the heads of military fraternities and who function only in war, and *peace chiefs*, who are the civil governors, who supervise internal tribal relations and have judicial powers over certain classes of crime.

This may still be compatible with a considerable measure of democracy, for no decision is merely imposed upon his followers by the chief. Complete unanimity of opinion is always sought. There is in all primitive communities a strong impulse to defer to general sentiment.

The emergence of the headman who still largely offers no more than the authority of his experience and reputation passes over by degrees to the council of elders.

In the Trobriand Islands the leader of the most important sub-clan in the village becomes the headman. On him devolve all the honorific titles as well as the ceremonial functions, offices, activities, and powers vested in the village community as a whole: more important, he wields any magic of which the sub-clan is possessed, on behalf of the whole community.

Among the Akamba (Africa) the council of elders has great authority. It contains women as well as men. It acts as a court, in which all cases are tried and decided. It decides on plundering raids. It is responsible for the maintenance of religion, the offering of sacrifices, and the ceremonies of purification on the advent of public misfortune.

This council is the custodian of the tribe's tradition. It sees that it is maintained, and has on the other hand, authority to prevent the rise of customs it considers harmful. Anyone who is in doubt as to how he ought to proceed according to the custom of the tribe goes to a council member for information, for which he pays a small fee, such as a goat.

Such are the prestige and authority of a tribal council among primitive peoples.

Long before the institution of central government emerged, primitive groups and tribes worked out systems which maintained peace and cooperation among their different units. How this was done is a matter of great interest.

Social ties were formed which linked together people who in other contexts were enemies. This, as we have seen, may be based upon kinship, for exogamy requires that marriage shall only be with someone from another group or clan. Or a tribal fighting unit, based on age groups, may be conscripted from a number of villages. Other ties were established by the loan and giving of land or chattels to strangers. The *kula* system of exchange in the Trobriand Islands links a number of islands between which there were at one time hostile relations and which are still 'foreign'. *Kula* partners are allies in enemy territory.

People from many districts or diverse groups may be linked together by a common ritual, as in the totemic rites of Australians, and among the Tallensi in Africa. The people participate in ceremonies to secure the good things of social life—food, children, health, and peace. Often these ceremonies are so constructed that every representative of a political group has ritual powers, but these powers are exercised in a cycle of ceremonies in which representatives of every group take part. *All have to act if each is to be prosperous.* The ceremonies aim at collective prosperity. Thus they imply the recognition of a moral order which will allow the society as a whole to enjoy prosperity. They enforce lawful rights against individual interests and make the political structure something sacred.

LOYALTIES ACROSS FRONTIERS

If a family is a member of a clan and its interests are bound up with the interests of that clan, some of its members may, nevertheless, belong to another group or organization (military, religious or even related by blood) belonging to quite a different clan or tribe. Thus a *cross-cutting* bond exists, which can operate to keep the peace if the clan falls out with another clan, because many of its members have relatives among them, or are fellow members of some special organization. This is what has been called *cross-cutting systems of alliance*.

In each system of relations individuals and groups might come into conflict, but that conflict will set up disturbances in the other systems where the disputants share membership or have common partners. This joint membership or these common partners exert pressure to bring about the settlement of the conflict. The redress of injury must be worked out in various ways without open conflict, usually by the pressure of persons related to both disputants.

GOVERNMENT IN STATELESS SOCIETIES

These very primitive communities enable us to see that our examination of the institution of government must begin where no visible organization to exercise authority and enforce law is to be found. Such societies we may call stateless. On the other hand, particularly in Africa, there are also states with established governmental officers, and councils with executive, judicial, and legislative powers. But our first inquiry must be directed to those communities who are without the usual governmental apparatus.

Such societies never act in common as a state, its various tribal or territorial sections act independently. An example is a 'tribe' which is an independent group of a population with a common culture. It must be regarded as a political community, no matter how it is governed. We have already seen how such communities carry out what is perhaps the primary function of government—the redress of wrongs, and the maintenance of peaceful relations. They do this entirely without the exercise of force by authorized persons, and this means government without *a government*.

This process is carried out in such stateless societies everywhere in the world, and it works entirely by the operation of kinship relationships and the obligations and restraints which they impose. We have already seen how they operate to heal a break between exogamously related groups. However ties of friendship and kinship, or other bonds which work against hostile actions, come into existence, they have political functions and take the place of political institutions. These may be trading relationships like the *kula* of the Trobriand Islanders and their neighbours. But, as Gluckman points out in his *Institutions of Primitive Society*:

> Particularly important are the linkages set up by intermarriage between groups, because ties of kinship enjoining co-operation—or ties of co-operation which are based on other considerations but which are stated in kinship terms—have a high value in primitive society. Kinship ties and marriage ties were spun into an elaborate network which constrained people to co-operate in order to maintain customary rules and group survival.

It is impossible to conceive of a society of this sort without exogamy. These restrictions on marriage will drive men to find wives where a prohibited relation does not hold and that may demand that they go far afield, which establishes relationships with very many groups. It gives a man friends among his enemies, since he and his in-laws have a common interest in the welfare of a woman and her children. It is quite possible too, where there *is* a common interest, to *invent* a single genealogy, as among the Bedouin tribes of Cyrenaica. The (imagined) common descent in such cases demands friendship and co-operation. There are many ways in which cross-links within and between groups can be established. Ultimately common rituals are devised so that participation in ceremonies can cement social bonds—for the rule in all such rites is that none can participate who harbours enmity against others celebrating with him. The principle is always that cross-cutting systems of alliance must be organized so that a man's enemies become as friends or allies in some such relationship.

In all these methods we see not a conscious and deliberate planning of the whole system, but the unforeseen consequence of a series of single arrangements which each has its own purpose. There is no external, coercive authority to enforce peace and good-neighbourliness. The authority is only a strong desire and intention in individual minds, and *acknowledged* as authorative universally.

THE IROQUOIS

The League of Iroquois shows some special features of this stage of government. It was a *federation* of five tribes: the Mohawk, Oneida, Onondaga, Cayuga, and Seneca. Each was autonomous in local affairs, but in matters involving relations between tribes a council of 50 representatives acted for all. Unanimous decisions were required.

The council was highly responsive to public opinion, since anyone could argue before it concerning any question under discussion. Its functions were the preservation of peace, the making of treaties, and the settlement of intertribal disputes.

Women played an extraordinary role in the government of the Iroquois. In fact it might almost be described as a **gynocracy,** a state governed by women. The 50 chiefs who constituted the council were representatives of the *clans,* but were elected by the *maternal family.* When a chief died, the women of his tribe and clan held a meeting at which a candidate for the vacant place was decided upon.

The women kept a close watch over the ways and actions of their delegate. If he deviated from the accepted code of behaviour, a representative of the women appeared before him and remonstrated. If her appeal had no effect, she repeated the visit. If that also proved of no avail, she was joined by a warrior chief of her clan and together they endeavoured to reform him. If all failed, the women of the clan met and deposed him.

Women played an important part in other forms of government and tribal life. Of the six ceremonial officials in each clan, three were women, and women ran some of the most important ceremonial societies. Speeches were often made in council by women, some of whom were reputed to be skiful orators, wielding strong personal influence.

Women among the Iroquois were the property owners; the men owned only their weapons and wearing apparel. The children, of course, belonged to the mother. In marriage arrangements the mothers made the match. In fact the entire social structure of the Iroquois was permeated by a maze of channels through which women guided the affairs of the people.

THE BEGINNINGS OF ORGANIZED GOVERNMENT

At last there appear certain groups with effective authority and definite responsibilities. In some African societies this may be an age-set (all who went through the initiation ceremonies at the same time) who at a certain age qualify as elders. A typical series of grades would be *warriorhood, junior elderhood,* and *senior elderhood.* This provides the organized exercise of at least some political authority by the council of senior elders.

Another method is for a privileged lineage to appear with special responsibilities among the other lineages, a kind of hereditary élite or caste. And then there may be succession of individuals who have ritual powers, though they never give orders, like the members of the Clan of the Fishing Spear among the Dinkas. Certain clans claim authority because they possess certain emblems which are passed down from generation to generation. In some tribes the holder may even be called 'king', though he has no special power and even passes the emblem on to another, so that there will be found in the tribe a limited number of people who have in their day held the emblems and have great authority of a customary and moral kind. There are many other ways in which a certain diffused power emerges though no person or body of persons is recognized as having general authority to take decisions in matters affecting them all.

African States. But alongside these stateless peoples and societies with diffused and incomplete systems of government, we have properly organized African States with kings and a subordinate feudal nobility of chiefs. It is probable that this position is obtained by conquest in certain cases, but before that an élite probably emerged from a privileged lineage, or a class of nobles such as the emblem-bearers we have mentioned. At any rate one group of people who are united by common descent establish some kind of superiority over others who do not belong to their group.

Another essential feature is the sacred element, the belief that ritual powers are hereditary. When these two factors combine we are on the way to kingship. Such a line of hereditary rulers is a symbol of the unity of the state and can exercise considerable power in settling rival claims and minimizing internal conflicts; but it now does so by the definite exercise of power emanating from acknowledged and sacred authority.

The Priest King. Everywhere in the world the head of state supports his prestige and authority by assuming supernatural powers. In some communities he becomes a shaman, in others a priest. Among the Outong (Java) the position of headman in a group of joint families carries with it the office of priest. The chief of the Wabena (Sudan) is not merely a secular ruler. The main feature of the tribal religion is ancestor worship, and the chief, as the living descendant of the most powerful of the spirits (i.e. the former holders of his royal office), is not only the temporal but also the religious head of the tribe, binding religion and law into a firmly united whole.

The warrior's sword and the magician's wand are different in origin and function, and a man may wield one or the other. But if he is skilled enough and if his culture permits, he may seize the sword in his right hand and the wand in his left. Then indeed he becomes a powerful force.

Shamans and priests are specialists in controlling the action of the supernatural; headmen, chiefs, and kings are specialists in controlling the actions of man. But the actions of men must be controlled in their relations to the supernatural, and so the priest has temporal influence. The politician uses religious means for political purposes when he is able to control religious power; the priest in turn is apt to use political means to attain religious ends. The rivalry and hostility between church and state may become acute, as it did during the Middle Ages. But frequently a compromise is worked out, as is the case in many primitive societies.

In general, supernaturalism is so ubiquitous that it colours all government to some degree. Political officers invariably possess some magic power or religious sanctity. War-making, legislation, and judicial procedure inevitably involve religious ritual.

In agricultural communities *the chief is usually the high priest of the rain, fertility, and garden cults.* As he is the supervisor of political and legal relations, so he is also responsible for the economic well-being and religious security of his people. If his society is composed of ancestor worshippers, he is also the ancestral viceroy on earth. He himself is a direct descendant of the gods and has godhood in him. In Africa, again and again, he symbolizes the tribal soul.

Kingship in Africa. Kingship in Africa was highly developed. It showed the following characteristics in addition to the recognition of the king as the supreme authority and also a sacred figure.

1. Other men, his deputies and appointed chiefs, exercise authority in his name.

2. Every person in his kingdom is subject to some superior authority, so that a feudal system exists.

3. Those in authority can punish disobedience not only against the laws but against themselves, try cases, collect taxes, organize public activities, and take positions of leadership in war.

Kingship however is never exercised without a council of notables which is consulted and whose support is essential; and there will always arise the problem of succession and the necessity for bringing an unsatisfactory exercise of kingship to an end.

One matter of great importance which shows a fundamental difference from the stateless system of government is that the administration of the law by officials with external authority means punishment, and perhaps the chief purpose of this is to assert and compel submission to authority, to make the king's name and his deputed authority in his chiefs and agents feared.

Kingship among the Ashantis. The great African monarchies were among the most interesting forms of primitive government known to anthropology. They are to be compared with Europe of the Middle Ages more than to the common conception of the primitive state.

One of the most important of these was the kingdom of Ashanti on the Gold Coast of West Africa. Others were the kingdoms of Dahomey, the Yoruba, and Benin.

There are three basic principles of Ashanti government:

1. The patriarchal rather than the aristocratic principle.

2. The principle that office involves obligation rather than right.

3. The hierarchy of loyalties—a feudal conception in which every lesser loyalty is a means to achieving a greater loyalty.

We begin with the household. Grouped into large wholes, each social unit is represented by its head in the councils of the village, and so on right up the scale. Only in emergencies does the decision of the authority come down from the top through the succession of councils to the households at the bottom.

In normal times regional leaders may act only with the consent of the members of their councils, and they in turn must consult those whose deputies they are, and so on down the line to the individual family member. Thus every Ashanti felt that he had a right to participate in government.

Ashanti was divided into five territorial divisions, each ruled by a paramount chief guided by a group of elders.

The kingdom had most of the institutions of a well-organized state—a system of collecting revenue, courts to administer the laws, and an army. Court cases were heard by a chief and his elders, and appeal was possible to higher authority. Punishment was severe—execution, maiming, and flogging were some of the penalties.

The individual Ashanti knew that he lived under an ordered system which protected him so long as he adhered to custom. He knew that all religious and ceremonial precautions were taken care of and would be punctiliously carried out. If charged with crimes, he could have recourse to the orderly processes of law. He was strongly defended by his army.

Of course there would be injustice and exploitation, but this was not due to defects in the constitution but to the human imperfections of its workings. Within its limits, the Ashanti state functioned well and efficiently performed its task of regulating the behaviour and assuring the peace of its many citizens.

King and Council. There is no king and no government without a council. No tribe or nation does without it. The most authoritative king has his advisers. In many cases no final decision is reached unless unanimity is obtained.

Even the African monarch can rarely act without full approval of his council, and this is not forthcoming until the elders have tested public opinion.

Monarchy, like every other social relation, rests on reciprocity. If the exalted ruler receives great social privileges, he must give service to the people in return. Some kings and dictators may ignore this precept, but it is difficult to ignore for long the principle voiced in the Balinese proverb: 'The ruler owes his might to the people.'

TOWARDS AUTOCRACY

Undemocratic Government on the American Northwest Coast. Government on the American Northwest coast was by hereditary village chiefs, supported by their ownership of slaves, fishing sites, and hunting areas. They were thus able to appropriate larger shares of the products of all communal fishing, hunting, and food collecting. They also profited by fines, tribute, and forced gifts. They were served not only by their wives but by other persons attached to their households and by armed retainers.

In effect the chief was a kind of monarch on a small scale.

It was here that the potlatch (see p. 78) flourished.

Class was more strongly marked here than in most primitive communities. The slaves consisted of unfortunates captured from other tribes and were reduced to the level of productive capital. Slaves could be killed, just as blankets could be destroyed, to show their masters' unconcern for wealth.

The Natchez. The Natchez tribe in Mississippi had a peculiar and abnormal history. They were sun-worshippers, and small pyramids were found in all their towns on which were built the temples of their priest chiefs.

Each community was divided into two halves. This in itself is a common way of dividing the clans, but among the Natchez it meant a class division between aristocrats and commoners.

The aristocrats themselves were divided into Suns, Nobles, and Honoured People. The commoners were all referred to as 'stinkards'.

The Natchez retained the basic rule of exogamy and every aristocrat had to marry outside his *class*. Not only so, but all the children except those of Honoured People and 'stinkards' became aristocrats. When a Sun husband married a 'stinkard' woman, their children went down one degree and were only Nobles. 'Stinkards' did not have to maintain the rule of exogamy. They could marry one another; or a 'stinkard' man could marry an aristocratic woman of any rank.

This would eventually lead to the disappearance of the inferior caste, but in fact it was replenished by absorption of the shattered remnants of neighbouring tribes decimated by enemies.

This culture arrived about A.D. 1600. It was broken by the French between 1716 and 1731. It would seem that this social monstrosity was inherently incapable of maintaining itself. Nothing like it was found anywhere else.

The Incas. The Incas were governed by an absolute ruler who saw to it that every man, woman, and child was cared for, and that each laboured according to the capacities with which his age, strength, and training endowed him. But class lines were strictly drawn, and neither economic nor political democracy existed. *The system was totalitarian to the last degree. Even consultation among equals was unknown.*

FIELD STUDY NO. V—GOVERNMENT BY THE ELDERS IN SOUTHERN IRELAND (1937)

(*From Arensberg and Kimball's study of 'Family and Community in Ireland', 1937. See also earlier reference to this study on p. 103.*)

In every village there is an informally constituted but very select and exclusive gathering of elderly men. They meet frequently in a particular house. This is called going out on *cuaird*. The young men, of course, do not enter this assembly; they gather elsewhere to play cards and gossip. The old men discuss everything of importance to the village. One farmer said, 'There is never any bad blood between any of the village, and one reason is because we talk things over'.

This meeting is a tightly-knit group of males of similar status and interests, operating within a traditional setting. One man always takes the lead; he is the 'judge'. He is regarded as a wise man. All must defer to his opinions. He initiates nothing but comes out from time to time with a slow, measured judgment upon a current topic. It is under his guidance that any issues raised are passed round for comment and, when agreement is finally reached, it is his quiet 'so it is' that settles the point for good. Another old man, with a shrewd tongue, is known as the 'drawer down'. It is he who seeks information, who brings up points of importance and questions of the day. A third man is jocularly known as 'the public prosecutor'. He cross-questions and criticizes and leaves no argument from anyone untested. He clears the issue and brings out the right and wrong upon which all can agree.

The fourth man is nicknamed 'the senator'. He is an imposing man, full of precedents and references to the past. There are several others, some silent, some voluble and not taken too seriously, but they help to keep things going. Finally there is a middle-aged man who has just 'moved in'; he is not yet fully accepted but he intervenes from time to time, if only with a question.

The 'old men's house', as it is called, includes all the farm fathers of complete families in the village. Informal as the meeting is, it is highly responsible and unites the most respected members of the community. It is built around discussion and decision, and discussion and decision are the rule for the community at large. *In the persons of these elders, in their deliberations, the integration of the community is accomplished.*

The community's relation to the outer world takes its form here. Petitions for relief, road work, and a hundred other topics, all concerned intimately with the official county council, are *here* deliberated upon by the local community and nowhere else. It is here, too, that the community reaches unanimity in voting. It is strongly felt in the village that there should be no dissension on the score of politics.

The community reaches agreement upon its internal affairs through these discussions. Here public opinion is focused *and made*. The *cuaird* is both the centre on which public opinion hinges and ultimately the most powerful force in creating or changing it.

The members of the *cuaird* are the living repositories of tradition. They are all great storytellers; they know the legends, saga, and folk tales of Ireland. They will tell you all there is to know about 'the little people', and 'The West Room' in every farmer's cottage. The pattern of local life retains its continuity and preserves what it can of its conformity with the past through them.

The *cuaird* unites the old men as recipients of the respect and loyalty of the community. Its decisions are accepted without debate or demur, quite naturally and finally. It may settle the times of sowing, reaping, and harvesting. It may bestow praise or censure. It formulates, consolidates, and expresses village opinion on every question, domestic and political. It is, in fact, the closest approximation we have to the deliberation of the elders in the most primitive societies known to us. And it is here in our midst, on the fringe of a great industrial civilization.

FIELD STUDY NO. VI—POLITICAL ORGANIZATION AMONG THE BOTSWANA

Botswana is an immense territory in South Africa, comprising 270,000 square miles. It is part of the great Central African plateau, which is 4000 ft. high. (It was formerly known as Bechuanaland.)

The chief tribe is the Bamangwato. Each tribe is a politically independent unit and tribal populations exceed 100,000. The chief is not only the supreme ruler but also the visible symbol of cohesion and solidarity.

District Government. Within the village or town the households are clustered to form family groups, while related groups form a ward. The wards in turn make a tribe. A large village may contain several wards. The leader of the household is, of course, the father, and of the family group the senior male descendant of the paternal grandfather. His position is hereditary.

The headman of a ward also holds his position by hereditary right and acts as the ward's representative to the chief, for whom he collects tribute. He acts in consultation with a ward council made up of the senior members of his own family group and the leaders of the other family groups in his ward.

The headman of a village is the headman of the senior ward. His duties are on a larger scale but similar to those of the headman of the ward.

Villages are grouped in districts, and the headman of the most important village of a district will represent it in the capital.

Central Government. The chief is hereditary. He is at once ruler, judge, maker and guardian of the law, dispenser of gifts, leader in war, priest of the people. His time is his people's. He is always accessible to all who have complaints. He acts as chief justice, presides over the tribals council, and performs the major religious rituals.

The male relatives of the chief form a nobility. The chief has an informally constituted body of confidential advisers, drawn from among the important men of the tribe. There is also a tribal council of all the ward headmen, who meet when convened by the chief. The chief is chief by grace of the tribe. He is subject to representative checks and balances.

Affairs of importance cannot become official policy until they have been discussed and approved in open tribal assembly.

We have previously mentioned cross-cutting alliances as a method of building unity across clan divisions. We find this in Botswana where the age-sets constitute regimental associations and are also units of political organizations, extending across the whole country. This counteracts the parochialism and clannishness that stand in the way of natural unity.

The Balanced Interests of a Harmonious State. In this advanced primitive society the state, as a political system, balances kinship, territorial, and associational groupings and weaves them all together. It shows how the devolution of authority in group leaders is balanced by the necessity of consultation with those being led. Here we find the essential elements of monarchy, democracy, and even theocracy. But it has no elective procedures, and yet seems none the less democratic for that. The system works; government secures the well-being of the governed.

SUGGESTED FURTHER READING

Beattie, J., *Bunyoro, an African Kingdom*. Holt, Rinehart & Winston: New York, 1960.

Evans-Pritchard, E. E. and Fortes, M., *African Political Systems*. Oxford University Press: London, 1940.

Mair, L., *Primitive Government*. Penguin Books: London, 1962.

Middleton, J. and Tait, D., *Tribes without Rulers*. Routledge & Kegan Paul: London, 1958.

Rattray, R. S., *Ashanti Law and Constitution*. Oxford University Press: London, 1929.

Schapera, Isaac, *Government and Politics in Tribal Society*. Watts & Co.: London, 1956.

PART FOUR

THE MIND OF THE PRIMITIVE

CHAPTER TWELVE

MORAL STANDARDS IN PRIMITIVE SOCIETY

What has the anthropologist to say about the moral systems of primitive people? He must of course examine them in all their variety as he finds them in different forms of society. He will study the way in which moral ideas are reflected in the rules and customs intended to control human conduct. He will look for the source to which these moral ideas are attributed. Above all he will relate the moral system to *the particular form which the institutions of that society take.*

When he engages in this task, he will discover an immense variety of required morality, not just one simple code of right or wrong. What is permitted without question in one society is a sin demanding the death penalty in another. It becomes, therefore, increasingly difficult for the anthropologist to regard any system of morality, even his own, as rooted in the nature of things, *as absolute,* or to regard any particular moral feelings about moral standards as an essential and unvarying expression of human nature.

Consider the Eskimos. We recognize that they have a co-operative way of living that reflects a high moral standard. They are a friendly, likeable people, not given to war and violence. Yet they allow many acts which we consider heinous. Certain forms of homicide are socially justified and legally privileged. The killing of infants, invalids, and the aged, and also suicide fall into this category. The necessity of killing old and sick members of society very easily arises with a limited food supply, for those ailing persons might fatally cripple the tribe in its often desperate struggle against adverse conditions. Under these circumstances killing becomes a moral act. We also know that they lend their wives to visitors as a necessary act of hospitality, without any thought of this being a departure from morality.

Let us take another simple example. An educated Navaho boy of our times would not dance with a Navaho girl because, although not related, she would be a member of the same clan. Among primitive peoples as we know them, exogamy and the customs allied to it create moral situations which give rise to the strongest feelings of guilt, though the same conduct even in terms of our strictest codes would be regarded by us as perfectly innocent. Among primitives, breaches of the laws of exogamy are the most serious in their whole moral code.

Morals a Reflection of Culture. These strong moral feelings are not

141

instincts, and hence they are not universal. They are found in people because they were brought up that way or, as the anthropologist would put it, these ways of behaving belong to *special culture patterns*, to the total way of the life of a people. The individual acquires from his group a social legacy of customs, values, habits, attitudes, and strongly felt prohibitions and obligations. He is *conditioned* not only to have these moral principles, but to feel deeply about them. To understand a man's conscience, you must know the way of life of the group to which he belongs.

The Chinese dislike milk; some people eat large white grubs, ants, snails, and locusts. We eat oysters. What is a delicacy to some is repugnant to others. These value judgements are not innate, they are acquired. Similarly a culture supplies *standard orientations* toward the recurrent problems of life. The answers are all worked out and the rising generation learns them. The sum total of these attitudes (always, as we shall see, linked with very concrete methods of work and tribal institutions) is the very bond of union which holds men together, secures their orderly life, and makes possible the satisfaction of basic needs.

It puts constant pressure on men to follow certain types of behaviour. It regulates their lives. Eventually, from being an external pressure, it becomes part of their nature—*an acquired inner drive*.

In this way different cultures produce different moral codes and the values and ways of behaviour of one society seem strange and even repellent to another. Yet such ways are regarded by those who follow them as the best. They may be ready to defend them, and with reason, for they have actually proved their worth, since the group that lives in accordance with them continues to exist. These are the values set up in a particular society to guide its own life, and they have genuine validity to those who live by them, though they may differ from one's own standards.

Does this force us into a position of complete relativity? Are we to believe that all concepts of right and wrong are subjective?

This, as we shall see, is not the case. While there are no *absolute* standards, there are, beneath the changing customs and rules of different societies, certain prohibitions and requirements of very much the same kind which are found everywhere. They are universal. The forms they take are the products of the particular social and historical experience of the societies that manifest them. When we realize this, we can often come to see the sense in modes of conduct which we at first condemned.

An Example from Tikopia. Professor Raymond Firth, who has made a field study of the inhabitants of the Pacific Island of Tikopia, gives a simple but illuminating example of an habitual attitude which he at first condemned, but subsequently accepted. It concerns the morality of *giving*.

In Firth's *Elements of Social Organization* he says: 'To a European or American it would be strange and highly embarrassing to go to a dinner party after a wedding and then hand over a five-pound note to the host, who calls out the amount of the contribution loudly so that all the guests may hear, while a clerk sits by and writes it down. Yet this is precisely what happens in some primitive societies.' A gift must be acknowledged and implies a debt. In Tikopia no service is rendered without the recipient at once incurring an obligation which he may not forget. The people of this island do not believe in disinterested giving. If you give, you expect a tangible return of equivalent value. When Professor Firth found that he was being treated in this way, he was at first deeply shocked at the calculating greed and lack of generosity. Then he suddenly saw the native point of view and adopted it. He himself abandoned his early practice of behaving in a disinterested and generous manner. He gave gifts only if he thought that by this means he could establish a claim to something that he wanted, perhaps an ethnographical specimen. If someone did him a kindness, he at once offered a suitable return and clinched it on the spot.

He was no longer indignant at the attitude of the natives; it proved pleasant and simple to adopt this method and to cease looking for 'pure' sentiments. The foundation for friendship in Tikopia, he realized, was *material reciprocity*.

The Morality of Property Holding in Tikopia. The next thing that surprised Professor Firth with regard to these people was their extreme generosity in allowing other people to use their goods. Property is lent very freely. It is wrong to refuse the request of a loan. It is right for the hungry to be given food and for the thirsty to take coconuts or other drink at need. The line is drawn, however, between borrowing and stealing. What is the moral principle behind this? First, a generous use of one's goods increases one's prestige. Second, generosity will pay dividends later on, in indirect if not direct benefits.

Property has to play a dual role: it has to do social as well as economic work. The moral attitudes in all these things are a reflection of this particular type of small-scale farming, craft occupation, and property-owning system. Basic moral concepts are closely related to the requirements of the economic order. *The existence of a social system necessitates a moral system for its support.*

The Web of Custom. Culture and its web of custom establishes itself because of its survival value, and the particular form it takes is dictated by the demands of the social system. Conformity is, therefore, necessary, and the conditioning process is severe.

Primitive people conform more completely than we do. Their life is hazardous and they cannot afford the luxury of contradictory modes of behaviour. In such a society one may anticipate the behaviour of others under all circumstances, and this makes for the smooth functioning of daily life, the avoidance of unintentional offence, and the feeling that people can be depended upon. Custom provides the benefit of routine and regularity.

Changing Moral Standards. Because moral codes have a survival value, they must change with changing conditions. Darwin showed that *form must follow function.* The structure of the organism must undergo the modification demanded by changing conditions or it will perish. In the same way culture is always growing and changing to meet new needs, and customs which do not help people to adjust to conditions will fall into decay and be supplanted by new ones.

Thus a custom that has once been adequate may become less adequate, less able to satisfy not only man's present or past needs but his *growing needs,* for he may not be content with the more modest requirements of his father's generation. In consequence there may arise serious maladjustments such as were found in Central Africa, when the impact of Western civilization had not been accompanied by corresponding changes either in the reorganization of native life or in race relations. Hence there could arise a condition of grave disequilibrium leading to unrest, disorder, and rebellion.

Morals and the Social Pattern. In our sophisticated world we tend to think in terms of abstractions or general principles, and indeed these are important. The power to think in general terms is the hallmark of civilization. Nevertheless it has a danger; for we may come to imagine that these general principles have an existence of their own, are simply there for us to find, are antecedent to experience, and are immutable and eternal. This is not so, and particularly is it not so with respect to moral principles. These are *functional attitudes*—they arise in experience and are crystallized out of it; they are secondary, not primary. These functional attitudes must change, therefore, as the pattern of living changes, and above all *they do not first appear as principles* at all, but as *completely established ways of living,* very specific and practical. They are concerned with the special ways of living, working, marrying, and possessing life peculiar to any particular culture. Only long afterwards does the observant, philosophizing anthropologist abstract the principles from the practice. (We can only grasp this if we ourselves particularize and probe certain primitive cultures to find what makes them function.) We shall again consider the **Trobriand Islanders,** and a sharply contrasting culture with a different economic basis, a different set of institutions, and, therefore, a different morality, **the Crow Indians of Montana.**

THE MORALITY OF THE TROBRIANDERS

A man's attitudes, habits, and values arise out of his tasks and responsibilities. His way of thinking is formed by the dangers and achievements of his daily unending struggle with nature—not by his experience in general, but by the framework of his kinship relations, his marriage system, his farming procedures, his methods of exchange and barter, his magico-religious ceremonials, and all the peculiar relationships with his fellows which are unique for his mode of life.

Kinship and Marriage. The Trobriand society is one in which *the mother's brother* assumes special responsibilities for his sister's child. This involves him in a host of particular duties, and these press upon him as moral obligations. His motive is not his own interest, but the welfare of his sister and her family.

Marriage is a contract between two kin groups, bringing into existence a whole system of new rights and duties. These obligations, too, are part of the complex system of primitive family life.

The Hierarchy of Rank. Rank depends on one's clan and sub-clan. Rank determines one's privileges, one's taboos, and a whole range of duties, which in turn depend upon the whole series of village rites and ceremonies, feasts, organized communal tasks and so forth. This often means economic responsibilities as well as other specific tasks.

Work. This involves joining with others to construct canoes, build a house, clear the ground for a garden, go fishing, and so on. All these tasks are carried out according to rule and precedent. Different men are responsible for different tasks and each job is organized, paid for, the worker supplied with food and so on, according to a strict procedure.

Trading. This is an important institution centring round the gift exchange, the *kula*. It has the effect of integrating a great many activities of different kinds into an interdependent whole and is basic to the Trobriander's whole manner of life.

Ceremonial objects are exchanged with neighbouring islands, certain persons in a particular island receiving the gifts from their partners among the Trobrianders. These individuals act as hosts, patrons, and allies to one another and thus establish friendly relations with what would otherwise be hostile islands. Around these exchanges much normal intertribal trading of great economic importance has occurred. The natives concerned throw themselves with great enthusiasm into these activities, from which they personally get nothing in return, for as soon as they receive one of these gifts they must pass it on, but great prestige is acquired by this bestowal of rich gifts on other people.

THE MORALITY OF THE CROW INDIANS

Unlike the Trobrianders, these North American Indians were engaged in hunting the buffalo and in tribal warfare, and not mainly in trade and agriculture. The Trobrianders had an organized system of trade with neighbouring islands while among the Crow Indians the social bonds were between the different clans of the tribe. But in both societies the principle of reciprocity operated. Among the Crows this was to be seen in the system of exchange of services between the matrilineal clans, which imposed obligations on the clan members not only towards the fellow members of the clan but also to members of other clans.

A special feature among the Crows, which had parallels in other primitive societies, was the *joking relationship* between certain relatives. This made it a rule that one had to be constantly joking with certain relatives only, but never with others. It was apparently a method of maintaining peace between those liable to quarrel. It was regarded as an important part of regulated conduct and as conducive to good order.

As a society more concerned with war than the Trobrianders, the Crows belonged to military fraternities which extended across the lines dividing the clans. The special type of moral bond found in these fraternities is a good example of a cross-cutting relationship. In this warlike tribe, which has since been compelled to take to agriculture, social standing depended entirely on prowess in war.

The **ritual and ceremonial activities** of the tribe make for the strengthening of social bonds and give an added authority to tribal customs. In the resultant pattern, activities personal and social, peaceable and warlike, economic, political and religious are so intertwined that the benefits and privileges of one provide an incentive to perform the duties required by another.

The Crow Indians regarded as right that which they believed to be necessary to maintain and promote the smooth working of their way of life. Once more, though their main activities were hunting and warfare and not agriculture and trade, *reciprocity* became the basis of their concept of justice and their system of morality.

ETHICS

The Principle of Reciprocity. If you carry out a series of onerous duties, regardless of its cost to you, then at some time in the future the system will make you the recipient of like favours. In the system of exchange of goods and services the individual recognizes *that it is to his own ultimate advantage that he should comply with its requirements.*

Underlying the complexity of duties in this and all other primitive societies is the principle that the **rights and duties involved in tribal institutions are mutual.** The co-operation involved is the very lifeblood of the society, and from it there arise powerful social sentiments, a regard for the rights of others, and a strong sense of justice.

Thus the requirements of the principle of reciprocity are regarded as morally right because the natives recognize the form of life in which they operate as good both for themselves and for the community in which they live.

It is in this way that moral obligation arises in the social organization of primitive man. Here we have a moral principle of universal significance which underlies a wide range of duties and rules. But beneath these differences the same moral principle operates because *reciprocity* is fundamental to every form of human society.

If we examine a large number of such primitive societies, we can discern a definite pattern of morality emerging through the variety of tribal rules and customs. While obviously related to the structure of the societies where they are found, they reveal a real measure of uniformity. If a society is to survive, there must be some regulation of conduct among its members. These conduct codes reflect the following fundamental principles:

1. No human society can exist without some **regulation and restraint in sexual affairs.** This control is supplied by the kinship regulations and certain rules regarding marital fidelity which are supported by penal sanctions. Invariably, specific rules and customs are established to secure the stability of the marriage relationship and to provide adequate care for infants.

2. Every society must in some way or another place **a curb on violence.** This demands some general principles about the relative value of non-violence and of harmony in social action.

3. In every society **theft is prohibited, the sanctity of contracts and bargains enforced.**

4. In many rules of conduct we find the expression of **the value of human personality.** The saving of life and the caring for the sick reflect this, as does the sorrow accompanying the loss of friends and relatives. This principle underlies a very wide range of attitudes and norms of human behaviour in every society.

Are Moral Rules Absolute? No. They derive their value from social utility and not from any transcendental principles independent of actual human experience. Therefore when social utility is better served by setting aside the rule, it *is* set aside.

Although life is regarded as sacred and murder as a crime, not all types of killing are considered unlawful. But the decision of whether killing is justified does not lie with the person who performs the act. It rests with the governing authority of the community. The exceptions vary considerably from community to community and from age to age. It is the aged who must die among the Eskimos. It is he who commits incest who must die in an African tribe.

There are many empirical differences in the evaluation of the same or similar types of actions in different societies. Communities modify their moral standards in response to circumstances.

Sanctions. The legal institutions of primitive societies have already been dealt with under the heading of Law, but morality cannot be discussed without considering these sanctions in the form of punishments which give the necessary support to the moral code.

The force of tradition is itself very powerful and expresses itself in the approval and disapproval of the community. In small communities, particularly, this is usually enough except in extreme cases, and there may be no system of penalties. Among the Tikopia the public chanting of songs expressing moral disapproval or scorn is a way of bringing a negative moral sanction to bear.

The desire to be thought well of. This is a very powerful motive indeed. Loss of face may be the worst form of punishment.

Economic sanctions. That is, the belief based on experience that a particular line of conduct pays in the end.

Ostracism, expulsion from the tribe, fines, blood money, and death are among the other **penalties** found in such societies.

Religion and Morality. The relationships between religion and morality are not simple. The following considerations will demonstrate the way religion and morality react upon each other:

1. Religion does in many cases bring an *added sanction* to morality, but this does not prove that morality *depends* on such religious sanctions. If it is believed that a breach of the moral law is followed by disastrous consequences, perhaps for the whole community, then this belief will act as a powerful deterrent.

2. It may be believed that the rules of morality themselves have been promulgated by supernatural power; that will give them added sanctity.

3. Religion may require men to undertake specifically religious duties with respect to taboos, ceremonials, and sacrifices. These will be regarded as involving moral obligation. Moreover, if they are regarded as being useful to the community, then that fact itself creates a separate moral obligation to fulfil them.

4. In so far as religious ceremonials encourage tribal solidarity, they may be said to encourage morality.

5. Many religious ceremonials require the putting away of ill will and encourage a spirit of fellowship and kindliness which will indirectly lend support to morality.

Religious Authority and Moral Rules. Some examples may be given of the direct support which religion may give to moral law and social custom.

1. The Tallensi tribe in Africa has a strong tradition of filial piety. For a man to remain for years in foreign parts and neglect to make sacrifices at the ancestral shrines is dangerous. If his relations die or he himself has a run of bad luck, it is attributable to his having 'rejected his fathers'.

2. The Tikopia believe that marriage contrary to tribal law will result in the ghostly anger of the parents, after their death, and this will bring about the death of the children resulting from the marriage.

Morality without Religion. Nevertheless there are quite a number of cases in which (apart from the obligations to perform religio-magical rites) religion has nothing to do with moral laws either by their origin or their sanction.

1. The moral code of the natives of central Australia has no supernatural sanction.

2. Radcliffe-Brown's studies of the Andaman Islanders reveal supernatural sanctions against homicide only. The chief goddess of these islanders is not disturbed by moral faults; she is very angry, however, at certain breaches of taboo.

3. The moral code of the Murray Islanders, which is a high one, is purely secular.

4. The Bantu tribes of South East Africa have a keen sense of right and wrong and an excellent system of justice, yet their religion is non-moral and their morality non-religious.

5. The conduct prescribed by the religion of the Crow Indians is manifestly unconnected with their ethics, which in turn have no supernatural sanction.

6. Among the Tikopia, ancestral spirits and gods give support to some moral rules, but these often have a social sanction too. The rule against incest has a supernatural sanction but no social sanction. Many moral rules, however, are purely utilitarian.

Where a moral rule ceases to be of use, then, no matter how definite the supernatural sanctions, the rule will gradually fall into decay. In other words the really effective sanction is the realization of its necessity to the society.

We may conclude that supernatural sanctions may have their part to play in enforcing morality, but they are effective only because they compel people to conform to a living system of mutual obligations with corresponding rights. Custom unbacked by practical and rational sanctions fares badly when it comes into conflict with human nature; a man's observance of its rules, far from being automatic or induced by purely supernatural sanctions, is forced on him by sanctions inherent in the system of mutual rights and obligations of his group.

What then are Values? There is a tendency to erect these generalizations based on experience into moral absolutes, as if they could have an existence of their own. Lewis Carroll's Cheshire Cat disappeared leaving its grin behind it; but we cannot separate a sort of ethical entity, or moral grin, from the circumstances in which it is relevant.

Values don't attach themselves to objects; they are *relational*—right for someone in a particular relationship. Values are what people actually value for themselves and their kin, and people value what they desire. As Spinoza said, 'We do not desire a thing because it is good; it is good because we desire it.' Anthropologists are therefore interested in 'people valuing this or that', or 'people approving or disapproving such and such behaviour'. We don't say that value attaches to yams, but that agricultural people like to eat yams.

What we are chiefly interested in are, of course, *shared* values of this kind, by particular groups, clans, tribes and so forth. These are embodied in customs, habits, precedents, attitudes, and rules. We shall find a close relationship between these values and the means of subsistence—agricultural methods, ways of organizing cultivation or cattle herding. The approved behaviour and rules are strictly relative to the prosperity, safety and harmonious functioning of a particular community; what is thus established for, say, the Azande won't do at all for the Eskimos.

A most difficult moral problem arises when such a community becomes closely associated with a colonial settlement or an industrialized African community; these will have modern commercial moralities entirely different from that of the agricultural community. Problems like this exist in Africa, South America and many other countries today. What is perfectly clear is that *neither* system of morals can claim absolute authority, both are strictly relative, useful and 'true' in their own environment.

An interesting example of conflicting moralities has been noted among the Nyakyusa of Tanzania. Here there is a strong moral obligation of hospitality and generosity; but this is only possible in a polygynous household where there are several wives. Food production is mainly the woman's task; a man with only one wife cannot fulfil his duties as to hospitality. This traditional value, and the new value of monogamy, are mutually incompatible.

FIELD STUDY NO. VII—ON JOKING RELATIONSHIPS

All primitive societies maintain a strict system of etiquette controlling a person's behaviour towards other people. Everyone has a definite status, though as a man develops, he passes from level to level, from boy to initiate, from initiate to married man, from married man to father, from father to elder. At each stage he has to practise a particular form of behaviour (*a*) with his inferiors or equals, (*b*) with his superiors. Each step in the progression is marked by a corresponding standard of manners.

An important part of education is to train the young in the manners and deportment proper to their station in the community. Happiness, indeed, depends on knowing one's place and giving respect and obedience where they are due.

Joking. Among the rules of etiquette none are as important as those governing joking relationships. There is a person in a definite relationship to oneself whom one is permitted—or, indeed, required—to tease or make fun of without the other's being allowed to take offence or retaliate. It is a peculiar relationship, combining friendliness and antago-nism. What is said and done reflects a certain latent hostility and ex-presses it, but by the strictest rule this manifestation of hostility must be accepted without resentment.

Resolving Latent Conflict. There is a very good psychological reason for this. When new family relationships are established by marriage, there is a combination of antagonistic forces. A man is drawn into a new group, but he is an intruder. What does he do? How do people treat him? Conflict is latent, but strife must be avoided. Moreover the tension situation will never be completely resolved; it must find a permanent safety valve.

So hostility expresses itself in teasing, *and this is permitted and indeed required.* It is as though the man were told to let fly with his hostility and not to suppress it. It is much better to insult someone in a jocular way than harbour a corroding and sulky antagonism. The response must not, of course, be anger and resentment at the insult, but a good-humoured laugh. Friendliness is not the natural response to insult, but it is required on this occasion, and if it is forthcoming, the antagonism is brought out into the open and resolved on the joking level.

With Whom May One Joke? There are some people, however, to-wards whom one maintains an attitude of unvarying respect. A man is emphatically not in a joking relationship to his mother-in-law, but he is to his wife's sisters and their daughters, and to his brothers-in-law. He must not, however, joke with those of his wife's brothers and sisters who are older than she is.

There is sometimes a joking relationship between alternate genera-tions. One can joke with one's grandparents but not with one's parents. And it is to be remembered that this includes the entire parental genera-tion, not only one's own parents. A common form of joke is for a grand-child to pretend that he wishes to marry the grandfather's wife, or vice versa. A permitted joking relationship exists between a son and his mother's brother.

Etiquette and Its Uses. In the social system of primitive societies large numbers of relatives function as organized groups for mutual help. Tensions are bound to arise out of living in extreme intimacy and per-manence with so large a group. This has led to the stereotyping of behaviour patterns, which appears to be most useful where daily fum-bling and readjustment might develop into emotionally unbearable or dangerous antagonisms.

No interpretation of an act suggesting that it had been impolite or aggressive or suspicious would be permitted, according to the rule. Hatreds, passions, loves, frustrations, and aggressions are suitably toned down and regulated. Everyone, therefore, can manage his daily en-counters without too much pulling, tugging, hauling, and emotional strain.

SUGGESTED FURTHER READING

Firth, Raymond, *Elements of Social Organization*. Watts & Co.: London, 1951.

Hogbin, H. Ian, *Social Change*. Watts & Co.: London, 1958.

Macbeath, A., *Experiments in Living*. Macmillan: London, 1952.

Malinowski, B., *Sex and Repression in Savage Society*. Routledge & Kegan Paul: London, 1927.

CHAPTER THIRTEEN

MAGIC

Primitive man can sow, plant, hoe, and reap. He has a wonderful knowledge of the plants and animals around him. He can build houses and boats, make iron implements and pots, weave, and dress leather. He is no mean technician. But there are limits to his powers, and he reaches his limits fast. Hobbes declared that the life of man pitted against nature was 'solitary, poor, nasty, brutish, and short'. It is.

Primitive man cannot feed securely; one season of bad hunting or one poor crop might mean starvation. Disease strikes him unawares and he has few effective means of dealing with it; nor can he avert the blows of fate—accident, savage beasts or enemy attack.

It was once thought that in searching for some means of coping with what was beyond his means, man fell into the error of imagining that by *imitating* what he wanted to happen he would bring it about. If, for instance, he blew water with his mouth, or mimed in other ways, he would compel the rain to fall. This was Frazer's view; he also thought that men believed in *contagion*, that is, a man would believe that there was passage of power from the heart of a lion to that of a man if it were eaten, or that by possessing some portion of a man's person he could injure him. It is now realized that the motives of primitive man are not so illogical as this; but he needs to supplement all known ways of dealing with his external world, by making use of whatever forces there are that he cannot handle in a practical way. He does not, as we do, divide the world into natural and supernatural. If he can use these other forces, they are as much a part of the natural world as anything else.

It is strongly believed by primitive man that symbolic activity is effective when it expresses deep and passionate desires. A symbol stands for something, and what that something is, is always said—the importance of rain is asserted and so is the earnest desire that it may fall, then comes the mimetic symbol of rain falling. This is a way of expressing something, powerfully and dramatically, and it is believed to be effective in reinforcing and supplementing what as practical men they are doing to the best of their ability with known ways and means.

We might compare it with *artistic expression* in song, dance, instrumental music, cartoon or picture. These are not intended to be magical symbols, but are powerfully expressive of attitudes, desires and hopes. We rightly regard this expressive side of our feelings as playing an essential part in human life. It does not effect anything materially, but no one would say it was ineffective.

153

Nor is magical symbolic rite ineffective. Both art and ritual symbolism have important psychological and social consequences. Man may feel that the emotions expressed are flooding the world of reality. It does something in the way of putting heart and luck into his efforts. If associated with agriculture, as so many rites are, it holds out new hopes for the harvest, it gives men courage and heart for the lengthy labours ahead. It does this by the dance, the chant, the feast in common, the ritual act.

It may also help to order and co-ordinate everyday practical activities, like canoe-building, when each stage of the work is associated with a particular ritual. Duties involving social obligations are uplifted and sanctified. John Beattie sees one of the main functions of religion as being 'to express certain important social sentiments (or as we should call them now *values*), such as the need for mutual support and solidarity between the members of the community. Unless enough people held and acted on these values the society could not survive, and through the performance of ritual they are kept constantly in the minds of the participants, and so the maintenance of the social system is secured.'

The rituals associated with initiation rites strongly impress upon the youth the responsibilities they are now assuming. Kingship rites set aside the ruler as a superior being who should be respected and obeyed.

THE MAJOR RITUALS OF PRIMITIVE MAN

All rituals are stereotyped modes of behaviour; they are highly traditional, formalized, and organized. These rites are concerned primarily with **agriculture,** with such occasions as **birth, marriage, death, initiation** and, finally, with **tribal festivals.**

Agriculture. 'Give us this day our daily bread.' This is really the prayer behind all the rites which sacralize sowing and the harvest. They recognize the fact that spiritual powers are in some way responsible for the regularity of the harvest, and that when man has done his best there are still so many uncontrollable factors that it is necessary to utilize whatever chances there may be of enlisting supernatural aid.

There are innumerable forms of ritual associated with procuring food. In New Guinea the area cultivated by a lineage has a sacred spot, the abode of a colony of spirits dangerous to outsiders but not to the men of the clan. These spirits are venerated as the source of supernatural power, and appropriate rites and spells are utilized to guarantee that the cultivation of the land proceeds without disaster.

First fruits are offered; there are elaborate harvest ceremonies and seasonal feasts in which crops are accumulated and sacralized. Hunters and fishermen celebrate a big catch or the opening of the season by ceremonies at which food is ritually handled, the animals propitiated or worshipped.

As an example, we may mention the 'First Salmon Ceremony' among the Indians of California. After abstinence and prayers the shaman catches and eats the first salmon of the year. If the traditional rites are not performed the salmon will be antagonized.

A Pawnee Ritual. The Pawnee Indians of Nebraska have a special ceremony called the *hako*, which is held four times a year—in the spring when the birds are mating, in the summer when they are rearing their young, in the autumn when the birds are flocking, and in the winter when they are sleeping. The Pawnee hope, by this seasonal ritual, to obtain from some supernatural power the gifts of life, of strength, of plenty, and of peace.

The *hako* is composed of twenty rituals, consisting of dances, songs, and mimetic actions dramatizing the creative power behind nature. In the centre of the religious area devoted to the ritual is a fire surrounded by four posts. At the west end is a raised altar of earth, and at the east end is a mound. A priest is stationed at each of the posts and at the fireplace, symbolizing the spiritual powers of creation. Fire is the earthly counterpart of the sun, the symbol of life and of the orderly sequence of events. The sacred fireplace occupies the central position of the rite, while the posts represent the supports of the domed roof of the sky.

There is a myth explaining all this. The creative powers at the beginning of things placed the sun in the east to give light and warmth; the moon to give light at night; and the evening star to be the mother of all things. The myth explains in a complicated way how the four great spirits emanating from the supernatural world created in animals and men.

Spring in Ancient Greece. The life of the Year Spirit is a story of pride and punishment. Each year arrives, waxes great, and then is slain. The slaying is a sin, and hence the next year comes as avenger, or as the slain risen again.

At the great spring *dromenon* festival the tribe and the growing earth are renewed together: the earth arises fresh from her dead seeds, the tribe from its dead ancestors; and the whole process, charged as it is with the emotion of pressing human desire, projects its 'god' made in the image of man. He is a vegetation spirit, or Year Demon, a spirit that in the first stage lives, then dies with each year, and then rises again, *raising the whole dead world with him*. The renovation ceremonies were accompanied by a casting off of the old year, the old garments, and everything that is polluted by the infection of death.

Birth, Marriage, and Death. The rites associated with these events are universal, since the occasions are among the most important in the life of man. The ceremonial attaches religious significance to whatever concerns the vital interests of the tribe, as the generation of new men most certainly does.

The full account of such rites would be endless. An immense amount of investigation has gone into recording them. For our purposes it will be sufficient to draw attention to their great importance in maintaining the solidarity of tribal life.

This is well seen in the elaborate ceremonial connected with death, which seeks to counteract the centrifugal forces of fear, dismay, and demoralization let loose by the loss of some revered family head or chieftain. These rites have the effect of reintegrating the group's shaken solidarity and re-establishing morale.

Initiation Rites. These give ritual and dramatic expression to the supreme power and value of tradition. Initiation rites serve to impress this power and value upon the minds of each generation and are, at the same time, an extremely efficient means of transmitting tribal lore and maintaining tribal cohesion.

Among the Bantus, initiation rites constitute the youth's introduction to real manhood and are designed to impress upon him his new status as an adult member of the tribe. Initiation rites take place every four or five years at a lodge in the wilderness, where the boys are secluded for a period of three months. There they are exposed to a severe discipline and a series of hardships in order to teach them endurance, obedience, and manliness. They are also taught magico-religious formulas, but much of the instruction is by means of symbolism rather than precepts. The total effect is to impress upon the youth the virtues of obedience and discipline.

Clan Feasts. These have the effect of immensely enhancing tribal feeling. The collective feeling expresses itself in rhythmic dances and unified singing and chanting. What expresses also strengthens, and the men are carried away by an external power—a power from without themselves.

All this is much more exciting than the dull daily lives of the people, which is one of the reasons for the religious festival's being regarded as sacred, while the life of the individual is profane.

God and society are *one*. The supernatural force is the clan itself, personified and represented to the imagination in myth or totem.

In many tribal rites there is a sacramental meal in which the participants 'eat the god' and are themselves possessed by his spirit. Such events take place among hero cults such as in Tikopia, where, led by their chief, the members of the clan assemble in their temple and consume a ceremonial meal of hot yams. The proceedings begin in great awe and quiet. There is an air of great expectancy. Then the hot yams are rushed in and distributed. There is exciting competition to be the first to eat hot yam and there is much hilarity. An ordinary meal follows.

The contrast between the strained expectancy and hushed voices at the beginning of the ceremony and the relaxed ease and good fellowship afterward is very marked.

What is the significance of the rite? It is intended to demonstrate to the Spirit of the tribe that his people have cultivated their gardens and are perpetuating a custom which the Spirit himself initiated as a legendary hero. The Spirit himself is thought to be present and to descend for a moment to inhabit the body of the chief. When the men eat the hot yams, *it is the body of the god they hold in their hands.*

This is a primitive communion feast, like many similar feasts found in the totemic rites of the Australians. There is the same close association of a symbolic kind between a social group and a natural species. There is the same assembly of clan members to partake of the symbolic meal, the same aura of the sacred. There is the same tension, drama, and release, creating the excitement of religious emotion—a religious force ultimately given by the collective, anonymous force of the clan.

The Significance of Ritual. All these rites are public and collective. This is especially seen in the clan feast and the harvest festival. Here old friends meet, the whole community gathers, people are happy, and there is social harmony. The rite creates an atmosphere of benevolence and fellowship. All motives for quarrel and disagreement must be eliminated before the ceremony begins.

In such activities men are bound together socially; man is raised above himself and is made to lead a life superior to that which he would lead if he followed only his own individual ideas. Beliefs and myths express this life in symbolic form; rites organize it and regulate its workings. The ceremonial gives solemn and collective expression to the social sentiments of an organized community. These are affirmed, strengthened, and renewed by rites.

The ceremonies of birth, rites of initiation, acts of mourning, rites connected with burial, the rituals of totemism, and the magico-religious rites associated with agriculture are all public and collective. They affect the tribe as a whole, absorbing all its energies for the period of the religious activity.

At such times the spirits of the departed return, accept offerings, and mingle with the living in the acts of the cult and in the rejoicings.

This religious activity and faith fix and enhance all valuable mental attitudes, such as reverence for tradition, harmony with the environment, courage and confidence in the struggle with difficulties and at the prospect of death. This belief and these feelings embodied and maintained by cult and ceremonial have an immense social value.

Art and the Cult. The tie between religion and art is so powerful in primitive societies that some anthropologists have considered the origins of art in terms of the larger areas of religion and magic.

The aspects of religion which are treated artistically are many. Mythology, which we shall shortly consider, is a form of literature or poetry. Prayers, incantations, and chants are not simply recited in accents of everyday speech, but receive poetic treatment. Magico-religious dances are ceremonials of great complexity and ordered beauty. Songs which are addressed to divine beings are not sung casually, but according to the canons of an art style. Ceremonial regalia are often exquisitely designed and fashioned. The more beautiful the myth, music, dance, ceremonial, regalia, prayer, or other religious expression, the greater the spirit of *acceptance* in the worshipper and the more secure he is in his conviction that the objectives he seeks by supernatural procedures will be achieved.

CHARMS AND SPELLS

When a specific power is believed to reside in some tree or stone or fetish object, it can be drawn forth and utilized by pronouncing a formula, which must be exactly right and uttered under the required conditions.

The fetish is such a material object. It is believed either to possess *mana* or to be the abode of a spirit being, and it is venerated because of this, receiving special attention and care. The fetish helps to objectify and foster belief.

The fetish may be a small image or a curious collection of odd things contained in a skin bag; it may include parts of animals, herbs, bones, crystals, and the like.

Witch doctors in the Sudan make much use of magic whistles, which they hang round their necks. These are used for many purposes—they may make rain, they may guard against witchcraft. The whistle may have an accompanying spell.

> You are Whistle of *Mani*. I blow you. If any man attempts to do me evil let evil befall him, let him die. May a snake bite him. May he cut his foot with a hoe. May someone pierce him with a spear. Let evil befall him. If any man attempts to bewitch me may he sicken.
>
> (From the Southern Sudan)

There are whistles for summoning elephants. One Azande from the Sudan told Evans-Pritchard that when he and a friend went out to collect termites at night and his friend blew the magic whistle, they heard, soon afterwards, the trampling and trumpeting of elephants and next morning saw their spoor on the moist earth.

There are **charms** to ensure fertility, charms to give invisibility, magic pointing bones for cursing, and innumerable herbs and plants for 'medicine' of every kind—that is to say, for averting acts of sorcery.

Charms and amulets are not unknown in modern Europe. In rural England farm horses wear brass ornaments of varying designs, once intended to ward off the evil eye. They are much prized now by collectors. Blue beads are worn to prevent bronchitis, and motorists and airmen often carry little medallions bearing the image of St. Christopher.

Spells are not unknown either. An ancient spell runs:

> From witches and wizards and long-tailed buzzards; and creeping things that run along hedge-bottoms—Good Lord deliver us.

From ghoulies and ghaisties and long-legged beasties, and things that go bump in the night—Good Lord deliver us.

Many charms, amulets, and spells are *protective* and bespeak a great fear of witchcraft, sorcery, and the omnipresence of devils, spirits, and other malevolent forces. When Christianity came to Ireland, much of this belief was taken up into Christian practice, as the following hymn, called 'St. Patrick's Breastplate', clearly shows.

> I bind unto myself today
> The strong name of the Trinity
> By invocation of the same
> The Three in One and One in Three.
>
> Against all Satan's spells and wiles,
> Against false words of heresy . . .
> Against the wizard's evil craft,
> Against the death-wound and the burning,
> The choking wave, the poisoned shafts,
> Protect me Christ till Thy returning.

Magical Practices. Magic is never used in work over which the savage has concrete control. He separates strictly practical knowledge and magic. He may be an expert fisherman, craftsman, gardener. He can build a house or construct a canoe, conforming strictly to technical demands. But if magic has nothing to do with the result of efficient work, it nevertheless reinforces that work *to ensure against unforeseen accidents*.

But ritual does not take the place of proper work. Magic is not considered all-powerful. If it were, the savage would not work at all. His share is to deal with natural causes and conditions: he must dig, break the soil, sow the seed, weed, and harvest. The primitive agriculturalist knows when he should start cultivating. He has an equally scientific knowledge of soils and climatic conditions and finds no difficulty in selecting a piece of ground for the particular crop he wishes to grow. He has the necessary implements, and there is no concrete reason why he should not begin to dig when he knows that the correct date has arrived. But he does not understand the 'mysterious forces' which sometimes send a good season and sometimes a bad one. One year there may be a drought; another year excessive rains may destroy his crop. Insect pests and wild animals may attack the growing grain. There is always the dread of some unexpected happening.

Primitive man cannot estimate, foresee, and control the element of luck which is associated with agriculture. He dare not risk putting himself at the mercy of these 'unknown' factors. Consequently we find that every stage of agriculture is preceded by religio-magical rites designed to combat this element that primitive man cannot control, and to make it submissive to his needs.

The leader fells the first tree and performs a ceremony which will prevent anyone's being accidentally injured in the forest. Later, when the ground is ready for the seed, the magician *makes the rain magic* (which always includes the spraying of water to simulate rain) and thereby ensures sufficient rain and a healthy crop. No one may weed until the first weed has been removed by the magician, again with the appropriate rites, lest a blight should destroy the growing crop.

Last of all, the harvest must be preceded by a special ceremony to ensure fine weather for the harvesting.

In all these operations it will be seen that magic and technique are distinct, each with its special sphere clearly delimited. There is no trespassing from one category to the other and one cannot possibly supplant the other. Technique is governed by experience and reason. The contrast between the scientific and the non-scientific and the non-magical and the magical is always there.

MAGIC AND RELIGION

What is the relation between magic and religion? The distinction comes with more or less personified beings, but most religious rites contain examples of magical symbolism, and a good deal of magic includes reference to spirits. *In fact it is not really possible to distinguish clearly between magic and religion.*

Ritual Is Collective. All these rites are public and collective. They affect the tribe as a whole, absorbing all its energies for the period of magico-religious activity. This gathering together of large numbers for sowing rites, harvest feasts, and similar celebrations unites the whole community in a mood of happiness and harmony. It gives solemn and collective expression to the social sentiments of an organized community, sentiments on which the constitution of a society depends.

Some Examples of Magical Rites. Magico-religious rites are associated with the clearing of a plot for cultivation and planting. There are also harvest rites, and many rain-making rituals. Every form of disease will have its appropriate methods of averting or dislodging the visiting evil. The Lango of Central Africa always consult the omens before going on a journey. Should these predict danger from a lion, he moulds three clay figures. One represents a man lying dead and to this he gives the name of a personal enemy: the second represents his enemy's wife with her head shaved for mourning: the third is a lion which is in the act of devouring the man. He can now go on his journey happy in the thought that he has averted the threatening danger from himself.

Among the Omaha Indians of North America, when the corn is withering for want of rain, the members of the sacred Buffalo Society fill a large vessel with water and dance round it four times. One of them drinks some of the water and spurts it into the air, making a fine spray in imitation of a mist or drizzling rain. Then he upsets the vessel, spilling the water on the ground, whereupon the dancers fall down and drink up the water, getting mud all over their faces. Lastly, they too squirt water into the air, making a fine mist.

In Mabuiag, a small island in the Torres Straits, the rain-maker paints himself white in front and black behind. 'All along same as clouds,' he explains. 'Black behind. White, he go first.' Or he may put on a large grass petticoat to symbolize the rain clouds and direct the rest of the community to help him produce the storm. He is always a weird-looking specimen, often wearing a towering headpiece of skins or of bark, a hideous mask, rattles around each ankle, and a general outcrop of furs and feathers. A bone or stick is thrust through the gristle between his nostrils, and his ears are pierced and loaded with bangles. Very often he makes the women perform special rain dances; and nearly always water is poured over a sacred stone or a young girl. Perhaps, too, the wizard will fill his mouth with water and spurt it out to show what he requires.

Many magical practices concerned with hunting are designed to guarantee the successful killing of the animal being hunted. Some of these practices go back to the Old Stone Age and are recorded in the cave drawings which are now so well known. Almost all the animals portrayed are those on which palaeolithic man dined. The few exceptions are animals that were feared.

Before the hunter went off to the chase, he would have an exact portrait of the animal he wished to kill painted on the wall of the cave, and then he imagined that the animal would soon fall prey to his weapons. Of he would make clay models and go through all the actions of killing the animal.

Often the hunter went through the entire hunting performance as a ritualistic dance, wearing some part of the animal's skin. The imposing figure of such a masked man dominates the cave paintings of Trois-Frères in France, where it seems to represent a great magician performing such holy rites, as no doubt he actually did in that 'magic' cave.

THE WITCH DOCTOR

Magic is an hereditary craft, a guild. A man either inherits magic or, more rarely, acquires it. He may even possess it without knowing it, and among many tribes the magical property is believed to be responsible for certain recognizable changes in the internal organs which may be seen in a post-mortem examination.

A man suddenly falls ill. There is only one explanation that the savage knows: someone has bewitched him. His friends try one or two

Fig. 17 Lango rainmakers (Africa). The wavy lines painted ochre on their bodies, symbolize rain. The elbow switch is of buffalo hair. The baboon skin mantle signifies an elder. (From Driberg.)

homely remedies, but he rapidly grows worse. The symptoms are alarming; only one resource remains—the witch doctor. He is sent for with all possible speed. When he comes, he makes a powerful impression: in the first place, he seems to know just why the man is ill, and he looks awesome too. He has painted his face and body with bright-coloured clays; with him he has sacred images and a mysterious bundle made of skin, containing his magical paraphernalia. He burns mysterious perfumes around the patient; he mutters strange words; he twists his body; he shudders and dances in increasing frenzy. Everyone present feels strange powers streaming from him; and when at last he sucks at the part that causes the pain and produces from his mouth a quartz crystal, everyone believes he has sucked the sickness clean away.

Some witch doctors have confessed to knowing that their trade was pure trickery, but others say that though they started without very much belief, they saw such wonderful cures that they ended by believing. The witch doctor often works himself up into wild excitement until, as he himself would put it, a demon or spirit enters into him and he hardly knows what he is doing. He may, indeed, go on with the patient's cure automatically, like a sleepwalker. He only knows afterwards that the crystal is there, that the patient feels better, and that everyone is impressed and pleased.

Granted a magical category, a magical cause for unknown phenomena is not unreasonable. Since man has shown himself to be the master of what he knows and therefore of his practical environment, it is assumed that there is a *similar power possessed by privileged men* to master the magical environment. With this assumption the development of the system is entirely logical.

Witchcraft and Sorcery. Sorcery consists of associating oneself with supernormal powers to effect destructive and anti-social ends. It too is magic—*black magic*. It is the same as white magic, but used for evil ends.

Primitive peoples are so frightened of sorcery that they are prone to attribute all unpleasant occurrences to it. Among the Azande anything that goes wrong—an ache or pain, poor crops, an accident, loss of cattle —is attributed to the malevolence of some personal enemy, using witchcraft against them.

Sorcery is a hazardous and unpopular pursuit, and elaborate methods have been devised to track down the witch and compel him to remove the evil spell.

To work evil magic on an enemy, it is necessary to obtain something belonging to him and then to set in motion various spells using these things. As the magic works upon the bewitched, the unfortunate victim begins to suffer.

Sorcerers are sometimes so cunning that they do not require tangible relics, like hair or nails, on which to operate. They can utilize a man's shadow, his sleeping soul, even the personal aura which members of certain primitive tribes carry about with them.

The witch is believed to have evil substance in his body by which he does harm.

The Magician. The magician is a man of genius, of great intelligence, energy, and enterprise. He does not run away from emergencies; on the contrary, he brings to them a great sense of power, of competence to deal with them. This in itself spreads hope, restores confidence, and definitely helps his people to overcome the obstacle successfully. This in turn enhances his reputation. Stories of his wonderful powers are told throughout the countryside, and in the next emergency his encouraging and inspiring presence is even more eagerly sought.

Is it actually possible for a magician or witch doctor to work wonders?

In the first place there is a definite element of sleight of hand or conjuring in his procedures. This is freely admitted. But can he really work miracles? Can he restore the sick to health or cause a man's death? Modern psychiatry and psychosomatic medicine have taught us that we have powers of curing or killing ourselves which help or hinder the doctor. In primitive communities men may be so discouraged that they simply lie down and die. It is indeed possible for a man to be killed by magic—but by his own! And he may be healed by the same agency. Today, we know a little bit about the powers of self-healing and self-harming and of the power of suggestion. We know that these powers work. So does the witch doctor.

J. R. Crawford has shown in his *Witchcraft and Sorcery in Rhodesia* that there are quite definitely two kinds of witch: there is the nocturnal, malignant, and altogether nauseating creature that exists only in the native mind, but is nevertheless a powerful and terrifying force; and there is the sorcerer or practitioner in 'bad medicines', who most certainly exists. It has sometimes been suggested that witchcraft functions, or can function, as an effective social sanction to support good order. Crawford doubts this and believes that accusations of wizardry are more a means of marshalling public opinion against a rival than a curb on anti-social conduct. Psychologists have sometimes seen in these phenomena a way of getting rid of obsessive hatred and fears; on the contrary they are more likely to deepen the rift between the individuals concerned. Only a clear-cut proof—either of innocence or guilt—can clarify the social atmosphere and enable people to return to normal relations.

Of particular interest is the discovery of the role of a certain fundamentalist Protestant sect, the Pentecostal Church, still found in England and America. This believes in the sudden descent of the Holy Ghost upon the believers, with physical transports, emotional disturbance and 'speaking with tongues'. When someone is accused of witchcraft, it has been usual for him to undergo an ordeal. But in the area of Rhodesia where Crawford was investigating these phenomena, one's name could be cleared by joining the Pentecostal Church whose prophets also function as diviners of wizardry.

It has repeatedly been suggested that witchcraft and sorcery are symptomatic expressions of social tension and conflict so that when external political forces or other disturbances threaten to disintegrate tribal society, there is frequently a great upsurge of this form of superstition. The fact that they thus mirror malaise does not mean, as some critics have suggested, that they cannot become in themselves dynamic forces of some consequence. What begins as an effect can very well, and in fact does, become itself a cause.

Divination. Closely allied with witchcraft is spirit mediumship or possession. Here an individual, such as a witch-doctor, falls into a hypnotic condition in which he believes that he is controlled by some spiritual force external to himself. This spirit may pass on communications to others through him, in which case the witch-doctor is called a 'medium'. Just as it is possible to be trained as a witch-doctor, so one can learn the technique of a medium.

Divination reveals to a man the source of his misfortunes. The divine may use the oracles—so well described by Evans-Pritchard (see Field Study No. VIII, p. 167)—or may examine the entrails of an animal. Frequently the diviner indicates witchcraft as the source of trouble.

THE SHAMAN

The shaman is a more potent and important figure than the witch-doctor. He manifests the special interest and calling of some people in seeking access to such power. This requires not only training, but separation from the cares and distractions of ordinary life.

The preparatory stages of shamanistic inspiration are painful and lengthy. The novice, after feeling his call, leaves the world, ceases to work, and eats little. He often betrays signs of mental instability and is excitable and hysterical. Suggestibility and a great power of subjecting themselves to an invasion from the subconscious are essential traits of these men. They are all subject to hallucinations; without that capacity no man could be a shaman.

No doubt he is partly the dupe of his own beliefs, though his magical powers involve a good deal of sheer fraud, skill in conjuring, and the creation of optical illusions. The shaman is nearly always a ventriloquist, and this is of great assistance when conducting seances.

Yet he cannot simply be dismissed as an exploiter of primitive credulity. He can use his powers to discern evil-doers, to convince men that evil forces have been driven away, to give confidence in difficulty, to consolidate the authority of the elders. But for this he must pay a price in self-denial of many things, for his work is exacting and even dangerous, and the burden of shamanism is often hard.

It is sometimes very difficult to decide whether the shaman is acting a part or has by auto-suggestion or self-hypnotism induced an abnormal state of mind. Lévi-Strauss has recorded a remarkable confession by a shaman of how he became a member of the profession. This man did not at first believe in the shaman, but driven by curiosity about their tricks and a desire to expose them, he associated with them and was invited to become an initiate. He received secret instruction and learnt the routine of pantomime, conjuring tricks, simulated unconsciousness, nervous fits of an epileptic kind, sacred songs, and vomiting. He also learnt the importance of gleaning as much information from persons willing to reveal it about the private affairs of those consulting him. Finally they told him about the best trick of all, which was to keep a piece of wool in one's mouth, then bite one's tongue until it bled and spit out a ball of blood-soaked matter which would be described as the source of the illness. At this stage he was ready to practise and was asked to take a case. He was very successful, but not at all convinced that he

Fig. 18   Shaman's mask (Eskimo), one half representing a seal, the other the seal's spirit. (From Andreas Lommal.)

was using supernatural means. He believed he was really practising faith healing.

He now went farther afield and began to score successes, using the bloodstained-wool method, where the local shamans had failed. His rivals were bewildered and plunged into doubt. One of them in despair went mad and died. This shaman now became very famous, exposing impostors on every side and full of contempt for his profession, though he now believes that real shamans do exist. Lévi-Strauss feels, however, that he lost sight of the humbug of which he was originally convinced. His case ends on a note of ambiguity. Lévi-Strauss has his own way of explaining the cures which actually take place. The shaman constructs a myth to explain the illness, explaining how he, the shaman is himself battling with the evil in his own body. This he calls 'the fabulation of a reality unknown in itself consisting of procedures and representation', a myth. The shaman does himself induce within his own body psycho-somatic effects. The patient is induced to live out the myth too. All of the surrounding witnesses are also convinced, so that an atmosphere of intense conviction is built up. This often works because, says Lévi-Strauss, the *structure* of the myth is analogous to the actual structure of the organic disease. As a result there is a connexion between the organic level and the deep unconscious level of the patient, stimulated and set going by the myth and, above all, by the dramatic event of the shaman before him going through a series of experiences of a convincing character symbolic of the myth.

The shaman who confessed did not become a great shaman because he cured his patients; he cured his patients because he had become a great shaman. His rivals must have failed because they lost confidence and probably the public began to have doubts in them.

FIELD STUDY NO. VIII—WITCHCRAFT, ORACLES, AND MAGIC AMONG THE AZANDE

This important piece of field-work was carried out by Professor Evans-Pritchard among the Azande of the southern Sudan, between 1926 and 1936. Evans-Pritchard lived among them, spoke their language, and was completely accepted by them. His work remains one of the leading studies standing to the credit of British anthropology.

It is an attempt to make intelligible a number of beliefs, quite foreign to our Western ways of thought, by showing how they form a compre-hensible system of thought and how this system of thought is related to social activities, social structure, and the life of the individual.

Among the Azande any misfortune can be, and generally is, attributed to witchcraft, which the Azande consider to be completely real. The witch (a term applied to *men*, not to women) dispatches what he calls the soul, or spirit, of his witchcraft to cause damage to others. The sufferer consults oracles or a diviner to discover who is injuring him. This may be quite a lengthy and complicated procedure. When the culprit is revealed, he is requested to withdraw his malign influence.

If in a case of sickness he does not do so and the person dies, the kins-men of the dead man could, in the past, take the affair to the chief and exact vengeance, or they could make, as they do today, a countermagic to destroy the witch.

In addition to this form of magic the Azande have a great deal of magical knowledge and many techniques, giving information, in most cases, only to those who are members of special magical associations used largely to protect their own persons and activities from witchcraft.

Witches and Witchcraft. A witch can by a psychic act injure anyone and gradually bring about his death. This power arises from a certain *substance* in the body of the witch. In former times when a witch died, he was cut open to verify his witchcraft. Illness and death are attributed to witchcraft. In such an eventuality the first thing to do is to consult an oracle to determine whether the illness or death can rightfully be attributed to witchcraft. The oracle is asked whether a particular person is bewitching the sick person or the deceased. If the answer is yes, the bewitcher is considered to be a witch. How do the Azande arrive at a suspect? Presumably suspicion will fall on anyone who bears the victim ill will.

Witchcraft explains all unfortunate events. It plays its part in every activity of Azande life—in fishing, agricultural and hunting pursuits, in the domestic life of the village as well as in communal life. Witchcraft plays a prominent part in the total life of the community and forms the background of oracles, magic, and countermagic. It is prominent in technology, law, morals, and even religion.

If the groundnut crop is diseased, it is witchcraft; if the bush is vainly scoured for game, it is witchcraft; if women laboriously bale water out of a pool and are rewarded by but a few small fish, it is witchcraft; if the termites do not rise when their swarming is due and a cold, useless night is spent in waiting for their flight, it is witchcraft; if a wife is sulky and unresponsive to her husband, it is witchcraft; if a magical rite fails to achieve its purpose, it is witchcraft; *if, in fact, any failure or misfortune falls upon any one at any time and in relation to any of the manifold activities of his life, it is believed to be due to witchcraft.*

The Azande do not exclude natural causation. But why did the accident happen just when it did and to that particular man? That is where witchcraft comes in. A man is injured by an elephant. Why this man? Why by this elephant? We would say it was bad luck. They say it is *witchcraft*. Witchcraft is a causative factor in the production of harmful phenomena in particular places, at particular times, and in relation to particular persons. If a tree falls and kills a man, that is natural—but why did it fall just as he was passing?

How to Find the Witch. An oracle is consulted to determine whether some individual is bewitching another individual. One of the most popular kinds of oracle is the poison oracle. Fowls are taken into the bush and poison administered to them. The man making the inquiry makes certain that the oracle fully understands the question put to the fowl and is acquainted with all the relevant facts. This may take quite some time. The man making the inquiry then says something like this: 'Poison oracle, poison oracle, if X has bewitched my father, kill the fowl. If X is innocent, spare the fowl.' After the first decision has been reached, a second attempt is made with another fowl, reversing the order in which the *instructions* are given.

If, in the two tests, one fowl lives and one dies or both fowls die, the man is adjudged to be a witch. If both fowls live, the man is adjudged to be innocent.

The Rubbing Board. This is not the end of the matter. The suspicions which now fasten on a particular man must be tested by another kind of oracle—possibly by the chief, to whom the complaint is taken.

The chief, or confirming oracle, may use a rubbing board. The rubbing board is a three-legged stool with a flat, round piece of wood on top for rubbing. This flat piece has a little knob on top for moving it about. The man rubs the top of the stool with a mixture of medicines and oil and proceeds to rub the movable piece backwards and forwards. It may stick or it may not stick. Now you can ask it any question. Is the suspected man guilty? If so, let the board stick. If it does, then the poison oracle's decision is confirmed.

This may appear very simple, but in fact the making of a rubbing board requires conformity to many taboos and elaborate ceremonies, and the working of it must also be strictly according to rule.

Removing the Witchcraft. If a man is now definitely charged with witchcraft, he will in all cases deny it. What is to be done? An emissary of the chief will bring him a bone from the poisoned chicken and the man, strongly protesting his innocence, will nevertheless *blow a mouthful of water over the bone* as evidence of good will. This removes the witchcraft and everybody is satisfied.

Questions for the Oracle. Here are some of the questions which a man will put either to the poison oracle or to the rubbing board. The answer will indicate 'yes' or 'no', 'here' or 'there' and so on.

1. Where shall he dig his pit to trap animals?
2. Where shall he sow his crop?
3. Shall he marry a certain woman?
4. Is he likely to become ill?
5. Who is causing him sickness?
6. Will he encounter misfortune if he goes on a certain journey?
7. Will he receive a gift of spears if he goes to his chief to beg for it?

Witch-doctors. These are not people who work evil (or black) magic. Quite the contrary. They are the men who counteract it. The witch-doctor is a diviner who exposes witches and a magician who thwarts them. He also acts as a leech, or doctor.

The witch-doctors are organized in a corporation—a specialized profession with vested interests in the knowledge of a great number of medicines. Medicines are used not only to cure illness, but for every kind of counter-witchcraft magic.

Because they can resort to these powerful men, the Azande are a cheerful people. The Azande believe that they have rational means for controlling the conditions that produce misfortune. So do we, but our concept of controlling these conditions differs from theirs.

FIELD STUDY NO. IX—WITCH-DOCTORS IN SEANCE

A seance consists of a witch-doctor or group of witch-doctors dancing and singing in accompaniment to drums and gongs and answering questions put to them by the spectators. Seances may be held when a man has suffered some misfortune such as sickness, failure in hunting, difficulties in agriculture, social difficulties with wives or relatives. To consult a witch-doctor is a more impressive thing than consulting an oracle, and it brings considerable prestige. Even more important is the fact that the witch-doctors are visibly and actively engaged in war against witchcraft.

The dance is weird and intoxicating. It is a very picturesque performance (and an excellent show to watch). It provides material for comment and gossip for a long time. Preparations include marking out an area of operations with horns containing magic 'medicines', from which dangle magic whistles. Among the horns are gnarled pieces of magic wood. These 'medicines' play a very important part in all the activities of a witch-doctor. His supernatural powers are derived from his knowledge of them and from the fact that he has eaten the right ones in the correct ritual manner. His inspiration comes not from spirits but from his medicines.

When their preparations are completed, the witch-doctors proceed to dress up in straw hats topped with large bunches of feathers of geese and parrots. Strings of magic whistles made from particular trees are strung across their chests and tied round their arms. Skins of wild cats and other animals hang around their waists like a kind of skirt. Over this hangs a string of dried gourd-like fruits with wooden tongues to make dull-sounding bells. In their hands they hold rattles and bells. Each witch-doctor is capable of making a considerable noise when he gets all these contraptions going at once.

A great crowd gathers for the occasion and all play their part in what follows. But the drummers and chorus of boys are the most noisy and necessary collaborators. There is keen competition to play the drums on these occasions. There are also gongs, which are beaten with sticks.

A crowd of young boys is especially recruited as a chorus, and they are required to sing lustily. If they do not, a witch-doctor will (pretend to) shoot a black beetle into one of the boys and then, to prove he has done so, extract it for all to see, perhaps from his back, with great shouts and gesticulations.

At these seances nothing happens until the performers are thoroughly warmed up, and that takes some time. It requires much frenzied drumming and singing, and the witch-doctors will reprimand the choir and orchestra until they are putting all they have into it.

The magicians then take turns dancing in front of the drums. Then the members of the audience, especially the man who has organized the seance, ask questions.

Now come the revelations which are the whole purpose of the occasion. The drums cease, the witch-doctor begins to give an oracular reply in a strange, remote voice. He utters his words with difficulty. Then something takes possession of him and he vigorously shouts his utterances, perhaps dancing himself in a state of fury and gashing his chest with a knife, or even cutting his tongue.

These revelations may actually mention certain names. Following the proceedings, the oracles will be consulted to verify the charges.

Are his findings likely to be correct, and if so, how does he reach them? As we have seen, there are two modes of utterance—the truculent shouting and the exhibition of mediumship. No significant revelation will be reached unless the witch-doctor has produced in himself a heightened form of consciousness (which we perhaps would see as a kind of hysteria). But there is a very rational basis for whatever intuitive guesses are made. The witch-doctor first assimilates all the local gossip, and since all black magic is worked by enemies, he takes great pains to smell out surly-looking and hostile people. He then divines 'successfully' because he says what his listeners wish him to say, and because he uses tact. He asks his client for the names of his neighbours and wives and then dances with the names of these people in mind and discloses, usually by implication, that one of them is working evil sorcery against some innocent person.

The witch-doctor also puts his listeners into a suitable frame of mind for receiving his revelations by lavish use of professional dogmatism. He struts about telling everyone that he will hear the truth today because he has powerful magic which cannot fail. He reminds them of his previous successes. He will then begin to make veiled insinuations and trial guesses *to see how they are received*. This is not a speedy proceeding; it often takes many hours. Thus the discovery of the culprit follows a long process of elimination which narrows the direction in which the revelation points to fewer and fewer persons.

The layman is really helping the witch-doctor all the time. He suggests the first set of names, and at the end he puts a name to the innuendo of the magician. As the witch-doctor proceeds, he watches very carefully to see whether his suggestions are meeting with acceptance. He becomes more definite only when he is assured on this point. Nevertheless he uses a measure of intuition in addition to his shrewd reasonings. His selection of the man to be accused of guilt is largely unconscious mental activity following a state of dissociation (hysteria) and intoxication into which he has worked himself accompanied by the wild, rhythmic music.

The witch-doctors also rouse their audience to sympathetic frenzy. Music, rhythmic movements, grimaces, grotesque dress, all lend their aid in creating a proper atmosphere for the manifestation of esoteric power—the audience is watching not merely a performance but a ritual enactment of magic. It is more than a dance, it is a conflict with the powers of evil, it is exorcism. For the Azande the supernatural is there in their midst in every such seance; and the witch-doctors succeed by their extraordinary powers in investing themselves, their hearers, and the whole occasion with an exalting feeling of common possession by the actual and very mysterious force of power usually hidden, but now manifest.

One of the most interesting examples of divination and possession outside the more generally known examples in Africa is to be found in Siberia and among the Eskimos and is known as the shaman. The name is now applied to men who perform the extraordinary feats so well described by Lévi-Strauss and Evans-Pritchard.

SUGGESTED FURTHER READING

Beattie, John, *Other Cultures*. Routledge & Kegan Paul: London, 1964.

Evans-Pritchard, E. E., *Theories of Primitive Religion*. Oxford University Press: London, 1965.

Evans-Pritchard, E. E., *Witchcraft, Oracles and Magic among the Azande*. Oxford University Press: London, 1937.

Frazer, Sir J. G., *The Golden Bough* (new edition). Macmillan: London, 1962.

Fortune, R. F., *Sorcerers of Dobu*. Routledge & Kegan Paul: London, 1963.

Malinowski, B., *Magic, Science and Religion and Other Essays*. Glencoe Press: Illinois, 1948.

Middleton, J. and Winter, E. H., *Witchcraft and Sorcery in East Africa*. Routledge & Kegan Paul: London, 1963.

Radcliffe-Brown, A. R., *The Andaman Islanders*. Cambridge University Press: London, 1965.

Steiner, F., *Taboo*. Cohen & West: London, 1956.

CHAPTER FOURTEEN

THE SUPERNATURAL

While a substantial measure of agreement is reached on the basic theories of any science—*always on the basis of testing the theory by further observation*, not by appealing to its plausibility—there inevitably remains a considerable area still open to extension, correction or total replacement. Even fundamental concepts are challenged, and recognized authorities called to question. What is meant by *testing* is not gathering more instances; a tested theory is one which the facts *could* contradict, and if a theory is so framed as to be consistent with all possible facts, it is not a very wonderful theory, but a totally unacceptable hypothesis.

In no field more than that of magic and religion has controversy raged so fiercely among anthropologists, and we shall now discuss some of the much-debated topics, which centre on the idea of the supernatural. Herskovits, in his important work on *Cultural Anthropology* says that magic, animism and religion are all 'part of a single mechanism that helps to assure man his place in a scheme of things so vast and so complex, that without these varied controls he would be hard put to it to make meaning out of his life or to achieve a sense of security in it'. Perhaps the beginning of this quest for supernatural aid begins farther back than either religion or magic; it can begin in a feeling of awe, amazement and thrill, sometimes described by other writers as a sense of the *numinous* or the 'spooky'. It is a kind of impersonal power associated with magicians, witch-doctors, chiefs and kings, which is actually dangerous to ordinary people unless dealt with according to strict propriety.

To this 'something not ourselves' the name *numinous* is given because the *numen* was for the Romans the vague feeling of the supernatural from which all religion springs. The *numen* presided over marriage, over agriculture, over the domestic hearth, over each man's person. It is formless, sexless, and cannot be represented, nor does it need a temple or statue. The *numina* influence the lives of men and arouse feelings of awe and often of dread, when we feel ourselves in their presence.

THE SENSE OF MYSTERY

Man often becomes conscious of the *numinous* in some special place—in some dark wood or deep valley, by some lonely lake, on a hilltop set about with great stones. These are 'haunted' spots, and here he experiences a terror which no material thing can arouse. He is in the presence of 'something' mysterious and tremendous, *the nature of which is indicated by the feeling it evokes.*

This is felt as the perception of an object outside the self, an object of a singularly daunting and awe-inspiring character. It is beyond our apprehension not only because of the limitations of our knowledge, but because in it we come upon something 'wholly other', whose character is incommensurable with our own, and before which we recoil in wonder. The *numinous* is not only mysterious and weird—it is imposing, horrifying, fascinating; it is something monstrous. It has its aspects of the sublime, of majesty, augustness, and terrifying might.

Considered as *mana* there are recognized means of acquiring and using it which entail the performance of special rites. Beattie points out that it is related to the special potency which attaches to the symbols which play such an important part in all ritual. Durkheim relates it to *totemism* and says that the totemic principle is a form of *mana* which incarnates itself in each individual of a clan. The Spirit of the Clan thus *possesses* each individual. All tribal rituals are concerned with manipulating this form of collective *mana*.

It is only fair to say, however, that Professor Evans-Pritchard is highly sceptical of these theories. He does not like the idea of deriving any form of ritual, magical procedure or religion from *feeling*. He prefers to describe it in the following terms:

'It should be understood as an efficaciousness (with the allied meaning of truth) of spiritual power derived from gods or ghosts, usually through persons, especially chiefs—a grace or virtue which enables persons to ensure success in human undertakings.'

TABOO

The numinous must be handled with care. If improperly approached it may be offended, it may strike back. Supernatural power does not work according to natural law; it may not be dealt with casually or irreverently. Hence there arises a set of *negative rules*—things one must *not* do, or disaster will follow. These are *taboos*. The function of taboo is predominantly psychological, originating in man's fear of dealing with forces he does not wholly understand. It engenders respect and cautious fear for the supernatural. Inasmuch as supernatural power always involves taboo, no man can ever take his possession of power wholly for granted. It sustains the awesomeness of the supernatural by reinforcing attitudes of care and mystery, and by punishing attitudes of carelessness and profanity in dealing with it.

It may also be used to separate higher groups from lower groups, attaching to the kingship or the priesthood a certain essential holiness absent in the commoner.

When travelling in a foreign country, it is important not to break taboo or great offence will be caused. The violator of a taboo is the object of communal vengeance in primitive society. The most striking instance of such a taboo breaker is the man or woman who disregards the prohibition against marriage within the kin—in other words, violates the law of exogamy. To be guilty of incest is to incite in the entire community a feeling of horror and a reaction often leading to the death of the offender. Other examples of transgressions that are severely punished include the damaging of a grave and the eating of forbidden meats.

Taboos Concerning Birth and Death. The mystery of life and birth is supernatural to primitive man, and taboos grow up accordingly. No doubt many ceremonies were originally the results of natural care for mother and child, but it was the mysterious nature of the processes of reproduction that caused them to be viewed with such great reverence and awe, as objects of unusual sacredness.

From the attainment of puberty women are hedged around with innumerable taboos at all times, particularly during pregnancy and childbirth. So sacred, and therefore so dangerous, is she at these times that it is sometimes necessary for her husband to go and live elsewhere, lest he should come under her mystic influence.

Taboos are also associated with death. Contact with a corpse renders a person taboo. So contagious is the taboo that the prohibitions relating to death extend to the whole house, the whole family, the whole clan. The Jewish law held that 'whosoever is unclean by the dead: both male and female, shall be put out, without the camp shall ye put them; that they defile not their camps, in the midst whereof Jehovah dwells' (Num. V : 2, 3). All persons present at a Roman funeral were sprinkled with water and forced to step over a fire.

Taboos and the Warrior. A number of taboos and rites have centred around the warrior. The vessels he uses are sacred, continence and personal cleanliness must be observed before battle, care must be taken lest the enemy get hold of anything by which they might work magic against him.

The Indians of North America hang the warriors' eating vessels on trees so as to prevent their sanctity being contaminated.

Blood is so potent in primitive society that the warrior who has slain his foe in battle is as dangerous as a pregnant woman. He may touch nobody, not even his wife, nor go near the rest of the tribe until he has performed the necessary purificatory rites.

Taboo and the Thing Feared. If the supernatural can be our 'very present help in trouble', it can also be a source of danger and disaster if not handled circumspectly, propitiated, and 'insulated' as if it were a live wire. If the ancestral spirits come to us in our spring feasts, we must, when the rites are over, purge them with tar and buckthorn from every corner of the village until the air is pure from the infection of death. If the crops failed it is felt that some taboo must have been broken; it was a matter of pollution, of unexpiated defilement. Hence the cruelty of many primitive rites, the human sacrifices, the scapegoat, the tearing to pieces of living animals. Its roots were in terror, terror of the breach of taboo—the forbidden thing.

Taboo and the Priesthood. The priest (and often the king) is regarded as a sacred person. He must be guarded against contamination by profane things and care must be taken to prevent his sacredness from being injuriously communicated to other persons or objects. The priest is often required to abstain from a flesh diet. The hair and nail parings of such sacred persons must not be touched by common folk. He must not shed blood. Even the Christian Church, at a much later date than the primitive religion we are considering, did not permit priests to bear arms; though militant bishops at one time went to war armed with maces which killed but, unlike the sword, did not spill blood.

Every kind of sacred rite and mystery requires of the worshipper a somewhat similar ritual purity to that demanded of the priest. Prior to participation there must be a period of preliminary purification and abstention from forbidden things.

Among the sacred things are the temple, the sacred stones or trees, the sacred images and objects used in worship. When Uzziah put out his hand to prevent the Ark of the Covenant from falling, he fell dead. It was taboo.

Beattie says that the concept of ritual taboo is as widespread as the idea of ritual power; indeed it is an aspect of it. It rests on belief in *the efficacy of symbols*. Taboos can prove very effective indeed. Placing a taboo on things may discourage theft, placing it on a person enhances his prestige. In relation to all ritual it is an essential part of a process which reinforces certain values upon adherence to which the smooth running of the society depends.

ANIMISM AND THE SPIRIT WORLD

The early anthropologists believed that primitive man thought all things were in some sense alive—this they called *animatism*. If man eventually came to believe in souls (as they thought he did on the basis of dreams in which something in one seems to leave the body), then he believed that the life in a thing is a kind of spirit of that thing. These views are now regarded with considerable scepticism, and we may probably be content with the ideas of *Mana, Magic* and *Ritual* to account for what was once explained as animism. It is also doubtful whether early man personified the forces of nature. This appears to be a somewhat later procedure.

But ancestors most certainly have some sort of existence; they are associated with certain shrines and sanctify tribal land. Among the

Talensi of Northern Ghana there are animal totems or symbolic creatures representing the power of the lineage ancestors, and most certainly these and other spirits play an important part in the life of primitive man. People frequently have a special regard for the spirits of dead ancestors. Sometimes this is not a matter of great importance, but in other cases it is. It may help to quell quarrelling among lineage members since that may anger the ancestral spirits. Thus an ancestral cult may act as a social sanction for good behaviour and help to maintain the social system. Ancestors may be considered as entities who must be propitiated, either as individuals or in the lump. Such ancestors-as-a-whole demand a cult of a rather different kind from that required by individual ancestors.

There may be a multitude of other spirits, as there were for the Western world in the Hellenic and Medieval periods—often extremely terrifying and dangerous, but divisible into good and bad spirits. Spirits have been thought of as immaterial personifications of *mana*, and therefore endued with power. In fact they have immeasurably greater control over the environment than man has. They serve a useful purpose. For if we believe that they can be on our side, that they can use this power for our good, then they make it easier to adjust to our environment because they humanize it. Man thus projects himself into his environment, and, as John Beattie explains, the spiritual powers which he enlists to help him representing an extension of his human mastery of the world.

> Everyday existence is surrounded by unpredictable and sometimes terrifying hazards, of which mortal illness is not the least. And there exists no adequate body of empirical knowledge which might enable man to cope with these hazards, or even to hope to cope with them, by means of practical, scientifically proven or provable techniques. So they must cope with them symbolically and expressively instead. One answer is to spiritualize the universe.

If they can endow the universe, or that part of nature which *we* call supernatural (but they do not), with human qualities, they can try to persuade it to help, or, if it is hostile, to desist from harmful actions. By invocation and sacrifice they may try to avert malign intervention and secure help. These spirits are eventually united until they constitute important gods. We can see that this belief, and the worship and rituals which give it real existence, takes a valueless, purposeless, indifferent, and shifting environment, and turns it into a world that has intrinsic value, purpose, solicitousness, and order. Thus man's environment becomes, in part, at any rate, benevolent, human and social.

THE ORIGIN AND FUNCTION OF RELIGION

Religion is closely associated with belief in spirits and with the rituals associated with man's relations with them. The difference between religion and magic appears to be that between the notion of a magical power made available through symbolic actions and declarations, and the idea of more or less personalized spirits who can *listen* to one, spirits that can be cajoled or persuaded, and can take up an attitude of hostility, indifference or benevolence.

There develops a close relationship between the group and certain spiritual powers with obligations on both sides. If the rites are performed and the sacrifices offered, one may expect a return. The precursors of the Greeks performed rites *to drive the spirits away*—'I give that you may go'; other communities, and no doubt these people on other occasions, 'give that you may give'. If the rites are neglected, even the benevolently inclined spirits may be harmful.

SACRIFICE

Sacrifice is an essential element in religion. Robertson-Smith interpreted it as 'eating the God' in a sacramental and totemistic fashion Others have thought of it as *sharing* a feast with the Gods, which is appropriate in good times; but propitiating the supernatural powers by shedding blood or by human sacrifices in bad times, or on occasions of getting right with neglected or offended powers. Offences are seldom what we would call *moral* offences, they are more likely to be mistakes of a ritualistic nature or the breaking of taboos.

The importance in every case is the powerful effect of the dramatic symbolization on the worshipper. In other words it is a way of expressing deep emotions and desires.

Supernatural beliefs, as we have seen, are creations of man, expressive of his hopes and fears, of his precarious life in a dangerous world and his earnest desire for succour and encouragement. They may *in this way* (and not philosophically or theologically) provide answers to otherwise insoluble questions, diminish the area of doubt and uncertainty, give confidence in time of trouble. Religion provides an institutionalized means of coping with life's pressing problems.

Radcliffe-Brown sees one of its functions as asserting and reinforcing the values, that is to say socially accepted goals and ideals, on which society depends; it also translates uncontrollable natural forces into symbolic entities which, through ritual, can be dealt with. Through these symbols man expresses his apprehension of the universe and of its meaning. Indeed is there any other way of expressing this except through myth and symbol?

DURKHEIM

The French sociologist and anthropologist Émile Durkheim made a contribution of such great importance to the theory of religion and at the same time to an understanding of the communal sense of unity, that special attention must be given to his theories. Durkheim believes that religion is strong group feeling, this being absolutely necessary for survival. Group solidarity and the maintenance of the social system demand a strong reinforcement of attachment to the rules and principles of social obligation. The gods men worship are then the man-made symbols of society itself, for is not society the indispensable condition of human life?

Religion is therefore a social fact, and is thoroughly objective. It stands for something over and beyond individual minds and lives. What gives it objectivity is:

1. That it is transmitted from one generation to another. It is something we grow up into and then pass on to our children.

2. It is accepted and believed by all. In such a primitive community dissent is inconceivable.

3. It is obligatory. To neglect the rites of religion is as impossible as rejecting the language that is spoken. In fact it is part of that language and of the ordinary concepts of social life.

Religion is thus a social fact. It arises out of the nature of social life itself and is indissolubly bound up with economics, art, morals, marriage laws, agricultural procedures, and so on.

As Evans-Pritchard explains, 'Religion is the way in which a society sees itself as more than a collection of individuals, and by which it maintains its solidarity and ensures its continuity. . . .' It is a unified system of beliefs and practices which unite into a one single community all those who adhere to them.

Durkheim therefore seeks for sacred objects of a totemic nature to act as the symbols of this unity. The revered object is not a fiction, *it is society itself*, which men worship in its ideal representation.

We have seen that if collective life awakens religious thought on reaching a certain degree of intensity, it is because it brings about a state of effervescence which changes the conditions of psychic activity. Vital energies are over-excited, passions more active, sensations stronger; there are even some which are produced only at this moment. A man does not recognize himself; *he feels himself transformed and consequently he transforms the environment which surrounds him*. In order to account for the very particular impressions which he receives, he attributes to the things with which he is in most direct contact properties which they have not, exceptional powers and virtues which the objects of everyday experience do not possess. In a word, above the real world where his profane life passes he has placed another which, in one sense, does not exist except in thought, but to which he attributes a higher sort of dignity than to the first. Thus, from a double point of view it is an ideal world.

It follows that for a society to become conscious of itself and to maintain its sentiments at the necessary degree of intensity, it must periodically assemble and engage in communal religious rites which arouse great excitement, compel men to feel that they are possessed and exalted by the tribal spirit, and that it has complete authority over them. The rites *produce* the religious ecstasy and the feeling of solidarity.

FROM POLYTHEISM TO THEISM

Polytheism belongs to a higher level of social development than that of tribal and village life. We find it in the more advanced cultures of ancient India, Egypt, Mesopotamia, and Greece. It implies, in the first place, some degree of emancipation from the fixed tribal community. This comes with increasing wealth and prosperity and the appearance of a society with an organized priesthood. Man projects more and more of his own growing individuality upon the spirits, and they themselves become individuals after his own likeness. The spirits become *personal* deities.

The One God concept is generally regarded as a very late development in which religion merges with philosophy. Even the Hebrews were not monotheists at first, but henotheists, believing initially that Jehovah was their tribal god, and later that he was more powerful than other gods, who nevertheless existed. Only in the later Jewish religion and under the influence of the great prophets did the concept of a single deity emerge.

From what could the concept of 'high gods' have developed? Either there had been a forerunner to the idea of deities, or we must assume that the different gods revealed themselves in the early days of man on earth. If this were the case, how would we account for religions in which deities are but minor expressions of the power phenomenon that we have found present in all the varied beliefs and rituals concerned with the supernatural and the numinous?

We must conclude that *monotheism, in any real sense of the word, is the culmination and not the origin of the religious quest.* It is dependent not only on that great expansion of civilization which united many nations in one empire and equally subdued the many gods to one Supreme God, but on the appearance of great religious geniuses like the founders of Buddhism, Islam, and Christianity. One of the greatest religious reformers was Akhenaten of Egypt (1385 B.C.) who was one of the first to conceive of a deity as being universal, supreme, and ethical. Aten, the sungod, is the creator not only of Egypt, but of other lands as well.

Monotheism. The Supreme God has human characteristics: he is made in the image of man, and the consequences for man himself are great. Consider the following thoughts:

1. If natural events are brought about by spiritual beings or a spiritual being with human attributes, then the forces controlling

human life may be *persuaded* (since they are humanlike, they can be reasoned and pleaded with) to help us.

2. If the gods are akin to man, then man occupies a favoured place in the scheme of things. Man comes to believe that events are produced by a being with a benevolent interest in human affairs, that he lives in an environment basically friendly. Moreover this environment now becomes comprehensible. Everything that happens must have a reason, and all things work together for good.

SUGGESTED FURTHER READING

Durkheim, Émile, *Elementary Forms of the Religious Life*. Collier–Macmillan: New York, 1961.

Forde, D., *African Worlds*. Oxford University Press: London, 1934.

Harrison, Jane, *Prolegomena to the Study of Greek Religion*. (New edition.) Merlin Press: London, 1967.

James, E. O., *Primitive Ritual and Belief*. Methuen: London, 1917.

Lowie, R. H., *Primitive Religion*. Owen: London, 1921.

Otto, R., *The Idea of the Holy*. Oxford University Press: London, 1926.

CHAPTER FIFTEEN

TOTEMISM AND MYTHOLOGY

Totemism. Totemism, the understanding of which we owe to Elkin, Spencer and Gillen, and Radcliffe-Brown for their exhaustive studies of the Australian aborigines, was the system which provided that the identity of the social group was dependent upon a certain intimate and exclusive relationship towards a particular kind of animal or plant. Originating in this early account of Australian tribes it has been seen all over the world, in Africa, in North America, and elsewhere, and has become, principally in the hands of Durkheim and his followers, a basic principle of all religious and social life. The totem appears to stand for the unity and solidarity of the group to which it is attached, so that we have the *Kangaroo Men*, or whatever it might be.

It may be believed that the primeval ancestor of the group was closely related to this animal, so that he and his descendants are *in some way* themselves kangaroos. But no native regards himself in any literal sense as a kangaroo, whatever he says. It is for us to enter into the unique way of thinking and speaking that finds nothing odd in speaking in these terms.

The totemic group will usually be exogamous. Its members will only marry those of another totemic group. The particular animal will not, in developed forms of this system, be an item of diet of the group, but the totemic rituals may be thought of as maintaining the species to provide food for other groups, while *their* totem animal is maintained and multiplied to provide food for the first group.

As we have already seen in discussing the views of Durkheim, the totemic belief and ritual exists to strengthen and symbolize the solidarity of the group, and therefore has a considerable survival value. Radcliffe-Brown has argued that the totem animal must be of importance to the tribe. It is so in Australia, but not in Africa where it appears to be no more than an arbitrary symbol of the social unit.

Totemism certainly plays its part in providing a common body of values, beliefs, and customs, which every individual in a particular society learns, accepts, lives by, and transmits to his descendants. Such universal, unquestionable values and assumptions, Durkheim calls 'collective representations'.

Lévy-Bruhl, the distinguished colleague of Durkheim, went on to argue that the whole system of beliefs of primitive peoples *reflects their social structures*, and in so far as the patterns of society differ—as for example between the food-gatherers and hunters of Australia and the farmers of

Central Africa—these beliefs and categories of thinking differ too. This view has been considerably developed and modified by Lévi-Strauss.

Totemism and Classification. Lévi-Strauss sees totemism basically as a system of *classification* which is mentally necessary, as the Greek philosopher Aristotle believed when he first defined *species* and developed the system of logic based upon classification. Man himself is man and the world of men is therefore continuous. The imposition of species creates a disunity within this continuity, a differentiation within the unity. This is seen, for instance, in the caste system, which, in effect, is a method of securing the division of labour. On this is based the *exchange of services* necessary for social life. If totemism divides men into clans, then the practice of exogamy is another method of exchange, but this time the commodity is women.

In so far as totemism is another, widely spread and important form of division, it does not involve a real relationship between men and animals; it is only an intellectual scheme to help grasp the natural and social universe as an organized whole. Mankind *must* classify in order to *think*; and he must think in order to act. Everything in his world—men, animals, and plants—must be named and classified.

The Superstructure. This system of classification can be considered as a superstructure of a linguistic or logical character, which actually attributes and gives to all known things *their name and nature*. They are *constitutive*. Things as known are constituted, made real, and recognizable *for us*, by the act of thought and the apparatus of names and classes with which we organize our world.

This, and nothing less, gives meaning to existence in the objective world. The superstructure is therefore a sort of mediator between *matter* (objects, the external world in the raw), and the world of intelligible and factual entities.

Lévi-Strauss is emphatic that this system of thinking, or superstructure, by which we know everything, *is not final*. In the first place, as Lévy-Bruhl said, there may be several simultaneous systems in different parts of the world. Secondly, such a system may itself go through a process of change and development, perhaps owing to radical changes in the method and technique of production or trading.

But at the same time such a superstructure is essentially conservative and strongly resists change. This is because the superstructure is not *seen* as a superstructure. *We* are responsible for that process of abstraction. It is the natural way of seeing things and talking about them, *and behaving*. This is why the field anthropologist has to shed his own carapace and wriggle into the hermit-crab shell, which is not his own, in order to understand any people he lives with and wishes to investigate. This is why symbolic systems of magic, religion, and totemism are natural to the primitive and make complete sense, but unnatural to us, and often seem to be nonsense.

THE ROLE OF MYTH

The most usual role of the myth is an explanatory one, along the lines of Kipling's *Just-So Stories*, such as *How the Leopard got its Spots* or *How the Elephant got its Trunk*. Frankfort, too, has written of *The Logic of Mythopoeic Thought*. Primitive man is, however, not only seeking an explanation. According to Frankfort, he is personally involved in a never-ending conflict between natural and supernatural powers in a world which, for him, is not understood because he has little knowledge of scientific law. Thus one such power may be hostile to the harvest upon which he depends, another, frightening but beneficial. When a sudden storm overcomes the drought, this is seen as a highly personal conflict, in which he is *involved*. The mythological beings thus playing such an important role in his life are often seen in striking and fantastic form, capable of artistic representation, and not mere fantasy. This is nothing to do with legend, fable, or fairy tale. The mythical image is presented with a compelling authority. It is part of the personal revelation and intervention of a 'Thou'.

Our categories of thought are different and cannot properly handle this world; and yet it has a logic of its own. Primitive man expresses his 'emotional thought' in terms of cause and effect. He could reason logically; but in these matters he uses other forms of relating himself to reality, because ordinary logic is not compatible with his most significant experience of reality. Frankfort elaborates a number of such myths, expressing a dramatic conception of nature which sees everywhere a strife between divine and demoniac, cosmic, and chaotic powers, and does not leave man a mere spectator. It involves him deeply in the struggle.

Most anthropologists believe, however, that human *thinking* everywhere proceeds in the same logical manner, even if the basic assumptions, or structural pattern of the conceived universe, may take radically different forms. The *mentality* so shaped by varying cultures is something that is shared by everybody, and its laws are universal.

There are many other views of the importance and universality of myth in human life. These tend, on the whole, to unite it with ritual and art in serving the function of adapting man's emotions to the necessities of social life. One of the most widely found is myth as folklore.

MYTH AS FOLKLORE

Folklore contains many different elements. It consists of myths, tales, legends, proverbs, riddles, and verses, together with appropriate music when they are sung. The elements of folklore are often very closely linked with ritual and dance, which they explain.

Folklore presents a penetrating picture of a given way of life; it reveals much about the aspirations, values, and goals of different peoples. In its more poetic and imaginative forms, mythology reveals some of the deepest emotions and conflicts in the heart of man.

We must distinguish the different kinds of myth or folk tale.

1. There is the myth that explains a ceremonial dance or cult. This may not only be told but may be recorded pictorially on temple walls, vases, seals, shields, and the like. An example of this is the myth of Demeter and Persephone.

2. There is the embellished and romanticized story of some historical figure. This type of myth is called a *legend*.

3. The *allegory* is a type of myth which reads animal or human causes into natural events or seeks to explain them as the actions of supernatural persons.

4. Carl Jung has tried to persuade us that myths symbolize not cosmic phenomena but subconscious urges which, if not expressed, can destroy us. These, he maintains, are common to all men in all ages, which accounts for the great similarity of fairy tales and myths throughout the world.

5. Myths may be sentimental *fables*, as in the story of Narcissus and Echo; or minstrel romance, as in the story of Cephalus and Procris; or even simple melodrama, as in so many Greek myths.

Behind such stories one can always discern elements of history, of tribal organization, of religious belief and political activity, of invasions and migrations. Most often the true myth will rationalize and describe in personification archaic magic-making that promoted the fertility of the soil.

The Great Goddess. There are perhaps more myths about the Great Goddess than about any other supernatural person. She is the Mother, the Earth, the symbol of fertility, worshipped all over the ancient East in the many female deities of India. She is also worshipped in the fertility and mother goddesses of the eastern Mediterranean, the Phrygian Cybele, Astarte, Aphrodite, Gaea, Demeter, and the rest.

The *moon* is one of the goddess' celestial symbols. The moon's three phases of new, full, and old recall the matriarch's three phases of maiden, mature woman, and aged woman. Then, since the sun's annual course similarly recalled the rise and decline of her physical powers, spring becomes a maiden, summer a nymph or marriageable woman, winter a crone. The goddess thus became identified with seasonal changes in animal and plant life, and thus with Mother Earth, who at the beginning of the year produces only leaves and buds, then flowers and fruits, and at last ceases to bear. She could also be conceived as yet another triad: the maiden of upper air, the nymph of earth or sea, the aged woman of the underworld—typified respectively in classical mythology by Silene, Aphrodite, and Hecate. Thus do myths originate, proliferate, and change.

Mythic Themes. There are innumerable symbolic figures and plots which recur in every culture from North America to Central Africa:

(*a*) Two antagonistic beings argue and decide what will happen in the future.

(*b*) A discussion in the council of the animals. (There is an excellent Russian version of this in Krylov's fables.)

(*c*) The trickster hero's travels and adventures, as in the story of Till Eulenspiegel.

(*d*) Stories of dangerous animals and ogres that attack people.

(*e*) Stories of women who marry non-human beings.

(*f*) The magic-flight plot in which the fleeing hero successively casts small things over his shoulder and magically creates formidable obstacles which have to be surmounted by the pursuing ogre.

(*g*) Themes such as that of the Swan Maiden.

(*h*) Stories in which the weak prevail over the strong, where evil meets an avenger, or where the less pleasant conditions of life are resolved in ways that are not of the workaday world.

> The giant laughter of happy men
> That roars through a thousand tales,
> Where greed is an ape and pride is an ass,
> And Jack's away with his master's lass
> And the miser is banged with all his brass,
> And the farmer with all his flails.
>
> (G. K. Chesterton)

The Psychology of Myth. It is clear that many of these myths have a therapeutic effect similar to that of the novel or film in our day. By transporting men and women into a realm where problems are solved as they rarely are in actual life, folklore shows itself as a means of psychological release of tension and creative self-expression on both the conscious and unconscious levels.

Often, as Plato observed when discussing the education of the Greeks, the gods behave badly by human standards, and their myths are hardly for young ears. This may be explained by the hypothesis that we derive powerful satisfaction from *identifying ourselves, unconsciously, with characters who transgress the codes we ourselves may not violate.*

More fundamental still is the fact that the great myths, the universal myths, strike right to the roots of the question as to *what is man,* how did he come to be, why is life, why death, why evil—and good. Once developed by primitive myth-makers, then refined and shaped through generations of telling and retelling, their appeal became so elemental that they spread smoothly and quickly from primitive hearth to primitive hearth until the whole world was girdled with these common stories.

Myth also *explains the social order* and the right of the ruler to govern and the necessity of obedience. As Malinowski says:

> It justifies by precedent the existing order and it supplies a retro-spective pattern of moral values, of sociological discriminations and burdens and of magical belief. The myth of magic, of religion, or of any other body of customs or single custom is definitely a warrant of its truth, a pedigree of its filiation, a charter of its claims to validity.
> (From 'Culture' in the *Encyclopedia of the Social Sciences*.)

Myth, Poetry, and Collective Emotion. Myths, expressed in poetry and song because of their rhythm, are sung in unison and are thus capable of expressing collective emotion. Why should the tribe *need* a collective emotion? The approach of wild beasts, of a foe, of rain and storm, of an earthquake, will naturally elicit a conditioned and collective response. All will be menaced, all will fear. The artistic form is not so necessary in these circumstances, but when there is some long-distant objective—fields to be sown, a harvest to be reaped—something is needed to weld men together. This is achieved by group festivals and ceremonials in which the chanted myth helps to free the emotions and canalize them in a collective channel. The real object becomes an imaginative object; the crop to be reaped in the future is symbolically reaped now, and this *spurs man on to the labour necessary for its accomplishment in reality.*

Thus myth in poetic and chanted form, combined with dance, ritual, and music becomes the great switchboard of the instinctive energy of the tribe, directing it into trains of collective action whose immediate causes or gratifications are not the actual work but its imagined out-come.

Thus *the tribal individual is lifted above the present reality into a world of emotion* which drives on the whole machine of society. He is changed, educated, by having participated in the collective illusion.

This collective emotion organized by art at the tribal festival, because it sweetens work and is generated by the needs of labour, goes out again into labour to lighten it. The primitive conducts such collective tasks as hoeing, paddling, ploughing, reaping, and hauling to a rhythmic chant which has an artistic content related to the needs of the task and ex-presses the collective emotion behind the task.

Without the ceremony portraying in imaginative anticipation the granaries bursting with grain, the pleasures and delights of the harvest, men would not gladly face the hard labour necessary to make the harvest a reality. Sweetened with song, the work goes well. This is ritual's dynamic role in society.

A Typical Social Myth: The Circus. The circus, as we all know, is a ring. (The word comes from the Greek *kirkos* m. and *kirkē* f., meaning a ring.) Few people, however, realize that there is a connection between the circus and Circe the enchantress, but there is; they are the masculine and feminine of the circle, the ring.

The first circus was at Rome in the year 800 B.C. In the centre stood a ritual pit, which was opened at the time of the races. Running from the pit down the middle of the oval circus ran a low wall on which statues and trophies stood. This pit was the supposed entry to an underground cave where the stored fruits of the earth and their potencies were found.

The races were part of a religious festival concerned with this mother cave and its fruits. It was held on 21 August. There was a god connected with this pit called *Consus*. Here, then, is a ritual symbol of Mother Earth, a centre of life and the powers of generation.

Where does Circe come in? Circe is the Earth Mother, as she appears in the ritual circle of dance and race. Her island is the Earth itself. What of her spell that turns her wooers into beasts? It indicates that the dancers of the circle are fertility dancers, and so disguised as stags and bears and horses. By becoming these, they partake fully of the earth magic of her fertility.

In Homer's *Odyssey* when Odysseus with his voyagers reached Circe's magic island, all but Eurylochus and Odysseus were turned into swine. What has happened to the ancient myth? No longer do the dancers enter into the life of nature in its fullness; they are damned and doomed, and the Earth Mother becomes a temptress and enchantress. The offer of love and fruitfulness becomes a thing of fear and pollution. The beast mask will not come off. The dance will not stop.

Now we know what a circus is. It is the Earth conceived in artistic and ritual form, in the dance that brings men together in the rhythms of a new purpose—to increase the sources of fertility. And Circe is its spirit, its incarnation.

Yet the circus became something different, not the centre of a fertility dance, but the theatre of the death wish, of gladiatorial conflict, of beast fights and men thrown to beasts. The fertility ritual was distorted by the decaying Roman Empire in the days of its corruption and decline.

The Myth on the Threshold of History. Lévi-Strauss sees the role of myth in a fundamentally different way: when natural man makes the transition to culture, myth bridges the gap. It is therefore concerned with three main types: the coming of fire, and *cooking*; the elaboration of *kinship* relations and rivalries; and the waxing and waning of the seasons, which involves *the myth of the limping man*. The concept of the seasons is concerned with one of the fundamental polarities or disfunctions with which man is confronted: the wet and dry season, *plenty and famine*.

It is around such disfunctions, the framing of the totemic groups, and the uses of fire (Promethean Fire) that man builds up his interpretative way of life, with its rituals and myths.

A series of myths that concern totemic exogamy not as a system of rules (which is how the anthropologist comes to view it), but as a theme for mythical thought is concerned with *incest prohibition*.

The Myth of the Indian Girl and her Brother. This is an American Indian myth and concerns the adventures of a girl alarmed at the nightly visitation of one whom she fears is her brother. In the daylight he bears the signs of the visitor, including a scratch on his face, witness to her defence of her virtue. But the brother declares that he has a double, so close that any injury to him appears on the twin. To convince his incredulous sister he kills his double before her. The mother of the double cries for vengeance. To escape this the youth declares that he is *not* the brother but is himself the double; and proves that he cannot be the brother by marrying his sister. The mother is hoaxed, but she is a sorceress and the mistress of the owls. The owls know better and denounce the guilty ones, who, however, succeed in escaping.

This has reminiscences of the Oedipus myth—the incest between mother and son and a contingency arising which makes the incest inevitable. In the Greek myth the Sphinx plays an important role; Oedipus guessed her riddle and she slew herself. Now among North American Indians there are riddle myths and one of them very neatly put the myth of the girl and her brother. The owls set riddles to the hero which he must answer on pain of death.

What is the riddle? Lévi-Strauss suggests this *is a question to which one postulates that there is no answer*; or inverting this suggestion let us say *an answer for which there is no question*. Is this nonsense? Far from it. Mythology is full of myths which derive their whole point from *the answer for which there is no question*.

Lévi-Strauss exercises incredible ingenuity in linking these themes together, but his ultimate aim is really to show the universality of mythical themes all over the world and in widely different cultures. There are not many persons who could in so few pages simultaneously illuminate the story of Oedipus, an Indian incest myth, and the legend of the Holy Grail. What he hopes he is revealing is an obscure psychology, underlying social reality which anthropology unveils as the common heritage of man. As Strauss says 'Men communicate by symbols; but they can only have these symbols and communicate by them because they have the same instincts.'

MUSIC, DANCE, AND DRAMA

Song as a part of ritual changes one's subjective attitude to reality, and so indirectly it changes reality. Sung music must have preceded instrumental music by hundreds of thousands of years, but it must always have been closely associated with ritual dances, in which it immensely enhances every aspect of the psychological experience enjoyed.

In modern society the various arts are separate. Painters, sculptors, poets, musicians, and dancers only occasionally integrate their activities, as in a ballet or opera. But in primitive society the arts are an adornment for public festivity, and on such occasions music, dancing, poetry, and the plastic arts all come together in a single complex.

The drama gives opportunity to affirm some of the deepest sanctions of living. The myth declaimed and acted, the rhythm of the dances and drums call forth responses that bear profoundly on the emotional re-actions of the spectators and participants and facilitate their adjustment to tribal life. They give assurance that the rains will come, that crops will be abundant, that the hunt will succeed, or that victory over their enemies will be obtained.

The dance may be all-important after hardship and calamity have spread discouragement. If the magician explains this by discovering witchcraft behind the misfortune, steps must be taken to expel it. The dance brings the gods of the village among the worshippers. In particu-lar the magician himself is *possessed* by the gods, as his wild and yet per-fectly rhythmical dancing suggests. Tensions mount with his possession, as he indicates that he has found the source of evil and is about to drive it out. Then the whole dancing community goes wild with excitement. The dance lasts well into the night until all are exhausted. It is a cathar-sis, a purging—it heals and restores.

Primitive Music. Vocal music probably first consisted of rhythmic work songs which originated with the use of tools and the need for joint effort. Later came spinning songs, reaping songs, and hauling songs. Such songs go back to the very beginning of human life, when men were actually becoming men.

The first *instruments with strings* over a sounding board probably did not appear until neolithic times. Carved and hollowed flute-like instru-ments were probably among the first, and the myth of the piper Pan reflects their influence on the emotions.

Percussion instruments, such as rattles, tambourines, and drums appear at a very early period.

With the metal age the advance of technology made more complex instruments possible. The *lyre* spread from the Near East to most parts of the Old World. Stringed instruments were brought to America by the Spaniards, for the American Indian had never developed a true stringed instrument.

Where people lack instruments with fixed pitches, *the human voice controls all tonal patterns* and there are no mechanical factors to limit their variety, complexity, or range. Quarter tones or intervals other than half or whole tones are found under such circumstances. This is why it is impossible to record folk music on paper without doing violence to what is actually sung by forcing it into our scale. Our octave is divided into twelve equidistant tone intervals, the Japanese into five, the Siamese into seven.

In most cultures not only is singing in a fixed key not the rule, but deviation from true pitch is not regarded as incorrect; on the contrary it adds originality and interest.

Our music is *polyphonic*—that is to say, many notes, often on many instruments, are sounded in harmony. This is *not* the case with most primitive music, where richness is obtained by an extended scale, quarter tones, and great *flexibility of melodic line*, coupled with a complex rhythm.

The importance of rhythm is reflected in the large number of instruments used for percussion compared with those that carry the melody. If one breaks down a three-beat rhythm (waltz time) into a five- or seven-beat rhythm, it would be difficult for Europeans but easy for Africans.

FIELD STUDY NO. X—TOTEMISM AMONG THE AUSTRALIAN ABORIGINES

(This is a study based upon the work of Elkin, Spencer and Gillen, and Radcliffe-Brown.)

Totemism is a religious system in which a group depends on an intimate and exclusive relationship with an animal or plant for its identity. Such a totem provides the social group with *a name*—e.g., the men of the Kangaroo. In the second place this name tends to be the outward and visible sign of a supernatural force that binds the tribe together. In the third place the totem may be thought of as the ancestor of the tribe, a sort of fund of life force out of which all the members of the tribe are born.

Totemism, however, is by no means a one-way relationship of dependence upon the supernatural, for in turn the totem requires the sacred rites of the tribe to give it strength and fecundity. The elaborate rites maintain the life force of the totemic animal and ensure that it will multiply and be available as food for all the other tribes. The members of the *Kangaroo* totemic group, however, will normally refrain from slaying and eating the totem animal unless it be in a specially solemn and sacramental way. The other tribes have their own sacred animals and they in turn will look after them in the same way, so that all of the tribes together ensure that a wide range of animals, birds, insects, and plants are in plentiful supply for all their needs.

Thus when the time of the year arrives at which certain foods become fit for eating, a ceremony has to be performed before the food may be eaten freely. A ceremonial eating or sacramental meal must take place. In the Witchetty Grub Totem, for instance, when the grub is plentiful after what might, among an agricultural people, be called the harvest time, large supplies are gathered and brought to the camp, cooked, and stored away. Later, members of the totem eat a little and then distribute the rest of the store to those belonging to other totem groups.

This is not merely a magical rite. The solemn preparations, the reverential awe about the proceedings, bear evidence of a consciousness of the sacred, of genuine religious feeling. As Émile Durkheim has pointed out in *Elementary Forms of the Religious Life*, the sacredness which inheres in the totem is transferred to the men of the totemic group. Every member of the clan contains a mystic substance within him of which his very soul consists and through which he obtains his social as well as his religious status.

The Totem and the Sacramental Meal. One important kind of primitive sacrificial rite is the communion feast, in which the worshipper, by partaking of food and drink enters into fellowship with some supernatural force, thus establishing a union between the human and the divine by the mediation of a victim eaten by the worshippers. A remarkable example of this kind of sacrifice, which in fact takes many different forms, is the totemic ritual in which the men of the tribe periodically strive to enter into sacramental relations with the fountain and source of their tribal life. To whom else can they go for the all-important quality, and how else can it be obtained than by assimilating the sacred flesh of the species?

The Regeneration of the Kangaroo. The religious significance of such a ceremony is well seen in the *intichiuma* ceremony of the Kangaroo Totem. On this occasion the men proceed to the foot of a hill. On the slope two blocks of stone project, one above the other. One of these stones represents a male kangaroo, the other a female kangaroo. The headman of the totem clan with his mother's uncle, or a man of that generation, climbs up to the two blocks of stone and rubs them with another stone. They then go to a rocky ledge, supposedly haunted by the spirits of ancestral kangaroos, and paint it with stripes of red and white to symbolize the red fur and white bones of the kangaroo. When this is done, a number of the young men sit on the top of the ledge, while the men below sing of the increase of the kangaroos. Blood-letting follows. The men open veins in their arms and allow the blood to fall on to the sacred ceremonial stone where an ancestral kangaroo went down into the earth long ago. The purpose of the ceremony is to drive out in all directions the spirits of the kangaroos and so to increase their number. After the rite has been duly performed, the young men go and hunt the kangaroo. The old men eat a little of the flesh and anoint their bodies with its fat, after which the meat is divided among all the men assembled. The men then decorate themselves with totemic designs and the night is spent in singing songs about their tribal exploits. When this is done, the animal may be eaten sparingly for the rest of the year.

Here is a ceremony that provides men not only with their food but with something else. These ceremonies are penetrated by quickenings of sacrifice, prayer, and communion. They bring to bear on the need of the hour all the promise of that miraculous past which not only cradled the race, but still yields it the stock of reincarnated soul force that enables it to survive.

Ritual and Tribal Life. Elkin thus describes the effect of these ceremonies upon the participants:

> When they return from their ceremonies to the world of secular affairs they are refreshed in mind and spirit. They now face the vicissitudes of everyday life with a new courage and strength gained from the common participation in the rites, with a fresh appreciation of their social and moral ideals and patterns of life, and an assurance that having performed the rites well and truly, all will be well with themselves and with that part of nature with which their lives are intimately linked.
>
> (*The Australian Aborigines*)

The Totem and Tribal Unity. Totemic religion is an expression of social solidarity. Man alone is nothing. He realizes his significance and worth only as a member of a social group. Religion is social—for all its entities, its gods, the whole field of the sacred and the supernatural are nothing more or less than the tribe divinized. God and society are one. The totemic principle can therefore be nothing else than the clan itself, personified and represented to the imagination under the visible form of the totem.

During these rites the collective sentiment expresses itself in everything that is done, from the tribal dances to the sacred meals. This expression of tribal spirit strengthens it, and the men who participate find themselves carried away by a power outside themselves, the very presence of which and the power of which they can never afterwards forget.

The Totem and the Individual. Man gets all that makes him a man from society. It is the religious cult, the totemic ritual, that recreates him, imbues him with the life that is the life of the tribe, and therefore simultaneously regenerates the tribe. Thus the individual is raised above himself to make him lead a life superior to that which he would lead if he followed only his own individual whims. The totemite receives his very manhood, his essence as an individual, from the tribal spirit which possesses him in the ceremonies and rites of this form of religion.

FIELD STUDY NO. XI—FOLKLORE AND THE SUPERNATURAL IN SOUTHERN IRELAND

The activities of every primitive community are interpenetrated with a sense of the supernatural. The unseen is not, for them, either something remote or for the sacred occasion only. It is always there; it is in everything. At every stage of washing, dressing, eating, or working, the primitive resorts to the aid of friendly spirits or tries to drive away evil ones. When things go wrong, he suspects the interference of demons; but he is equally on the alert for happy omens and signs of grace.

Not only are there actual spirits—or, in Ireland, fairies known locally as 'the good people', or simply 'them'—but in early times kings and chiefs were regarded as being endowed with supernatural power. Even today certain people are credited with close acquaintance with spiritual beings and are therefore to be feared or interceded with for help. Certain objects or materials are also believed to be allied to the supernatural— iron in particular; indeed smiths form a special caste, are still credited with some faint tinge of the unusual, and almost always marry within the trade. 'There is great power in iron,' says the Irish countryman, 'and if the butter does not come in the churn, take a ploughshare and hold it in the turf fire and it will come all right.' There is power, too, in a hazel stick, and if necessary it will drive 'them' away.

Irish folklore is rich in butter stories. Churning, especially by hand, is a tricky process. 'And queer things do happen to butter, and it's a fact that it often wouldn't come and you don't know why.' Belief provides both explanation and remedy. The fairies have taken the butter and must be induced to bring it back. Two men come home and find a woman churning, but no butter will come. Are 'they' holding it up? The woman now tells them that an old woman had borrowed some milk. They are deeply concerned and at once close the door and put a ploughshare in the turf fire. Soon there is a knock, and after the third knock an old woman's hand passes a jug of milk through the door and a voice says, 'Put this back in the churn.' The woman does so and the butter comes immediately.

Are the 'good people' friendly or hostile? It is difficult to say, for there is no very clear distinction between good and bad spirits. In general they are a law unto themselves, sometimes good and sometimes bad; it depends on what you do. It is possible to offend them and then they will plague you. But if you treat them properly they will help you. 'If we knew how to be neighbourly with them, they would be neighbourly and friendly with us. Therefore it is advisable to leave food and water for them at night, and one must be careful not to throw out dirty water at night, for it might drench them.' The good people particularly favour clean and tidy houses and good household management. An old fellow of North Clare speaks thus (1937), 'They very often put up at a house in the night. They would come to certain houses, and if they liked the house and it was good and clean and everything swept for them, they would come often to the same house, and that house would be prosperous. If it was dirty and they found no comfort in it, they would not stop.' In this way the values of daily life are projected into and reinforced by the supernatural world.

The fairies are not entirely friendly beings; indeed they will spirit away anything, from hens to men and women. The common Irish belief in changelings has its roots in taking by fairies. The real person has been taken away and someone else, or something else, left in his or its place. The fairies mysteriously sap the strength of an old man, leaving him weak and listless, little recognizable as the strong helper of former years. The vitality has gone out of him. The real person has been spirited away, and left in his place is 'some spent old man that they had with them for a long time.'

Precautions must also be taken about cattle. 'The good people have cows and sheep and chickens out in the raths, just as we have, for it is they that have taken them when bad luck is on us, and whatever we do won't stop them.' When danger of this sort is abroad, precautions must be taken, the necessary rites must be performed. If cattle fall sick, other rites will drive off the threatening good people and restore the cow to health.

Ghosts and the Dead. Death is a great disturber of social habits. It shakes emotional equilibrium. What will help, however, is a reformation of the bond between the living and the dead. So the dead join the fairies. On the borderline between the mundane world and the hereafter they find a place in the ranks of the good people.

One must always act towards these spirits of the departed (who are never far away) as one acts towards the living. They tell a story of a man who was walking along the road and saw the ghost of his brother. He didn't say anything to it and it walked home with him all in silence. They sat at the fire for a long time, the living man waiting for the other to go, so that he could go to bed. Finally the dead man said, 'You have put me to great trouble tonight by not saluting me when we met. I must go now and I won't be able to defend you in the council of the rath.' And it was true for him, too; the cow that was ailing with the man was taken the next week.

'Cowls' are ruined, deserted cottages where the family has died out. You often see old people sitting in them. 'What people?' an anthropologist asked a countryman. 'The people that used to be in it,' he replied. 'Do you mean ghosts?' He answered scornfully, 'You might see lights in the cowl and you going along the road at night, and you pass people you don't know and you can't tell if they are ghosts or not. Of all the people you pass in the town, how would you know what it is they are?'

In the treatment of death one can see the social system of rural Ireland in the full perspective of its deep-rooted strength. In the flashes of poetic genius which seem so prone to trip from an Irish tongue, death seems to acquire an increasingly poignant meaning.

The Significance of the Fairy Cult. This cult serves a definite social purpose. It provides a symbolic order overlying the values of social life and clothes them in emotional terms in much the same way as do unofficial dogmas and cosmologies among all peoples. What the countryman's belief is doing for him is something belief always seems destined to do wherever it is found. Tradition is bearing upon him to keep alive and organize the regard his group must feel for the codes of conduct and the way of life of the local community. Belief focuses his attention and his emotions upon them. It gives security to his conventions, his needs, and his goods. It infuses them with emotional associations far beyond their normal capacity to carry sentiment. It gives them symbolic form.

In this way the fairy cult holds before man, in emotion, in ritual act, in hope of cure and defence against evil, the important place that traditions and ritual have in the social life, which is dependent on habit and sentiment. It provides him with the secure and stable order of traditional life.

SUGGESTED FURTHER READING

Durkheim, E., *Elementary Forms of the Religious Life*. Collier–Macmillan: New York, 1915.

Elkin, A. P., *The Australian Aborigines*. Angus & Robertson: Sydney, 1964.

Frankfort, H., *Before Philosophy*. Penguin Books: London, 1949.

Lévi-Strauss, C., *The Savage Mind*. Weidenfeld & Nicolson: London, 1968.

Lévi-Strauss, C., *Structural Anthropology*. Penguin Books: London, 1968.

Lévi-Strauss, C., *Totemism*. Merlin Press: London, 1967.

Levy-Bruhl, L., *The Soul of the Primitive*. Allen & Unwin: London, 1923.

Smith, W., Robertson, *The Religion of the Semites*. Macmillan: London, 1966.

Spencer, B. and Gillen, F. J., *The Northern Tribes of Central Australia*. Macmillan: London, 1904.

Radcliffe-Brown, A. R., *The Social Organisation of Australian Tribes*. Oceanic Monographs No. 1: Melbourne, 1931.

CHAPTER SIXTEEN

LANGUAGE AND WRITING

Tools and Speech. Tools and speech are distinctive features of mankind, and these two great human functions are causally interdependent. One theory of the origin of speech maintains that speech came into existence in conjunction with the aid of implements; thus the first forming of words was a collective process. The tool creates speech, and speech, because word symbols have a meaning, produced the forming of clear conceptions and logical thought. A tool is a thing used *as a means to consequences*, instead of being taken directly and physically. It is *anticipatory and predictive*. The most convincing evidence that animals do not think is found in the fact that they have no tools, but depend on their own body structures to achieve results.

Animals make signals and express emotions—often the expression of the emotion *is* the signal, but they do not use symbols for general ideas relating to either objects or actions. There is a physiological reason for this: the brain of the animal is not adequate to the task of framing such concepts and associating them with sounds. The appearance of speech requires a development of the association centres in the rest of the cortex, which is the real meaning of the great enlargement of the human brain compared with that of the anthropoids.

Abstract thinking, speech, and the use of tools are inseparably connected. As tools differentiate into new and more appropriate forms, so language differentiates into an ever-growing wealth of words, sentences, and thoughts to further general ideas. Thus speech became increasingly adequate as a means of imparting information. The ability to think improved man's capacity to investigate the world and enlarged human possibilities.

Speech and Society. It has been supposed that changes in the environment drove our ancestors, who had just descended from the trees, out into the plains. There the final differentiation between hand and foot took place, together with the upright posture.

Under these changed conditions of life, with a more difficult food supply and greater dangers, man grappled with the world in three new ways: by tools, by fire, and by a closing of the ranks into groups—and these groups engaged in continuous co-operation in the utilization of new tools and new techniques. This demanded speech.

Animals living in isolation cannot arrive at such a stage of development. *It is only as a social being that man can reach this stage.* Outside the bounds of society language is just as useless as an eye in darkness.

Language is possible only in society, and only there is it needed, as a means by which members may understand one another. All social, tool-using animals possess some means of understanding, otherwise they would not be able to execute plans jointly.

The use of tools also presupposes a society because it is only through society that attainments can be preserved. In a state of isolated life everyone has to make discoveries for himself; with the death of the discoverer the discovery also becomes extinct, and everyone has to start anew from the very beginning. *It is only through society that the experience and knowledge of former generations can be preserved*, perpetuated, and developed. In a group individuals die, but the group as such does not; it lives on.

LANGUAGE AND CULTURE

Sturtevant defines language as 'a system of arbitrary vocal symbols by which members of a social group co-operate and interact' (*An Introduction to Linguistic Science*). Such symbols must, of course, be learned, and they are learned as part of the culture of which they are a part, a culture which, in all its aspects, must be assimilated by every new generation. We may therefore add to Sturtevant's definition '. . . and by means of which the learning process is effected and a given way of life assimilated.'

Language is therefore more than a means of expression: it cannot stand alone, but must be taken in relation to the whole background of tribal and natural life—in relation to a whole culture. This is why it is so difficult to translate an African language directly into English. **Words can be understood only in relation to the culture of which they are a part.**

Take the word 'uncle'. To us it means one thing, to the African it conveys quite a different set of ideas. Among primitive peoples the mother's brother and the father's brother are strictly distinguished, and the same word will not do for both; for the duties and privileges of the former are much nearer those exercised in our society by a father than by an uncle.

The point to note is that language both depends on culture and explains culture. It is limited by the culture of which it forms a part and is moulded by the knowledge and requirements of its users. Some primitive tribes do not use numbers beyond six, while others can count to sixty or more. This has nothing to do with intelligence, for the same people who can count only to six can play complicated games using what are really mathematical principles.

Hence the idea of the speech community—a group of people who share a culture, its categories, concepts, and unique modes of behaviour. All the higher activities of man spring from the close adjustment among members of society, and this is based on language. The forms of speech, therefore, are so deeply imbedded in the habits of a people that they provide an excellent means of investigating the culture as a whole.

Vocabularies. The first step in analysing a *culture language* is to study the vocabulary. This often has surprising results. It was previously thought that primitive peoples had primitive vocabularies of two or three hundred words. This is not so. The vocabulary in general use among savages may run to 20,000 words, of which 2000 words is the normal vocabulary employed in ordinary conversation. This is actually greater than the vocabulary of many Europeans. Moreover, because social stratification is less developed, the widest range of words is shared by everybody.

The number of words used has practical significance, and so have the different words used for different varieties of the same thing. Some tribes have a name for every kind of fish and yet no general name for fish. To speak of 'fish' in general has no significance, whereas to speak of a certain kind of fish means a great deal. Similarly a European carpenter, when he wishes to purchase wood, does not ask for 'wood', but states the exact kind that he requires.

Does this mean that these languages are lacking in abstract terms? This is not so. These languages have whole classes or categories of words devoted to the abstract; they are fluent and lucid vehicles of expression. They are precise, and for every concrete substance or activity there is a corresponding abstract; moreover, grammatically they have an exceptionally wide range of moods and tenses to express the special qualities of different actions.

Grammar without Grammarians. The languages of primitive people are not only rich in words but highly complex in structure. However, the rules of grammar are not formulated, in spite of the fact that they are rigidly kept. To the native the immense range of speech structures seem obvious and logical, just as ours do to us; but we would regard them as difficult and even unnecessary.

Let us consider the word 'cut'. We can say: I am cutting; I cut (past); I cut myself; I shall cut—but the Liberians have many more forms of this word, all of them quite different. Here they are:

PRESENT

I cut now.
I am through cutting just now.
I am continuing to cut now.

RECENT PAST

I did cut a little while ago.
I cut several times a little while ago.
I kept on cutting a little while ago.
I had the purpose in mind of cutting a
little while ago, but didn't.

DISTANT PAST

I did cut a long time ago.
I cut several times a long time ago.
I kept on cutting.

And so we continue with four different forms also for the Near Future and the Indefinite Future until we come to the Present Reflexive and the—

RECENT PAST REFLEXIVE

I did cut myself a little while ago.
I cut myself several times a little while ago.
I kept on cutting myself a little while ago.

The way action is conceived in this series of tenses and modes is clearly different from English, for *distance in time* is also taken into account; and further, it is specified whether action is continuous or intermittent, whether it is to take place at a given moment or at an indefinite period. All these shades of meaning are embodied in various forms of the simple word for 'cut'.

Interesting speculations are suggested over the strict relationship of categories, ideas, forms of thought to the peculiarities of social and technological organization. Is it possible to conduct an argument on democracy in our terms using a language devised in a matrilineal, agricultural clan with a magico-religious ideology?

THOUGHT AND LANGUAGE

An entirely new approach to the problem of primitive ways of thought and the language and symbols in which this is expressed has been made in recent years. The early anthropologists, to whom we owe a great debt for their pioneer work, proceeded on the assumption that they could understand primitive belief-systems only by putting them into their own terms and then trying to see how a reasonable person (the anthropologist of course) could possibly come to accept them. The result usually was that savages were supposed to live in a welter of absurd and irrational superstitions. The problem was how the anthropologist would have reached these beliefs were he a savage. This was answered in terms of intellect. So Tylor argued that when men tried to explain dreams they produced the theory of a soul which left the body in sleep, and thus primitive man endowed all things, including inanimate objects with souls. Frazer saw magic as an attempt at scientific explanation which did not work, so that rational explanation shifted to religion, and produced the hypothesis of spiritual beings who could be invoked. These rationalistic explanations then gave way to psychological ones, like

Freud's *Future of an Illusion*, asking why men came to believe in palpable absurdities, and putting it down to their emotional needs.

It is still all too easy to say, in the words of the hymn, 'the heathen in his blindness, bows down to wood and stone', or to attribute religion to fear, or defective logic. This tendency should be resisted, because modern anthropology is convinced that this is to misrepresent the whole mental background of primitive people and seriously distorts the whole of our anthropological thinking.

In the first place savages are highly intelligent, secondly they know perfectly well what natural causes are at work and must be utilized to secure desired results; but beyond that they have complex ways of thinking and acting, involving an elaborate symbolism, which operates side by side with their practical techniques. Durkheim and Lévy-Bruhl came nearest to understanding this, and have taught us not to try to interpret magic, religion, rituals, kinship and so forth, in terms of categories derived from an analysis of ideas of our own culture.

> The scientific procedure, on the contrary, would be to start from distinctions made by primitive peoples between two kinds of thought and action, and then to determine what are the essential features of each and the main differences between them.
>
> Evans-Pritchard, *The Institutions of Primitive Society*

This demands a much more thorough and patient inquiry into the facts instead of a hastily constructed pattern of thought *on our terms*. Above all, religious and magical practices must be construed not by isolating them as if they were only primitive attempts at *explanation*, and rather poor ones at that; but by closely integrating them with the full social context of primitive life in all its complexity, with the whole system of social, economic, sexual, moral, and religious conception of a people. This in turn will bring us up against *a people's entire range of thought*. This constitutes their world, and their language, and in this we shall find the proper place for ritual, magic, and religion. It has thus come to be understood that the old anthropological stereotypes about primitive modes of thought were inadequate and misleading, mostly because they translated the beliefs of a pre-literate, non-Western people into twentieth-century European language. We are at last discovering the vast complexity and rich symbolism of primitive languages and the thoughts they express—and there is nothing illogical about it at all. It is highly sophisticated; in many cases too sophisticated for us, and that is why we find it so difficult to understand.

Beattie has tried to simplify this by speaking of *instrumental* thought (ordinary technical cause and effect), and *expressive* thought operating through ritual and symbolism. Both are contained within *one* world, and do not represent a dichotomy into natural and supernatural which is totally foreign to the minds of these people.

The Influence of Language in Thought. We generally assume that we think in a particular way first and then frame a language in which to express our thoughts. But linguistic inquiry is beginning to understand that what we know and feel is influenced by what we say, by the language forms in which we have to speak *and think*. Man can only think what he can say, and in the terms in which he has to speak, that is to say in the particular language he uses. For the categories of his language provide the categories of his perception, memory, metaphor, and imagination. This view implies that the categories of his language make one man's thought different from that of another. If this is so, speakers of different languages cannot think alike since there is a difference in categories and modes of thought which no translation can bridge.

Of course there are translatable signs for common objects and so forth, but it is when we come to the language of social relations, and what may be called the *implicit philosophy* of a people, that the difficulty of translation and comprehension really becomes insuperable.

Lévi-Strauss on the Savage Mind. This new approach to language and the savage mind is basic to the anthropological thinking of Lévi-Strauss.

Language begins with *classification*; and kinship rules are just that. Work out the intricate pattern of kinship linking you to hundreds of people and prescribing your obligations, behaviour, duties, and rights in regard to each and all in the community, and you have the significance of the terms, *the language* in which kinship is described, spoken about, thought about, acted about. Language also provides a way of transmitting experience in myth and symbol, and it is a way of thinking that works by *polarity*, by setting things in pairs, such as light and dark, dry season and wet season, and so on.

There is thus built up a conceptual scheme, a set of slots, into which all factual experience has to go, and we only see things and know them, *by the slot into which we put them*. All experience is realized as structure and only thus does it become intelligible.

What we seldom appreciate is that this is precisely how *we* have to reason, with our own *slots* or system of meanings; and this is far from that of the primitive. Our structural system of categories or slots is *constitutive* of our knowledge. The facts are *processed* in the act of knowing them. We never get them neat.

In future years this approach will have a profound influence not only on anthropological thinking, but on all our thinking about man, society and religion.

WRITING

Art is communication. Writing is communication by means of visual symbols substituted for spoken words. **All writing is symbolic and its origins lie in symbolic art and thought.**

Priests and Merchants. Writing is the art of civilization. Very many cultures with a rich language and a traditional mythology have no *written* language. It is possible to construct a written language for such people and to provide them with books. This was first done by Christian missionaries and has recently been done on a wide scale for formerly illiterate peoples in several regions of the world.

Writing has an early association with temples, which, with their priests, were of the greatest importance in the early centuries of Mesopotamian and Egyptian civilization and the whole of the Near Eastern culture. The priests formed permanent colleges or corporations, accumulating power and property, and engaged in much economic enterprise. They organized schools, which were provided with scripts and copybooks.

At first confined to the servants of the temple, the art of writing soon spread outside the temple walls; and when the monopoly on writing disappeared, the reins of temporal power began to pass from priestly hands.

The earliest writing is not very interesting from a literary point of view. It is almost entirely commercial or consists of lists of cities and of inventories of materials. Its origin lay in the necessities of accountancy rather than in any aspirations of the human spirit.

Pictograms and Ideograms. Very early forms of communication are not writing at all, but strips of pictures telling some kind of story or recording some event—a long trek, a battle, or even a peace treaty. There may well be a traditional interpretation of such a picture and when this is forgotten, no one can tell what the picture means.

We may later pass from a picture of an incident to a *succession* of fixed symbolic pictures, one representing a man, the next a fish, the next a fire and so on. We now have to interpret *the significance of the series*. This is a **pictogram.**

One stage beyond this is the **ideogram,** which is like a conventional traffic sign or other sign (such as a pointing hand). Signs can now represent ideas, qualities, and actions. Thus a rather conventionalized drawing of a leg comes to represent the idea 'stand', and an eye with lines below it means 'weep'. A goose represents a child, because both are valuable. A highly conventional mouth, with lines above it indicating vapour means 'words'.

The Phonogram. We are still a long way from true writing, but we now come to the first real step towards signs for sounds—the **phonogram.** Here the picture stands for a monosyllable, a sound. If the word for mouth is *ka*, as it is in Sumerian, then a picture of a mouth comes to represent *this sound*. Words other than 'mouth' may contain this sound and so, putting it together with other similar monosyllables, we may draw a series of pictures, each representing its own sound, and so make up a word.

This is what we did in the children's game of rebus. Thus a picture of a *pen*, followed by that of a *sieve* would represent the word 'pensive'.

The Syllabary. The next stage provided a separate sign for every possible syllable. The sign might have been remotely connected with an original phonogram, but perhaps this was originally in a different language, so the sign now comes to mean a *different* sound, that of the second language.

However there are no signs for single consonants, and if we want to use one, we must choose a syllable beginning with the consonant

A leg = stand

An eye with lines = weep

A goose = child
(= much prized)

A mouth with vapours = words

Fig. 19　Ideograms.

followed by some vowel. It was a remarkable discovery that led to signs for single consonants.

Syllabaries may contain a very large number of such syllabic symbols.

The Alphabet. It was a late development of Egyptian hieroglyphics, which were first ideograms and then phonograms, that led to the alphabet; for it was here that single signs were first given the value of *single letters* and not syllables containing, necessarily, a consonant and a vowel.

From this arose a group of slightly divergent Semitic alphabets, of which the Phoenician is the most important. These scripts ranged from Sinai to the Mediterranean coast. The oldest example of a Semitic alphabet yet found (1300 B.C.) was at Byblos in North Syria, from which we get the word Bible, which means the 'book'. *The Semitic names of* the objects depicted became the names of the letters; thus the Egyptian sign for an ox's head was called *aleph*; but each sign represented a *letter* and not a syllable. Thus aleph stood for A. There is a discoverable Egyptian picture for every letter of the alphabet and a Phoenician (Semitic) word for it. Thus a picture of a fish becomes by gradual transformation first in Phoenician an S (*samekh*) and then the Greek X (xi).

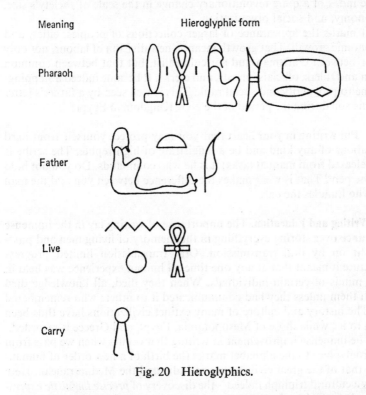

Fig. 20   Hieroglyphics.

There is **only one alphabet.** All existing alphabets are derived from the same original alphabet, whether we are speaking of the Devanagari script of India, Arabic, Hebrew, Persian, or Greek. There were thirty-two signs to start with, and no vowels (aleph, which is A, being a breathed consonant).

We are mainly interested in what the Greeks did with the Phoenician alphabet when they borrowed it in 1100 B.C. or earlier. They turned certain signs for which they had no use into vowels, and created a new sign for *ph*. The Greeks began by writing from right to left, like the Hebrews, but reversed it, going backward along each second line, thus going across the page like a ploughman crossing a field and turning at the end. Finally they adopted the idea of writing everything from left to right, and that is the direction in which all scripts except the Semitic and their Middle Eastern derivates run today.

The Romans took over the Greek alphabet, modified it, produced a cursive or running hand as well as the basic form, which consisted of capitals; and so writing as we know it arrived.

Writing and Civilization. Writing is a convenient and easily recognizable index of a quite revolutionary change in the scale of society's size, economy, and social organization.

It marks the appearance of larger collections of peoples, cities, and economic growth. That growth meant a new division of labour, not only that between craftsman and agriculturalist, but that between common men and rulers, officials, priests, and clerks. It became indeed a stepping-stone to prosperity and social rank. This is well seen by a father's letter to his son during the period of the New Kingdom in Egypt:

> Put writing in your heart that you may protect yourself from hard labour of any kind and be a magistrate of high repute. The scribe is released from manual tasks; it is he who commands. Do you not hold the pen? That is what makes the difference between you and the man who handles the oar.

Writing and Education. The importance of writing lay in the immense advance over storing everything in the memory of living men and passing it on by oral transmission. Oral transmission limited progress because it meant that at any one time all human experience was held in the minds of certain individuals. When they died, all knowledge died with them unless they had communicated it to others who remembered it. The history and culture of many extinct civilizations have thus been lost to us, while those of Mesopotamia, Egypt, and Greece is recorded.

The immense improvement in writing that occurs when we pass from hieroglyphics to the alphabet marks the birth of a new order of humanity, that of the great civilizations of India and the Mediterranean. Here was a cultural triumph indeed—the discovery of *precise linguistic expression through phonetically representative symbols.*

FORMS AND TECHNIQUES IN WRITING

But how did people learn the actual process of writing? Pictographs may be carved; they may be painted on some hard surface; they may be impressed in soft clay, then hardened; they may be written with pen or brush on papyrus—and that brings us to the pen and paper we know.

Hieroglyphics. The earliest Egyptian documents that survive, dating back to 3000 B.C., are names and titles on seals and vases, notes of accounts or inventories, and short records of events. The signs are recognizable pictures. The pictographs and ideograms of the Egyptians could be carved on stone and wood or painted on walls, especially on tombs, monuments, and other buildings. Later they were also written with pen and ink on papyrus, a paper made by felting, criss-cross fashion, the pith of the papyrus reed and then pressing it flat. There was surely a decorative emphasis in Egyptian hieroglyphics which obstructed the formation of symbolic letters of a more conventional kind. Nevertheless the Egyptians did develop two *cursive* forms—that is to say, writing in which one does not have to lift the pen from the paper after every letter.

Cuneiform. Before the well-known Babylonian records formed by impressing patterns on soft clay, the priests of Sumer kept the temple accounts by scratches on clay tablets. The marks consist of shorthand pictures—a jar, a bull's head, two triangles. You can guess what the signs mean just by looking at them.

After 3000 B.C. we find not only accounts and inventories but treaties, liturgical and historical texts, spells, and fragments of legal codes. The pictures are now completely conventionalized because they have to be made by pressing a straight, wedged-shaped piece of wood into soft clay in as near an imitation of a picture as possible. The clay was then baked in the sun.

This is *cuneiform*, and its use spread very widely in the Middle East and among peoples speaking quite unrelated languages.

Writing in North America. The North American Indians developed forms of communication which never passed beyond the ideogram. The simplest messages were recorded on *sticks* by cutting *notches* on them. These were made in the presence of the messenger, who received his instructions while they were being made. The notches were merely aids to memory.

Pictographs were widely used by the American Indians, who also used notched sticks to record various incidents, such as the number of days spent on an expedition, the number of enemies slain and the like.

Wampum belts, consisting of strung beads, were utilized as an aid to the memory, like the notched stick; but they were later employed in more intricate forms—e.g., white beads indicated peace, purple or violet meant war. Sometimes a pattern was made in the belt with beads of a different colour, as in the belt presented to William Penn on making his treaty with the Leni-Lenape chiefs in 1682. In the centre of the belt two figures, intended to represent Penn and an Indian, join hands, thus indicating a treaty.

Birch bark pictures were often used to indicate the order of a series of subjects in the song chants of a tribe.

The Record of the Years. The Dakota Indians invented a chronological table wherein each year was recorded by a picture of some important event which happened in that year. These pictures were symbolic—a black upright stroke indicated that a Dakota Indian had been killed; a rough outline of a head and body spotted all over indicated a smallpox outbreak.

Pebble Writing. We should mention **the Capsian culture** in Spain (see p. 222), closely connected with North Africa and represented by some remarkable drawings. This was a mesolithic culture; that is to say it lay between the latest phase of the Old Stone Age and the neolithic period with its polished axes and leaf-shaped arrowheads.

This culture was called **Azilian** (from Mas d'Azil near Saint-Geron in France); it produced implements fitted with small sharp flints in rows and also brightly coloured, patterned pebbles. The characters are of two kinds: (*a*) a series of strokes which possibly indicate numbers; (*b*) graphic symbols. These markings are certainly not accidental. They have been thought to represent symbols of an alphabet or syllabary, or perhaps ideograms—drawn or written symbols which stand for things or ideas.

Elsewhere in the Iberian Peninsula at Cogal, in Portugal, we find painted walls containing convincing pictures, but also conventionalized pictures which are coming to stand for notions; these are symbols. Like the more famous cave drawings of **Altamira** and **Lascaux,** they are probably magic hunting symbols to help the deer-slayer.

Whatever approximations to writing thus appear in Europe and North America, they never developed into a working syllabary, still less into an alphabet. For that great achievement we must turn to the Semites—to the Phoenicians—and to the alphabets derived from their discovery.

Shells, Bones, and Skins. In Egypt, Arabia, and elsewhere we also find writing on shells, on the shoulder blades (scapula) of sheep and, of course, on skins rubbed smooth. This parchment has preserved for us some of the greatest literature of the religious Middle East, notably the Hebrew scrolls, some of which were recently discovered in the vicinity of the Dead Sea.

Books Are Magical. It is hardly surprising that books were often considered to have some potency in themselves, especially if very old. The Egyptian or Babylonian student did not demand that a book be up-to-date. He valued it for its antiquity or as a faithful copy of a very old writing. The older the book, the more authoritative, and the words read aloud from it were so imbued with supernatural power that even of themselves they could produce strange and wonderful effects.

Something of this spirit is found in the reverence paid by Islam to the Koran, by the Jews to their Sacred Scriptures, and by Christians to the New Testament. The chained Bibles still to be found in old churches in England bear witness to the immense significance which was attached to the first Bibles put into general circulation.

SUGGESTED FURTHER READING

Bloomfield, Leonard, *Language*. Allen & Unwin: London, 1953.

Meinhof, Carl, *Structure and Relationships of African Languages* (translated by Werner, A.). Routledge & Kegan Paul: London, 1926.

Moorhouse, A. C., *Writing and the Alphabet*. Cobbett Press: London, 1946.

Sapir, E., *Language, an Introduction to the Study of Speech*. Hart-Davis: London, 1963.

Sturtevant, E. H., *An Introduction to Linguistic Science*. Yale University Press: New Haven, Conn., 1947.

CHAPTER SEVENTEEN

PRIMITIVE ART

Everyone knows what art is. We see it, hear it, even create it almost instinctively, and men have done so for tens of thousands of years. We know when we are engaging in aesthetic activities, whether we have ever thought about it or not, but what few people have ever done is to ask themselves *why* they do it. What is its significance? The anthropologist as well as the art historian, the art critic and the philosopher of aesthetics, does want to know why.

On reflection we have to confess that art is not the satisfaction of material needs on the one hand; and it is not a straightforward statement of religious or social ideas on the other. Is it then perhaps simply our dream world? There may be fantasy about such arts as poetry, music, and painting, but if it is only fantasy it falls short of what we are looking for and need. The world of artistic creation seems to be something in itself, though closely related to life and our deepest thoughts and our most sincere religious feelings. But it cannot be constructed without the imagination, without the dream, the 'going beyond'. And it plays an essential part in every culture in giving that culture a meaning, an emotional tone, in contributing a unifying force which at the same time exalts. It is in fact one of the basic elements which go to form a society.

We see it in the dance, with its vigorous rhythmic drum beat, in the chorus and chant, in the wall painting and sculpture, in the rich ornamentation in necklets, crowns, helmets, robes, and insignia, which are attached to those who lead, or are the people's priests or witch-doctors. It overflows into ornamentations, in the marrying of significant design to objects of a utilitarian kind, from pots and spoons, to door posts and gateways.

We have to ask ourselves what aspect of life is thus finding expression, satisfying us collectively, adding grace and dignity to life, making us proudly conscious of our culture. And what is the unique mode of apprehension whereby we feel it, enjoy it, in more than practical or intellectual terms, more than the terms of obligatory ritual?

We do not know of course what the forms of primitive art were, because everything must have perished except those few examples found in graves, buried with the dead, or painted or carved on the walls of caves. Those we have. But how much more there was we do not know. What we have strikes us at once as showing an almost obsessive concern with the large and magnificent beasts of those days—the mammoth, the

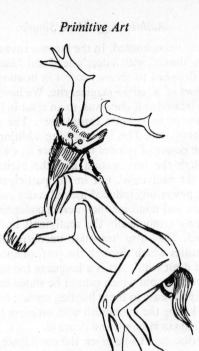

Fig. 21 The sorcerer of Trois Frères, Ariège (France), who wore the skin and horns of the deer to be hunted, and presumably conducted a magic hunting ritual. He dominates a cave decorated with pictures of animals.

bear, the bison, the ibex. Lévy-Bruhl says that this is not a matter of the animal's physical attribute alone, but of the invisible and mysterious powers associated with it. That it is not merely the animal as such that is depicted is clearly seen by the *highly selective stylization* of these pictures. This is, of course, an 'artistic creation of aesthetic force and influence, not a natural history lesson. One is not attempting to *explain* this art. One is trying to avoid some premature over-simplification which misses its highly original and potent significance. One is feeling the way *towards* an appreciation of the reality of the aesthetic experience to which these drawings and paintings are testimony.

ART AND MAGIC

There is considerable evidence that a great deal of art, though not all of it by a long way, was associated with magic. This seems the case especially in the cave drawings at Altamira, in Spain, and in the Dordogne and Aurignac in France. The walls are covered with paintings of mammoths and other animals, many with arrows sticking in their bodies, or actually being hunted. In the famous cave at Trois-Frères we have the sorcerer himself, with a deer's head and hide on him, leading a dance probably designed to secure success in hunting. This appears to depict, *or to be part of,* a religio-magical rite. We have already seen that magic cannot be treated as it once was, as an error in logic, a silly sort of pre-scientific attempt to operate causal laws. The savage knows the causal laws perfectly well. This is something additional and something different. It is the power of symbol to produce its own substantial reinforcement, through the imagination and the excitation of aesthetic emotion not in the individual, but in the participating group. Lévy-Bruhl calls these powerfully induced mental states *collective representations,* which assert and reinforce the interdependences which constitute society and express symbolically the sentiments and values on which their lives depend. They also 'translate uncontrollable natural forces into symbolic entities which through the performance of ritual, can be manipulated and dealt with'. Art is a language for saying things which are true and important, but which cannot be stated in prosaic terms.

This is certainly the case in these hunting scenes; for the heroic game of pursuing and killing the mammoth with no more than flint weapons demanded superhuman strength and courage.

How are the tribesmen to be given the confidence, the courage, and high spirits to confront the mammoth? It is through ritual, through dance and song, through the rhythmic beating of drums, the chant of *powerful words.*

Words are for us not only poetical but prosaic. Primitive man distinguishes practical instructions from song and prayer, but language is always a thing of power. The sharp separation of science and poetry has not yet arrived, nor is the natural separate from the supernatural, though the technical *aspects* of the unity are distinguished.

What happened in the magical rites so splendidly depicted in the drawing of the sorcerer in the deer skin with the horns upon his head? He was harnessing a group effort for a difficult task by a group ritual dance. The object, the killing of the quarry, becomes a fantasy object; it is conceived imaginatively as slain. The real deer or mammoth is far off, but the fantasy object is here and now. Man is projected into this fantasy world where his aim is accomplished. The result is that even when the ritual dance is over the accomplished deed still seems real, the accomplished future seems more realizable—spurring him on to the risks and labour necessary for its accomplishment. The tribal individual is thus changed by participating in the collective illusion.

Let us once again turn to Lévy-Bruhl who, in his interesting study *How Natives Think,* seems to be pressing these inquiries in the right direction, even if he has not arrived. This aesthetic experience, he says, is 'a *mystic* one, employing the word in the strictly defined sense in which "mystic" implies belief in forces and influences and actions which, though imperceptible to sense, are nevertheless real'. The natural and the supernatural, however, are not two separate realms, but two aspects of *one* realm in which the visible, the palpable, subordinate to physical law, is one aspect, and the other, invisible, intangible, 'spiritual', forming a mystic sphere which encompasses the first. But the mind of these cave artists did not recognize two worlds here. 'To him there is but one. Every reality, like every influence, is mystic, and consequently every perception is also mystic.'

At this stage in social development natural phenomena do not constitute the sole content of perception to the exclusion of other elements, which are then merely *associated* with the physical or animal object. This is what happens at a later stage and is rightly regarded as superstition. But the native mind does not dissociate the spiritual and the physical. What we might call occult power, is associated with all the objects which affect his senses or strikes his imagination.

The primitive, therefore, does not differentiate his aesthetic activity as such. It is simply part of his life-activity—a complex activity involving all his faculties in a world of mystic perception which is a single unity.

(Herbert Read, *Art and Society*.)

PALAEOLITHIC ART

The very earliest art that we know of is that of the late palaeolithic period, the last phase of the Old Stone Age. Here we find not only much-improved tools, but bone and ivory ornamentation, and paintings on cave walls. The painting was utilitarian, but the carving on ivory consisted of intricate and conventional patterns made from circles, dots, spirals, and entwining lines. We know that these primitive people painted in white, red, and yellow. Their grinding bowls and stones still retain the traces of colour. These people, who lived 50,000 years ago, also had necklaces and ivory beads. Thus primitive art was, from the first, both decorative and geometric as well as realistic and symbolic. There is no evidence that realism came before conventionalism, or vice versa.

No qualities that universally characterize primitive art can be deduced from the art of primitive peoples, but we can be certain of one thing: primitive does not mean childlike. This art is frequently advanced in technique and sophisticated in handling. Australian art is highly stylized, and much African art is abstract and symbolic.

REPRESENTATIONAL ART

While in basket-work and pottery we frequently have simple designs which might well be created just for pleasure, there is more often a well-thought-out content in primitive art.

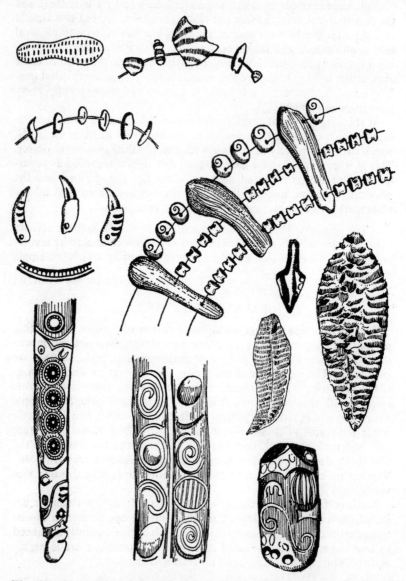

Fig. 22 Ornaments of the Magdalenian and Aurignacian peoples (Late Palaeolithic). They are usually found in cave graves. They consist of amulets, necklaces, carved ivory, pendants, shells used for embroidery, flint knives, ivory needles, engraved teeth.

If there is in every art product sheer technical skill and a definite quality of design, there is usually something *representational*—'every picture tells a story'. This has often been overlooked by contemporary art critics because they may have inadequate knowledge of the religious and mythological customs of the people who created them.

There is an indirect way in which art can reflect reality. It may indicate social stratification, especially the existence of an élite who wish to draw attention to their superiority. This seems to be the purpose of the totem poles of British Columbia, some of which are fifty feet high and covered from top to bottom with grotesque and intricate carvings. This is complexity and elaboration for its own sake and goes with the production of decorated versions of everyday objects which are not only flamboyant but technically useless. This is an example of ostentation, of the social climber's power to create expensive and useless things. As we know, this spirit expressed itself also in extravagant feasts and was the spirit of a society ruled by rich and privileged persons. The content of art products thus differs considerably, according to whether it is designed to display the unity of some tribal group or to assert the prestige of an individual patron.

Artists are servants in primitive society and they may be working to furnish religious ceremonial, decorate houses and boats, or provide memorials for the dead.

Much art is directly or indirectly religious or magical and is linked with the mythology and ceremony of the tribe, just as Greek and Christian art reflects the mythology, legend, and religious tradition of European civilization in their respective periods.

Many art forms are highly conventionalized representations of natural things, but they may be quite unintelligible to us, to whom they appear to be abstract designs.

Ornamentation. As soon as a people solves the fundamental technical problems of the production of tools and useful objects, the artistic impulse begins to assert itself. The more artistic individuals begin to experiment with the surface in an effort to increase the pleasure given by the object that is being made. This is the *embellishment of an artefact*.

Indians first decorated their moccasins with dyed porcupine quills and later with coloured beads. Basket-makers produce the most interesting and pleasing designs by using coloured fibres. Potters discover the potentiality of the decorated line and later of glazing and colouring. Handles of many implements are elaborately carved.

This may be purely formal, but as we have already suggested, it may combine a decorative and a representational intention. If the representation is faithful to the original, it may fail to serve a purely decorative purpose; for this, *style* must dominate the merely natural. The term 'style' means *a departure from absolute naturalism*—that is, from 'photographic' realism.

This is well seen on the north-west coast of North America in the carving and painting of masks, totem poles, boxes, rattles, canoes, houses, and other objects. The stylization still reveals the basic form, perhaps of the beaver or bear. Although much conventionalized, it is still possible to recognize the beaver by his flat, scaly tail and prominent incisor teeth, but the animal form is distorted or even dismembered to fit the surface which is being ornamented.

African Sculpture. Negro sculpture reaches a very high level and also reveals a high degree of artistic subordination of style to the hardwood or bronze material used. The wood is close-grained and invites a high polish. The glistening highlights of the smooth Negro skin are beautifully reflected in the finished statues.

Most African statues represent dead ancestors and must have a powerful emotional effect. It is not just a work of art, it is a personage, alive with the spirit of the man it represents.

Magnificent bronze heads were found in the western Nigerian town of Ife in 1938 and are comparable to Greek sculpture of the classic period. Brass figures from Dahomey, representing a man hoeing and a man in the grasp of an elephant, are really remarkable.

The Art of the Bushmen. In the Kalahari Desert we find the remains of a once numerous race, the Bushmen, now driven from their original lands both by the European settlers and by other African tribes. They are among the primitive food gatherers and hunters who are entirely without agriculture, like the Australian aborigines. They use a hand-rotated fire drill and keep water in large ostrich-egg shells, for water is scarce in the desert.

They have left painted on the rocks a most wonderful series of highly stylized paintings of running and hunting men. The last of these traditional artists were still to be found within recent years, but it is unlikely that the craft can continue.

The paintings we possess go back many thousands of years, and there are also remarkable rock engravings. The area of the Drakensberg Mountains in South Africa contains many of these paintings. The artists have succeeded in portraying vividly strong emotion and action. The men depicted are excessively tall and thin and are shown hunting, in procession, and dancing. The figures are almost always moving swiftly and violently. See Fig. 23.

In North Africa there existed a somewhat similar art, known as the Capsian. This extended to Spain, where vivid and exciting pictures of stone-age man fighting with bows and arrows have been found.

The Aurignacian Venuses. Quite in a class by themselves are the little statuettes of exaggerated female forms belonging to the Aurignacian and Gravettian cultures of the late palaeolithic. These have been found in Austria and France and almost certainly represent a fertility cult which existed 20,000 years ago.

Fig. 23   Rock paintings by the Bushmen of the Drakensberg Mountains in South Africa. Highly stylized, they depict very tall, thin men, hunting, in procession, and dancing. The figures are moving rapidly and violently. They show a remarkable similarity to the Capsian rock drawing of North Africa and Spain.

Fig. 24   A carved wooden dance mask from the Ivory Coast (West Africa).

These are all violently distorted, the head being treated in summary fashion, as are the arms and legs. The purely sexual features are much enlarged—hence the inference that they represent figures of a fertility cult.

African Art. In Africa masks are one of the most important forms of art and are, of course, in actual use and not merely to be looked at. As might be expected they are 'collective representations' of social and religious forces, and play an essential part in ceremonies re-enacting what the original myth really meant about human life. Such a myth does not recall the past, it communicates something latent in the existing and concrete situation here and now. If it represents a creation myth, it stands for the power structure of the society residing in the kinship system. 'Giving living reality to the myth through drama and art is the most vivid way of making people recognize their dependence upon the myth and upon the society whose members live by it and what it represents,' as Bohannan puts it.

FIELD STUDY NO. XII—THE ART OF THE HUNTERS

Palaeolithic Man, the first true man (*Homo sapiens*), lived some 25,000 years ago heralding the great surge forward of the Neolithic Age. His many remains are found chiefly in France, Spain, and Czechoslovakia, and although we have no written records of his thoughts, we have the remarkable pictures he painted in the recesses of deep caves, often in places which were very difficult to reach. Today even with climbing gear and electric torches it is no easy task to get to these paintings. The cave of Combarelles (Dordogne) is 726 ft long, and the drawings begin 350 ft from the entrance, in the pitch dark. The cave of La Pasiega in Spain is entered through a hole in the floor of an open outer cave. This leads into a labyrinth the walls of which are richly painted, and thence to another opening into the last chamber. Cro-Magnon men slipped, crawled, and scrambled down those dark, mysterious passages, where a false step meant disaster. The cavern of Niaux in France extends 4,200 ft into the mountain, with a subterranean lake barring access to the longest passage. One of the most interesting artistically is the cave at Altamira in Spain, the ceiling displaying coloured paintings of bison. The Abbé Breuil, to whom we owe much for his discoveries, drew them all and his volumes provide us with a conspectus of the whole, impossible to grasp when seeing them under the difficulties of cave exploration.

Trois-Frères in France has the fine painting of the sorcerer in horns and skin. It is possible to get at this figure only by swinging out of a window-like opening and resting the toes on a projecting piece of stalactite. One then realizes on looking down how the sorcerer dominates the frieze of animals below.

Figs. 25 and 26 Bison painted on a cavern wall at Altamira in Spain. The original is five feet in length. The legs are drawn in perspective.

In another cave at Tuc d'Audoubert (Aurignac), with a dangerous subterranean stream, clay models of animals and horses were found, and in the centre of the cave was a clay model of a bear. The models of horses are pierced with arrows and spears. The whole scene appears to be connected with hunting magic.

Figurines. As well as the drawings the Palaeolithic hunters made many little models a few inches in height. Some are of women and are clearly fertility symbols. Others are of mammoth, bear, ibex, and horses. The finest material, of course, would be ivory from the great tusks of the mammoth. They are remarkable not only as representing natural

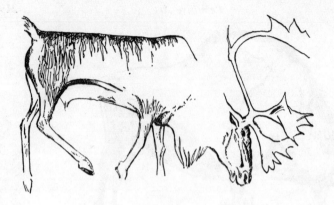

Fig. 27 Masterpieces of Magdalenian Art. Reindeer engraved on a round piece of antler from Kesslerloch, Switzerland. Below, an engraving of red deer and fish, from the cave of Lorthet, Hautes-Pyrénées, France.

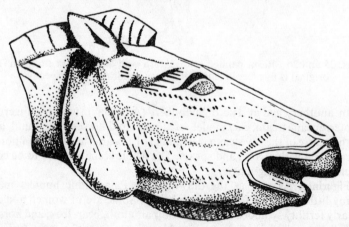

Fig. 28 Horse's head carved on the reindeer-horn or ivory handle of an implement.

objects, but for their abstract and schematic patterns, almost certainly expressing magical significance.

Bas-Relief. Many rock shelters have bas-reliefs carved on the walls, often just below the roof. At Le Cap Blanc, Dordogne, is a fine procession of horses some 45 ft in length. Horses, it will be understood, were

Fig. 29 The Capsian artists followed Magdalenian art but had totally different temperaments. Their work is found in North Africa and Spain. Their figures are animated—almost caricatures—intensely alive and busy. This painting shows deer being driven in a line towards four archers. It comes from Los Caballos, Cantillon (Spain).

neither ridden nor used as draught animals. They were hunted and eaten. At Charanti are reliefs of horses, bison, the primitive ox, and a bird's head.

Incised Drawings. As well as paintings and sculpture we have some very fine incised drawings on rock walls and on ivory or bone as, for instance, the reindeer head on an antler at Sainte-Eulalie in the Dordogne (France), or the magnificent startled horse at Hornos de la pena,

Santander (Spain), and the engraved aurochs (the wild ox) on a sand-stone block from Trou de Chaleux in Belgium. In the grotto dell'Adaura near Palermo is a large wall space covered by beautifully drawn human figures who appear to be engaged in some ritual activities.

Fig. 30   The Honey Gatherer. The man is climbing to reach a bee's nest. He is surrounded by bees (Capsian, Spain).

Capsians and Bushmen. South-east Spain was occupied during late Palaeolithic, Mesolithic, and even Neolithic times by roving hunters, probably of African origin, who have left some remarkable drawings on exposed rock faces. These are very like the quite recent work of South African Bushmen. The drawings were associated with a development of the flint industry which now produced very small sharp flint blades that could be fitted into bone or wooden handles.

These Capsian artists give us a strong impression of being caricaturists. Their drawings are immensely spirited and interesting, the little men looking like animated sticks, with very thin waists, and engaging in desperate encounters with themselves and their hunted quarry.

Art and Utility. The Palaeolithic hunters of the Old Stone Age were well-clothed in skin raiment, with sewn-on ornaments. They made

Fig. 31 Men fighting. In so few lines an exciting scene of activity and desperate encounter is brilliantly depicted (Capsian, Spain).

needles of horn, and hollow bone needle-cases. Ivory too was made into pins and buckles and there were necklaces of shells. We have found paint bowls in which colours were ground. The artists may have painted themselves as well as the walls of their caves.

These races had a higher standard of culture than any other early peoples. Of warfare there is no sign whatever. There are no pictures of fighting, no specialized weapons or broken bones, such as are found in later times when wars were common.

SUGGESTED FURTHER READING

Breuil, H. and Lantier, R., *The Men of the Old Stone Age*. Harrap: London, 1916.

Boas, Franz, *Primitive Art*. Constable & Co.: London, 1955.

Davison, Dorothy, *Men of the Dawn*. Watts & Co.: London, 1934.

Parkyn, E. A., *An Introduction to Prehistoric Art*. Longmans: London, 1915.

Powell, T. G. E., *Prehistoric Art*. Thames & Hudson: London, 1968.

Wingert, P., *Primitive Art*. Oxford University Press: London, 1962.

PART FIVE

SOCIAL EVOLUTION

CHAPTER EIGHTEEN

THE EVOLUTION OF CULTURES

We have considered the evolution of man and the successive appearance of Stone Age, Bronze Age, and Iron Age cultures. An important question now arises: can we trace, everywhere, the same pattern of successive food-gathering, pastoral-agricultural, higher agricultural, and city cultures? Is there an inevitable sequence from the first to the last wherever we investigate man's social development? No one would seriously advance the theory in such an extreme form, because the movement of peoples carries a new culture to a more primitive people so that they may jump one or two phases instead of laboriously learning each stage for itself. But, in spite of setbacks, there has been an almost continuous accumulation of technical achievements since the making of the first stone tools, though it has often been accompanied by the rise and fall of cultures with their arts.

The Lineal Theory of Social Development. This theory was enunciated by Lewis Henry Morgan in his *Ancient Society* (1877) and by Sir Edward Burnett Tylor in 1888.

Morgan's views may be summed up as follows:

Culture evolves in successive stages, which are essentially the same in all parts of the world; from which it is to be inferred that the order of the stages is inevitable and their content limited, because mental processes are universally similar among all peoples. In other words, when confronted with the conditions of stage A, men universally respond by inventing the cultural forms of stage B, in reaction to which they then produce stage C, and so forth through the ages.

Tylor expressed it this way:

> The institutions of man are as distinctly stratified as the earth on which he lives. They succeed each other in series substantially uniform over the globe, independent of what seem the comparatively superficial differences of race and language, but shaped by similar human nature acting through successively changing conditions in savage, barbaric, and civilized life.

(E. B. Tylor, *Journal of Royal Anthropological Society, London*, 1888.)

This theory was, like many great discoveries, too crudely formulated in its earliest forms. It ignores the great variability of cultures in the patterning of their inner details and in their adjustments to different types of environment. We cannot assume that every culture develops exactly comparable details in culture patterns on comparable levels of

technology. Nor can we formulate a line of specific detailed development through which all societies must pass. Contact of a developing
culture with another culture of a higher stage plays havoc with any
serial scheme of development *for particular cultures*. The steel axe may
be passed on to Australian aborigines with but the most primitive of
stone implements. The African native soon learns to ride his bicycle
through jungle paths worn smooth by bare feet. The Eskimo woman
rejoices in a sewing machine. Whether a particular people is exposed to
one or another impact is the result of sheer chance.

But there *is* a definite, lineal evolutionary development of the tool
itself, and also of society. Consider the axe. It does in fact develop from
the haftless stone axe through many stages to the polished neolithic axe
with a hole bored through it for a wooden haft. This in turn gives way
to a bronze axe which is cast in the same shape as a stone axe; and this
again gives way to the iron axe and then the steel axe.

Societies also have followed a certain basic sequence of forms, even
though many societies exposed to special influences or stimulated by
exceptionally favourable conditions may skip a stage, while others
missing such opportunities get bogged down in some regressive blind
alley.

The theory of multilineal evolution proposes the hypothesis that
similar sequences of cultural evolution occurred in the emergence of the
high cultures of Peru, Central America, Mesopotamia, Egypt, and
China.

A more modest and more factual form of the original theory attempts
once again, and with considerable success, to establish evolutionary
trends for culture as a whole even though no one culture ever embraces
all the cultural patterns. Therefore, in spite of the overall truth of the
succession of technological forms—stone axe, agriculture, pastoralism,
advanced agriculture, the surplus economy and corresponding forms of
social organization—the history *of a given society* cannot be told by
applying to it the total scheme as outlined.

Two contemporary theories, however, reject the evolution of cultures.
They are the **culture-pattern** theory and the **diffusionist** theory.

The Culture-pattern Theory. We owe an immense debt of gratitude to
Radcliffe-Brown and all the other functionalists who have drawn our
attention to the *unity* of each particular culture. We must note the interdependence and interaction of every phase of that culture, so that the
kinship system helps to determine not only the social pattern but the
ethical, legal, and ideological aspects of social life and so on. But *no
attempt is made by this theory to relate the culture to the stage of development in the control of nature.* Franz Boas, for example, denied any correlation between industrial development and social development. Lowie
finds no law of social development, but sees rather a 'planless hodge-
podge', a 'chaotic jumble'. This school of thought would argue that the

significance of social institutions is obscure, unknown—or even unknowable—and that therefore technology has no determining influence on social systems. Indeed social organization is *wholly different* from technological requirements, since it is determined by ideal ends and not by economic needs. In his *Introduction to Cultural Anthropology* Lowie observes: 'The purpose of an axe is to fell trees, but what is the purpose of art, communal life, belief, marriage?' Ruth Benedict inclines to the same view in her *Patterns of Culture*. She seems to think that a people *chooses*, apparently of its own free will, whatever type of social organization it wishes to have. The result of these theories is the emergence of a *psychological* interpretation of culture, which attributes the social forms to the chance appearance of different *ideas* (whether conscious or subconscious) and denies any necessary development of one idea into the next and so on, or any necessary sequence of cultures due to the progressive advance of technology.

The Diffusionist Theory. This theory, which was advanced by Elliot-Smith, W. J. Perry, and others, holds that all the major inventions were made but once by some chosen people—the Egyptians, it is supposed—and were then carried from land to land by the migrations of people or by voyages. This would advocate an Egyptian origin for Asian culture as well as for Central and South American civilization. Thus wherever 'pyramids' or anything like pyramids are found, there is unmistakable evidence of Egyptian influence, whether the pyramid is a structure on which to place a temple, as the Mexican pyramids were, a monument to a dead king, the stone platforms of Polynesia, or the earthen mounds of the Ohio Valley.

This is a theory which denies to all nations but the Egyptians any inventive capacity whatever. Everything of a culture higher than that of savagery must be Egyptian. Thus thighbones used for ritual purposes in Africa indicate a diffusion of mummification; other evidences for this were found among the Maoris of New Zealand and the Jivaros of South America.

Although this view is no longer held, it reminds us that diffusion over a wide area is not an impossibility. The permeation of the New World culture by maize cultivation is a good example, and so is the spread of the alphabet from Phoenicia and the megalithic tombs from the Mediterranean islands (Malta, etc.) around the coast of Spain and along the western shores of the British Isles and into France.

On the other hand modern anthropology believes that the diffusionists are mistaken in denying the possibility of independent invention. Fire is secured by different communities in different ways. It has probably been discovered on many different occasions. We may suppose, for example, that the isolation of the Inca civilization in Peru was complete enough to make the belated appearance of smelting there in the eleventh century an independent invention.

Convergent Invention. In connection with independent invention, we must note the tendency of human groups towards what is known as convergence or parallel development. This term helps to explain a marked resemblance between two societies which superficially appears to be due to close contact between them, whereas in fact there has been no cultural exchange of any sort. Sometimes the resemblance is extremely close and deceptive, though it is merely coincidental. The explanation of the resemblance is that societies may reasonably be expected to develop in certain respects in the same general direction. It is not surprising that, because of the universal need for some kind of vessel, sooner or later a number of widely separated communities should hit upon the notion of manufacturing baskets and pots. The case is similar with regard to institutions: the mental capacity and endowment of mankind once granted, it is understandable that primitive communities should manifest a general horror of such an act as murder. Exogamy—to cite another example—arises everywhere among primitive societies, as do magic and religion.

Whether discovered, invented, or introduced, each innovation responds to the propensity for conscious human experimentation and ingenuity and helps man to adjust more efficiently to the demands of his changing environment.

With regard to agriculture, it appears likely that there were three major centres of origin—south-eastern Asia, south-western Asia, and the New World. New World agriculture comprised domesticated plants which were unknown in Asia: e.g. potatoes, tomatoes, tobacco, Lima beans, and maize.

In the field of mathematics we find the invention of the concept of zero in India, Babylonia, and among the Mayas. Type printing was discovered by the Chinese five centuries before it was discovered in Europe. Did it reach the West by diffusion? It seems doubtful.

One of the most important kinds of diffusion is the dissemination of almost complete cultures by the superposition of one culture on another, such as the Hellenization of the Mediterranean by Greece, the imposition of British culture on India and Africa, and of American culture today not only upon its own Indians but all over the world. (This process, especially when a more advanced culture transforms a more primitive one, is called **acculturation,** and we shall consider it in detail in Chapter 19, p. 237.)

But in spite of the importance of acculturation as evidence of diffusion, the theory as enunciated by Elliot-Smith, Perry, Hocart, Lord Raglan, and others is today thoroughly discredited. But it is not dead, and even the Kon-Tiki expedition on a balsa-wood raft across the Pacific was designed to bring evidence of the kind of primitive voyages which might have been responsible for the diffusion of culture. We must therefore look a little more closely at this intriguing theory.

The Heliolithic Theory. According to Elliot-Smith, all the culture in both the Old World and the New World originated in Egypt. The Egyptians worshipped the sun, and therefore wherever they journey they are the 'Children of the Sun', hence the theory is called the heliolithic theory.

Primitive man, the diffusionists argue, 'shows no more innate tendency than do the manlike apes to embark upon the invention of civilization' (Elliot-Smith, *In the Beginning*). Lord Raglan goes even further, asserting that all available evidence proves that 'ancient savages when left to themselves, retrogressed just as modern savages do' (Raglan, *How Came Civilization?*). The creation of civilization must have been the result of special circumstances, therefore, and these were found only in Egypt, in the valley of the Nile. From this original point of radiation the elements of civilization and the social and political organizations that formed an integral part of it were subsequently diffused over the surface of the globe, through the agency of traders, migrants, and colonists. The aim of these traders was as much religious as economic, for they were scouring the world for gold and precious stones, which were required for purposes of *magic* and for their arts. Among the elements of culture thus diffused were, in addition to mummification and megalithic tombs, sun worship, serpent worship, tattooing, circumcision, irrigation, pottery, polished-stone implements, metalworking matrilineal organization, totemism, and exogamy.

Totemism and the Diffusionist Theory. According to this theory, totemism is found in Australia not because the Australian aborigines invented it but because about 3000 B.C. the 'Children of the Sun' arrived there looking for gold, met the food-gathering natives, married some of their women and taught them the laws of exogamy. Then they disappeared. The natives, having received this dose of culture, went on to elaborate totemism.

There is, of course, no evidence for this, and it seems far more probable that it arose all over the world not by diffusion but because the primitive group developed into the exogamous clan when co-operative production emerged as a useful means both of consolidating the group and establishing peaceful relations with other clans. Whatever its origins, there can be no doubt that totemism is a system corresponding with a definite stage in the development of primitive tribal society. It symbolizes the interdependence of the members of a hunting and food-gathering community. The totem is the living embodiment of a sense of community solidarity, and its magical mimetic ceremonies play a vital part in stimulating and organizing the tribe's community life. This social necessity explains the existence of totemism both among the primitive tribes of Australia and among those of predynastic Egypt and in America. There is no need to call in the theory of a single culture's being carried round the world by the 'Children of the Sun'.

The Beginnings of Civilization. The diffusionist theory of the origin of civilization contains one important truth, and that is its emphasis upon the special circumstances found in the Nile Valley—but also, and this the diffusionists ignore, in the other great river-valley civilizations which arose independently of it. The possibility of civilization followed the discovery of agriculture and the domestication of animals. But without favourable conditions its emergence might have been long delayed. Both in Egypt and in Mesopotamia circumstances were such as to favour the early adoption of irrigation; in both, natural inundations of the great rivers, on which life depended, increased fertility so markedly as to make evident the value of extending their benefits by artificial means, and in both the proximity of the desert to irrigated zones served to enhance the contrast.

But there was no 'civilization-building instinct'. Civilization was bound to arise, sooner or later, wherever *man* of whatever race met the challenge and the opportunity which drove him forward. That the event took place in Egypt, Mesopotamia, and the Punjab was a historico-geographical accident; but that it *could* take place was the result of thousands of years of slow development in productive technique and social organization.

The challenge to create civilization confronts man, when changed environmental circumstances face him, with the alternative of going unsatisfied or even enduring increasing poverty and ultimate extinction on the one hand, or, on the other, of inventing new means of satisfaction. But the latter course demands the transformation of his whole way of living—an opportunity that is also a challenge to which he may fail to respond, as many peoples did and perished or sank into decay.

The Decline of Civilizations. Why does society decay? We too frequently assume that existing primitive societies represent the early forms of now advanced peoples. That we have much to learn from them about our origins is undeniable, but we must remember that they have existed and developed or regressed (or remained static) for as many centuries as we have. What has happened to the Central African people during the past four thousand years? How similar to their present culture was their culture in A.D. 1000, A.D. 100, or 1000 B.C.? We do not know. We do know that in A.D. 1100 there were civilizations there with cities and arts comparable to European conditions, *but without the art of writing*.

The geographical and historical backwaters of the world, the tragedy of opportunity missed, of challenge refused, must present us today with fossilized and decadent cultures, paralysed by magical beliefs, frustrated by a bare subsistence economy and a declining agriculture, ravaged as were the African tribes by Moslem and African slave raids and internecine war.

But great civilizations have emerged in history and *subsequently* fallen into decay and stagnation. We must account for this too. The diffusionists have no adequate explanation of these disasters. All they can say is that a warlike people appears from somewhere and overthrows the older civilization.

This theory fails to note, as the whole diffusionist theory does, that civilization is not something static, something deposited somewhere as 'a present from Egypt', but that it is in a constant state of movement and change. Either it goes on, in response to its own internal development and the need for ever new adjustments to the environment and to other societies, or it declines. One such challenge is that presented by the development of the slave society.

The Collapse of the Slave State. What we do know is that when civilization itself emerges, in culture after culture it is slavery—on the basis of which the first administrative and organizing élite emerged to build the civilization—that is the cause, first of all of its economic success, but then of its decline and ultimate disintegration.

The growth of slavery by conquest and breeding slaves, the cheapening and degradation of free labour that went with it, the widening gap between mental and physical occupations with its consequent stultification of scientific inquiry and productive initiative, the increasing parasitism of the upper classes and the growing discontent and non-cooperativeness of the lower classes all contributed to destroy these ancient civilizations.

It was not the incursions of the barbarians that destroyed ancient civilizations. The warrior peoples simply hacked to pieces a dying body.

ADAPTATION AND SURVIVAL: THE EVOLUTIONARY THEORY

Vital to the evolutionary hypothesis is the contrast between the form of the living organism and its life processes, or modes of functioning. The life processes are carried on so that the organism may satisfy its wants; and to satisfy them, it must adapt itself to its environment. In the course of its adaptive activity it develops a form or structure corresponding to its way of life, and this form provides the means by which the struggle for existence is carried on. If the structure ceases to be well adapted to the preservation and activities of the living being, that being will become more or less unfit for the struggle of life and will be eliminated if the discrepancy between organism and environmental conditions becomes too great.

So in social evolution, this theory holds. As a culture develops its economic life, at a certain technological level *the forms it assumes become increasingly less adequate for the satisfaction of the needs of men.* The economic forms, however, may prove to be rigid and may resist modification because they are artificially preserved beyond the point where they are useful to society.

But in the case of the biological organism, changes take place through variation and inheritance. There is nothing to correspond to this willed human obstruction. In society reason, will, and passionate feelings play their part and interact with the economic and social forms.

The processes of nature, whether on the organic or the social level, are everywhere developing new forms as well as destroying old ones; in both cases the organization must undergo fundamental transformations to adjust the organisms to the demands of existence, or it falls into decay ultimately to stagnate or perish.

Evolution and Social Progress. While not denying either functionalism or the existence of diffusion, evolutionism does not regard either theory as sufficient to explain social change, or change of cultural pattern. Evolutionism notes the fact that communities progress from lower to ever higher stages; it seeks to discover *the dynamic processes of historic* change and does not rest content with accurate description and analysis of primitive cultures as we find them today, or with studies of the functional interconnections between the many features of living cultures. This is not the study of the *growth* of social organisms, but only of their present structure. These non-evolutionary studies lack historical perspectives.

One form of evolutionary view is set forth by Professor Leslie A. White in the following terms:

Man exerts himself to perpetuate his kind, to make his life secure and enduring. His primary and fundamental need is for food; his second need is for protection from his enemies. He must, at all costs, come to terms with the external world—the source of his food and tools, his enemies and his means of defence. Man has a means of adjustment to the external world unknown to the lower animals—it is the tool; by its means he develops *a culture*, and this is the real and effective method of grappling with the world. **A culture includes social organization, magico-religious ceremonials, kinship and marriage systems, behaviour patterns, institutions, beliefs, art forms, mythology, and feeling attitudes.**

Basically *the level of culture and the pattern and complexity of culture depend on the mechanical power made available to control the world* and produce the means of life by a particular technique (human muscles—the windmill—the steam engine—electric power), and the appropriate form of utilizing it. *Higher concentrations of energy and higher forms of organization produce higher levels of culture. In other words, culture develops as the amount of energy harnessed per capita per year increases*, according to this theory.

Degree of cultural development is to be measured in terms of human need—the need-serving goods and services produced per unit of human labour—amount of food, shelter, transportation, communication, defence, and control over disease.

(Leslie A. White, *The Science of Culture.*)

Social Transformation. It is clear that with the invention of a new source of power society makes a great stride forward, and its entire social pattern is transformed. But the amount of energy is not the only factor making for change. *The means by which the energy is harnessed is also significant.* This factor is expressed in the efficiency of tools and machines and in the social organization of their use. With the amount of energy remaining constant, the amount of need-serving goods and services produced will vary with the efficiency of expenditure of energy.

Improvements in tools and machines, resulting from the use of new materials or from changes in design, and improved ways of using the tools, whether through individual skills or through social organization, will therefore tend to increase the output of goods and services and consequently to advance the culture.

In particular the adaptation urgently required *after* the new technique has appeared, and also *as a consequence of its improvement and development*, is the reorganization of society to render it more appropriate to the developed technique. This is comparable to the adaptation of the animal form to the demands of the changing environment, as discovered by Darwin. It is a case of modifying *form* in order to fulfil the necessary *function*.

The bronze tool or weapon is not only a superior implement, it carries with it a more complex economic and social structure. The ship and the tools employed in its production symbolize a whole economic and social system.

It is the modification of the social system that leads to the great social struggles of history; for any particular form of social and economic organization becomes highly institutionalized and resistant to change. It appears to men to be something beyond criticism. There is in every society constant pressure to follow certain types of behaviour that other men have created in time past. It is by adhering to a system of related designs for carrying out all the acts of living that a group of people feel themselves bound into a social unity and constitute a community. Such institutionalized forms of organization also develop social, ethical, legal, and religious means of cementing the matrix into a solid block.

Aspects of culture, once adaptive, often persist long after they have ceased to be useful. As history and technology move on, either the culture changes or the society perishes. What survives goes to make up the changing pattern, combining that of the past which is still useful and the developments which the present requires as a new element in the pattern.

Social Transformation in the Atomic Age. Such transformations have occurred again and again in society. They first come clearly before our eyes in the formation of the first settled agricultural community, and then again in the formation of urban society. We have experienced them in the coming of the machine age and in the demands of its enormous contemporary development. But,

> as the Neolithic technologies induced a thoroughgoing revision of previously existing societies and drove the expansion of culture ahead in a great spurt, as the technological innovations of the industrial revolution forced similar alterations in the ways of men, so the atomic age will be one in which the old modes will become quickly outworn. We are destined to see such cultural changes in the new era that has burst upon us as will make all prior evolutionary development seem static by comparison.
>
> (E. A. Hoebel, *Man in the Primitive World.*)

SUGGESTED FURTHER READING

Benedict, Ruth, *Patterns of Culture.* Routledge & Kegan Paul: London, 1934.

Childe, V. G., *Man Makes Himself.* Watts & Co.: London, 1936.

Childe, V. G., *Social Evolution.* Watts & Co.: London, 1951.

Clark, Grahame, *World Prehistory.* Cambridge University Press: London, 1961.

Elliot-Smith, Grafton, *In the Beginning.* Gerald Howe: London, 1928.

Hoebel, E. A., *Man in the Primitive World.* McGraw-Hill: London, 1958.

Malinowski, B., *Dynamics of Social Change.* Yale University Press: New Haven, Conn., 1945.

Mumford, Lewis, *Technics and Civilization.* Routledge & Kegan Paul: London, 1934.

Raglan, Lord, *How Came Civilization.* Methuen: London, 1939.

Weber, Max, *The Theory of Social and Economic Organization.* William Hodge: London, 1947.

White, L. A., *The Science of Culture.* Farrar, Straus: New York, 1949.

CHAPTER NINETEEN

SOCIAL CHANGE

STRUCTURAL FUNCTIONALISM AND STATIC SOCIETIES

Structural functionalism shows us any particular society as a linked system of interdependent parts, each constituted by its relation to the other parts in this particular whole. When this pattern is understood, we can extract a model of social relationships and apply it comparatively to a great variety of societies. This is a matter of great interest and enables us to systematize our understanding of any one recurring phase, such as *magic*, as we find it in different circumstances.

There is no attempt here to ask *how* such a pattern came into existence, or whether it can change. It would appear that the functionalist would not consider it his business to ask the first question, and might consider the second to be covered by *acculturation*, that is to say the penetration, modification, and possible break-up of a primitive pattern under the influence of Western society, or by something like military conquest in times past. Thus the functionalist is content to record and compare the varieties of social pattern as he finds them. His task becomes a descriptive one, and follows the pattern of an empirical science which does not seek to go beyond accumulating facts, arranging them in order and classifying them, with statistical summaries where possible.

But there is a growing demand to know where these social patterns came from. They must have been established by men and have been the result of their ideas. This however raises an historical problem. That is to say it enters the field of *irreversible* phenomena, and here, it will be claimed, science has no place, because an historical event happens only *once*, whereas science is concerned with events which can be repeated experimentally. (But is this true of biological evolution, or of the evolution of galaxies and planetary systems?)

There is a further serious objection to resting on the functional system as observed. If this system is given the status of an *explanation*, as in many minds it will seem to do, it would appear to be arguing in a circle—the part is as it is because it belongs to this whole, and the whole is this kind of whole because the parts in it are so arranged and are what they are—a prefabricated sociological solution, that often appears to justify whatever is, and to support every existing social structure.

This raises the question of *equilibrium*. Every such society ought to be in equilibrium; and if not, measures should be taken to restore equilibrium. Any individual attempting to modify the structure, or not fitting into the organization in a docile way, would then be treated as a 'deviant'; steps would then have to be taken to eliminate him or re-condition him into what is called an 'organization man'.

But must we not ask both how such structures were formed and how they change? May unstable equilibrium indicate not the danger of fragmentation, but that of *re-adaptation to changing conditions*? Such changing conditions might be due to environmental changes, to the proximity and influence of other cultures, or to the development and improvement of technology to a point where the existing methods of production, or economic organization, have ceased to be the most appropriate for a more complex and more successful productive system.

Beattie, in his *Other Cultures*, has described this *radical* form of change in general terms:

> It is change in the character of the social system itself; some of its constituent institutions are altered, so that they no longer 'mesh' with other co-existing institutions as they used to do. This structural or 'radical' change, and the conflicts to which it gives rise are not resolvable in terms of the existing values of the society. They are new kinds of conflicts, and tradition provides neither precedents nor cures for them. If the social system is to persist, sooner or later further radical modifications will have to be made in it, and so the society will become something other than and different from what it originally was.

Are not all existing societies the result of such transformations occurring at certain moments in their history? If such change ceases, are we not confronted with fossilization or regression, as we are when we find a brachiopod which hardly differs from a fossil brachiopod of 400 million years ago, or an ant or dragonfly embedded in fossilized resin of 200 million years ago, indicating an animal that has reached the end of the road of a particular evolutionary line?

Lévi-Strauss characterizes such static social organisms as *Cold Societies*, which may be, in some respect, *farther* from the original social forms from which we and they evolved than we are—just as progressive evolutionary lines keep a certain flexibility and capacity to modify which is lost by specialization. If you want to be a whale, you can't, when you have succeeded, reverse the process, start again, and evolve into a horse!

Hot Societies got out of the rut of static functionalism by establishing a new relationship in production, a clear differentiation between castes based on specialization. Each caste represents a trade or special social function; and eventually the important *class* distinction between exploited and exploitees. Thus, says Lévi-Strauss, the city-states of the Mediterranean Basin and the Far East perpetrated slavery, a society in which the differential status of men, some dominant, others dominated, could be used to expand the forces of production. This created enough means of subsistence to allow large sections of the workers to become craftsmen, builders, soldiers, and servants, and other sections to become administrators, priests, and a ruling élite. The result was the production of an entirely new set of cultures in Egypt, Mesopotamia, the Indus Valley, and in China. The slave societies thus found *in social and economic organization* the dynamic force which produced their culture. Can the culture of our own society, which still perpetuates this condition, *transfer this dynamic function to the culture* so that we pass from 'the government of men to the administration of things'? Lévi-Strauss in his recent anthropological work has envisaged such a change and sees it as a change from the society which turned men into machines to one which makes machines the servants of men and thus achieves a manufacturing process which ceases to enslave man at the price of progress. He concludes:

> Our science arrived at maturity the day that Western man began to see that he would never understand himself as long as there was a single race or people on the surface of the Earth that he treated as an object. Only then could anthropology declare itself in its true colours: as an enterprise reviewing and atoning for [the first stage of civilization] in order to spread humanism to all humanity.

Acculturation. When different cultures come into continuous first-hand contact, they profoundly affect one another. When one of these cultures is definitely more advanced than the other, the weaker social system undergoes drastic alterations in the direction of conformity to the stronger, from which it borrows numerous traits and material elements.

This process has taken place all over the North American continent, where it is still in progress. It is in full swing everywhere in the Pacific. But it is in Africa where this process not only presents acculturation on a vast scale, but is raising social problems and even political problems of world-wide urgency and importance.

The 'oldest continent' has produced the 'newest' nation. This new Africa sometimes appears to Europeans as a threatening force; but as Bohannan so well says:

> It is fortunate that for most of the Western world, the new Africa does not constitute a threat—unless the job of creating smooth relationships with Africans be botched. European, Asian and American nations are all sending development missions to Africa. African leaders are spending vast proportions of their admittedly still small national budgets on education. But Africa is no longer a mere theatre of activities—a mere laboratory. Africans are now writing the drama and performing bold experiments. Within the European and American nations, vast new struggles in practical politics and scholarship

are opening up, because both the arts of diplomacy and the science of human interaction have found in Africa a new challenge.

(African Outline)

CENTRAL AFRICAN SOCIETY

Within living memory human relationships in Africa, south of the Sahara, were primitive; now they are rapidly becoming modernized.

Changes are currently and constantly being made in many major facets of life.

Economics. The economy of primitive societies was one of subsistence agriculture or pastoralism, with a few simple crafts. Each village community was virtually self-sufficient. Transport was very primitive. There were no wheeled vehicles. Money was unknown.

The economy of Africa today is part of a world organization. There is no longer any local self-sufficiency. Foreign clothes and shoes have become necessities of life; bicycles, sewing machines, tin utensils, and ploughs are found everywhere. Payment for these imports are made by the export of copper, tobacco, sisal, gold, tea, coffee, and cotton. The selling prices vary with world demand and supply. Railways and roads have been built. Money is in general use.

Within each African territory specialization of labour has appeared—some work in the towns, others in the country, and the latter alone produce food materials.

Language, Crafts and Dress. English is spoken by an increasing number of Africans, and native dress is giving way to European dress. Traditional dances still persist, but there is some European dancing too. The once unique patterns of local crafts are merging; all local differences are becoming less marked. The technical skills and materials of modern society are adopted everywhere. Books now make available the accumulated knowledge of a world society.

Politics. The once isolated tribes are now part of huge centrally administered territories, and these again are integral parts of the new African States.

Religion. The worship of ancestors, animistic beliefs, and witchcraft were, and still are, *local* magico-religious phenomena. But universal religions are appearing and their converts are conscious of being members of world organizations.

Migratory Labour. In many rural areas of Zambia and Malawi, 30 to 50 per cent of the able-bodied men were away at work in places as distant as South Africa. No proportionate flow of wealth came back to balance their going. The majority of these migrant labourers spent most of their working lives and most of their wages in town. Three-quarters of their dependents, however, remained in the country, where their economic position rapidly deteriorated.

PRIMITIVE AND ADVANCED SOCIETIES

The difference in scale is the fundamental distinction between primitive and advanced societies.

In a civilized community *we depend upon many more people* than does a Bushman, for instance, while our dependence on immediate neighbours diminishes.

In a civilized community *the area of communication is wider*, both geographically and in time. Primitives have little knowledge of distant lands or of the ancient past. With this greater area of communication goes a great increase in *mobility*, which means that the size of the group within which people move is immensely enlarged. With this goes the possibility of marrying outside one's own local group.

In a modernized community loyalty to larger political groups appears and world faiths emerge. Here, too, the range of social pressure is greater, for law embraces huge numbers and is often international in its scope, whereas among primitives it may be tribal or even limited to a few hundred families. Civilization leads to the loss of power by headmen and to the centralization of government.

Local patriotism declines as wider loyalties develop; the fierce patriotism of the city-state or the local tribe is weakened. But each local unit becomes more specialized and in that sense autonomous. A single town or area may be devoted to mining or some other industry instead of the practice of many crafts and a subsistence agriculture. As wider loyalties develop in large-scale societies, relationships between men become more impersonal; whereas in small-scale societies they are largely personal.

This produces, however, not less but more freedom in personal relations; the freedom of a primitive man is limited at every point by the pressure of neighbours and kinsmen, living and dead, from whom he cannot escape. He has little privacy. In many primitive societies even the *conception* of privacy is unknown. Primitive man's position in society is largely fixed by sex, age, and kinship. The freedom of the civilized man from neighbours and kinsmen, and from the immediate past, is much greater than that of a primitive. On the other hand civilized man is dependent upon distant groups—upon banks and industries, and upon world economic and political movement in a different way from primitive man.

Large-scale societies manifest specialization and variety to a much greater degree than do primitive societies. This is true in all fields—in the crafts, in the professions, in administration, and in the arts and sciences. With this goes an enormous increase in the control of the material environment.

Primitive people's knowledge of their material environment is infinitesimal compared with the accumulated knowledge of civilized society.

Primitive people may be skilled in the cultivation of certain crops and in the care of stock, in carving, or basket-making, but their techniques are always limited. There is no elaboration of skill comparable to that which produces aeroplanes and violins, modern textiles, and the many forms of radio communication.

The religious correlate of increasing control of the material environment is the decrease in magic. Magic is a characteristic of small-scale societies. The modern world does not believe that events are determined by metaphysical reality. If what are really technical errors are explained as being due to spirit intervention, then real causes will never be discovered and all our energy will be directed to conciliating supernatural powers. The presence of magic makes sustained scientific research impossible.

This is also reflected in the universality of scientific and civilized knowledge compared with the particularity of primitive thought. Savages and peasants talk about persons and particular events. Civilized people read books by authors they do not know, and their intellectual system is characterized by greater abstractions, which we see in science, in art, in political concept, and in the formulation of ethical principles.

SOCIAL CHANGE IN THE PACIFIC

Anthropologists in the past have been mainly concerned with investigating the customs of primitive peoples and have been relatively uninterested in their modernization under the impact of Western civilization. But another aspect of anthropology has come into prominence— *the anthropology of the primitive in transition.*

Western influence has now affected native communities in Africa, Asia, Polynesia, the Near East, and indeed in every part of the world. The results are not merely social but are beginning to have the most important political consequences, for they take the form of great social unrest coupled with nationalism and emancipation from European domination. Primitive peoples are taking over new tools, new crops, new processes, and new garbs. They are also finding new opportunities for acquiring and spending wealth. This has brought about profound internal conflict, as new values supersede or struggle with the old, and new institutions conflict with old methods of organization.

The effect of this struggle is not, as has been supposed, merely one of disintegration. The struggle has brought out new integrations, the building up of new customs, new institutions, and new values.

MODES OF SOCIAL CHANGE

There are three kinds of change which can overtake a primitive community: the first is **voluntary change,** as when the native adopts the steel tool instead of the stone implement and along with it such modern importations as sewing machines and matches, both of which are extremely popular and very useful. These, of course, are only simple examples of a great influx of new technical knowledge.

The second cause of change is **government regulation.** These regulations lead to the ending of tribal wars, attempts to eliminate the worst features of witchcraft, such as the murder of suspected sorcerers, endeavours to enforce regulations to prevent infectious disease and to compel people to bury their dead in cemeteries and not under the floors of their houses.

The third form of social change is economic and is due to **the introduction of money,** which is needed for many purposes and, in particular, to buy the new tools and other useful things imported from the West. Now money can be obtained by only trading with centres of Western occupation, or by wage labour on plantations owned by Europeans. This has led to the most fundamental change of all, the departure from the simple village communities of the young men for long periods of indentured labour on the plantations. And there have been a number of unfortunate results: the young men, removed from the pressure of tribal obligations, often degenerate morally; second, the village, deprived of their labour, declines economically; third, when the young men return with a little money at their disposal, they tend to break away from the old equalitarian society in which everything is shared, which is the basis of the primitive social order; they have also lost much of their respect for the old traditions and for the tribal or village headmen.

In order to understand some of the transitional changes currently taking place, we shall study the Melanesians, who occupy what is commonly called Melanesia. Melanesia is one of the three great divisions of the oceanic islands in the central and western Pacific. It includes the New British Archipelago, north-west of New Guinea, the Louisiade, Solomon, Santa Cruz, New Hebrides, and Loyalty islands, New Caledonia and Fiji and smaller intervening groups. Some Melanesians inhabit New Guinea.

New Tools and Techniques. Change begins when people recognize the superior efficiency of a new tool or method of working. The acceptance of the steel axe marked the first step in Melanesia. A steel axe cuts down a tree much sooner than a stone axe. Or consider matches. These are convenient, cheap, and reliable. They are more efficient and speedier than rubbing sticks together, which is a much more laborious job than most people, who have never tried it, suppose. The sewing machine, which is used everywhere, is one of the most common modern tools available in Melanesia.

On the other hand few primitive communities have adopted the steel plough. First of all it is very expensive, but also there are no draft animals, and tractors are out of the question. There is another reason in

Melanesia: there is a traditional bond between the farmer and the carpenter. The carpenter looks after the wooden plough and the farmer provides the carpenter with clothes, entertainment, and food. This social bond would be broken if the steel plough were introduced.

Objects are frequently adopted before the techniques for their manufacture. The Melanesians have not begun to learn how to make the steel tools they now handle daily.

Among these new tools and machines are some that are regarded as consumption goods, including pots and pans, beds and bedding, clothes, needles, and so forth. Others are regarded as capital goods or equipment, since they can be used to earn a living. Among these are carpenters' tools and sewing machines. With the sewing machine people can not only make their own garments, but they can make and sell clothes for others.

Carpenters are among the first specialist craftsmen of the Melanesians. Some men have even managed to buy trucks and set themselves up as carriers. They charge a set price for delivering loads and are also prepared to hire the vehicles out, with themselves as drivers, to building contractors, storekeepers, and others.

Government Control. A paternal government has certainly made great changes in the whole pattern of social life. *War has been abolished.* Although, in the beginning, the leaders gave up organizing warlike expeditions reluctantly, they are no longer anxious to fight. They have learned the advantages of living peaceably, without the constant fear of attack, and prefer to go on doing so.

Regulations designed to improve the health of the native population have been adopted. These include efforts to persuade them to build proper latrines, prohibition of the unpleasant habit of burying dead bodies underneath the earthen floors of their huts, keeping domestic pigs out of the villages, the proper treatment of infectious disease, and the eradication of sorcery.

The last two are closely connected. The inhabitants of all the primitive parts of Melanesia still oppose the regulations concerning infectious disease. This is because they have their own theories about disease and do not begin to have a scientific understanding of physiology and pathology, or any conception of what bacteria might be. On the contrary, they are convinced that sickness is brought about by supernatural forces set in motion either by sorcerers or by spirit beings. Ritual devices and countermagic are therefore, in their view, the only way to deal with illness. They dismiss all medical advice as pointless, possibly impious, or even harmful.

The proper burial of the dead is very difficult to achieve. The older method of burying the corpse in the house resulted in a nauseating stench which was endured as showing respect and affection for the departed. Patrol officers banned the practice and ordered people to set aside a plot of ground as a cemetery. This they did and neatly fenced it in. This seemed to present a real improvement, with tidy graves each with its headstone and flowers. But they were all empty. There were no bodies in them.

The disappearance of sorcery will mark a decisive change in the very basis of Melanesian life, since it will for the first time really open the way for a scientific appreciation of natural law. But there is still a very long way to go. The Melanesian islands are not as paradisal as we are asked to believe. There is a good deal of sickness. This is attributed to the malevolence of enemies who are thought to cast spells. The rites and spells which cause ailments such as headaches, toothaches, stomach-aches, boils, and so forth are well-known, and if people are angry they make use of them. Since these ailments are common, it often appears that the sorcerer has been successful. The patient, for his part, is not un-duly alarmed and does not make any considerable efforts to find out who is bewitching him (which is the main method among the Azande); instead he seeks out someone who knows the counterspells, and since he usually recovers, he is quite satisfied that the original illness was caused by sorcery and that he has found a magical remedy.

In the face of such beliefs and practices it is difficult to get people to understand the correct theory of disease and the right method of dealing with it.

Sorcerers may be quite well-known and the district officers have the authority to punish them, but the effects are not always what might be expected. The natives may interpret such action as a confession of the power of the sorcerer, since he is clearly being punished because he could indeed harm his victims. Imprisonment for a sorcerer is thus the equivalent of an award for his competence. In the old days the residents of his own village could laugh at the accusation that the man had really practised sorcery, but now they are really alarmed at this signal testi-mony to his power. He now becomes a figure of dread.

Wage Labour. There are many reasons for going outside the village to find opportunities for earning money by wage labour.

(*a*) There is the desire to see something of new places.

(*b*) There is the need for ready cash. The only way to get money is to take a job, and almost the only jobs are those on the plantations. (Money is needed to buy iron and steel implements, fishhooks, ham-mers and nails, saws and planes, lamps, oil, crockery, soap, bedding, sewing machines, and bicycles.)

(*c*) The government has imposed *a poll tax* of a few shillings per head per annum in order to induce the natives to offer their labour to the planters. This has proved very effective.

(*d*) Finally wage labour on the plantations or in the towns is an escape from village boredom, which has grown since the universal spread of Christianity has made the Sabbath a particularly dull day, with no dancing. It is also an escape from village discipline, and petty offenders avoid paying the penalty of their misdemeanours.

Young people usually leave the villages at the age of sixteen and spend an average of six years as paid workers with rations supplied. Most of them go to the plantations. Some few may eventually become clerks, truck drivers, or houseboys.

Life in the labour compounds is squalid. Detached from village influences, the men inevitably throw off moral restraints. Welfare institutions and night schools for native labourers do not exist anywhere. Apart from dancing and a little soccer, the chief pastime for the hours of leisure is gambling.

Meanwhile the effect on the villages they have left is disastrous. Labour is short; houses cannot be built or repaired; the gardens shrink in size; the old folk, women, and children may be inadequately provided for. Even in the most favoured villages the living standards are low, and they will never be raised while the fittest males are obliged to spend such long periods away from home.

On returning to the village, the men may have accumulated a fair sum of money in the course of six years. This they are expected to share with their relatives; but they are loath to do so. The men have by now lost all sense of tribal loyalty and discipline. They are not ready to accept the rule of the elders and instead of settling down to work, they sleep in the club huts until noon, until they can be persuaded once more to settle down to work.

Although they seldom share any of their earnings with relatives outside their immediate family, and only give them a few shillings, their sense of obligation to more distant relatives is not dead. A troubled conscience may persuade them that illnesses which overtake them are due to a resentful relative bewitching them.

CHANGING MELANESIAN INSTITUTIONS

Village Government. Government administration now overrides the authority of both chiefs and headmen, but the amount of money available for all purposes is very limited. Colonial expenditure must therefore be kept the barest minimum—public health, education, public works, agriculture and the rest all suffer. Only the senior officers are European or Australian and the native policemen under foreign authority are usually more in sympathy with their fellow countrymen than with their superiors.

In most villages natives have been appointed as government officials, and they are expected to maintain order or report the offenders to the nearest district office. The disadvantage of this method is that the real headman, who had much local support and real authority, is no more and only government representatives hold the field. These officials do not command the respect that is or was accorded to the traditional headmen. Village councils are now being formed in some of the more economically advanced areas.

The chief has lost his authority largely because it depended to a considerable extent on his supposed magical power. The natives today are not afraid of this kind of magic, though they continue to believe in sorcery; hence where the old type of headman or chief remains, his authority has diminished.

A very remarkable phenomenon is the appearance of new leaders with definite social programmes, and even the setting up of village councils without the consent of the government. This has sometimes resulted in the establishment of rival authorities, government and local councils. (These moves are really bound up with the Cargo Cults and similar uprisings which are dealt with on p. 248.)

Religion. Today practically every Melanesian below middle age who has had some years of European contact is a Christian. How can we account for this remarkable change? In most cases it was because the Europeans seemed more powerful and knew so much more that it was thought that their gods must be superior to the supernatural powers of the Melanesians. The missionaries were members of the politically and economically superior group; they appeared to be rich and had many possessions, compared with the natives, even when they lived modestly enough. Many natives decided to try the experiment of invoking the new gods to see if they had any better luck than when they practised their traditional rites. They hoped, by attending church services, to secure the goodwill of a mighty spirit. Many of them felt that the subsequent results justified their action.

There was another important reason. The natives wanted economic equality with the whites; but education is a necessary preliminary. The village schools are mission schools. Only Christians can learn reading and writing. Hence, giving up traditional religion is not considered too big a price to pay for the privilege of getting on the bottom rung of the ladder of social advancement.

Other natives joined the Church to satisfy their ambition. Church elders, catechists, and teachers all enjoy positions of some superiority in the village.

Finally, it was a relief to abandon the irksome restrictions, taboos, and ceremonials of a complicated pagan religion. The missionaries derided them and advised their Christian followers to take no notice of them. In a quite surprising way whole communities have abandoned at least the externals of primitive systems of animism and magic and accepted the creeds of Christianity. The resulting faith, however, bears little resemblance to Western Christianity and is much imbued with elements of the older paganism, as was the Christianity of early Europe.

THE CARGO CULT

Perhaps the most exciting and alarming manifestation of social change in the Pacific is the emergence of what is called the Cargo Cult. Whole communities of natives, driven by social unrest, poverty, and insecurity, organized themselves into new cults based on the powerful fantasy of coming deliverance in the form of cargo ships, or even aeroplanes, landing on the islands to bring them every good thing—that is to say, material wealth of every kind. Jetties are built, landing strips are prepared, and a wave of religious excitement passes over the entire population.

Very often the old religion is thrown overboard and with it all ancient customs. New and vigorously fanatical leaders emerge, often with great powers of organization and initiative. Quite considerable construction works are put in hand; new houses and often new villages and meeting halls are built. The movement is violently anti-European. Its leaders have frequently been arrested and imprisoned, but this has little effect upon the movement.

In some of its more recent forms a decidedly more political slant has been given to this movement, which in the Solomons is called the Marching Rule. Here a new code of ethics includes such rules as the following:

(*a*) No more making feasts for a man just dead.
(*b*) No more custom of child marriage.
(*c*) No more customs from ancient times.
(*d*) No more anger, no more fighting, no more stealing.

These movements have been described as the forerunners of Melanesian nationalism. Their adherents wish to throw out the Europeans so that they will again be masters of their fate; and they also want to recapture unity and common endeavour and to re-establish the dignity of their group. But the ideal they envisage is not a return to the past: it is a new world in which natives will live following the style of white men.

The administrative authorities are greatly concerned with this movement and particularly with the determination of the natives to secure effective power to control their own destiny and to manage their own affairs. The governments of Melanesia may in the future find themselves confronted with a Mau Mau cult or, if a Gandhi or a Nehru appears, with a serious attempt to obtain political independence.

The Origins of the Cargo Cult. Undoubtedly a powerful influence in the development of these cults was a deep desire for material betterment, which was reinforced when the United States Army landed in New Guinea and brought with it an immense variety of goods. American soldiers also assumed a more friendly attitude to the natives than most white people of the British and Australian colonial administration and business class. For the first time the natives were treated as human beings and made to feel their human dignity.

A belief sprang up among the natives that they were being deprived of goods being made for them by their ancestors. Cargoes of these goods were being sent to them but were intercepted by the white men. Now at last this was to stop; their ancestors themselves were going to bring the goods in a fleet of ships. There would be rice and bully beef for all, and much else besides.

They also believed that education had somehow cheated them of knowledge which the white men had, but which they were not allowed to obtain. Therefore they sought to obtain the 'secret' which the white man was concealing. This was declared to be *the first page of the Bible* which the Europeans, they said, had torn out of all the Bibles they had given the islanders. This was, of course, as mythical as the rest of the cargo cult beliefs.

Thus the natives wanted to adopt modern dress, customs, and ways of life, they wanted to enjoy what the white men enjoyed, but if they were avid for his goods and knowledge they saw the white man himself as the major obstacle between them and their goal. The movement was therefore anti-white, anti-mission, and anti-government in its general content. The whites had discriminated against and deceived the natives; therefore all obedience and submission to them must be renounced.

The fires of the Cargo faith were fed by the inexhaustible fuel of social dissatisfaction. To people desperate for some explanation of the irrational and unjust world in which they lived, desperate for a solution to their problems and for a faith to steer by, these fantastic myths were a source not only of passionate faith but of vigorous action.

The Effects of the Cult on Melanesian Personality. The effects of the cult were twofold: there was at first a great outburst of hysteria, but secondly there was a very real moral reformation.

Hysteria. When the cult reached any one of the islands, there was an outburst of hysteria. Men fell into trances or were possessed. They were thrown into physical contortions and saw visions and heard voices. These phenomena were obviously caused because the Melanesians lacked the means to satisfy their wants, their feeling of deprivation and frustration being heightened by the apparent irrationality of the white-dominated society in which they lived. Owing to their lack of technique and knowledge, they were unable to cope with the problems thrust upon them by the conditions of white rule. Not knowing any effective way of tackling these problems, their deep desires boiled over into hysteria. We must not forget, however, the powerful emotions engendered by conscious mobilization to overthrow the old, deeply established ways, and to adopt new ones.

Moral Reformation. An asceticism or puritanism characterized these cults. They all insisted on a new morality, on the abandonment of old ways, on cleaning up the dirt and untidiness of the villages, on clean eating, on washing, on better clothes—Western, where possible. They discarded their ornaments, even many of their amusements. Old ceremonies were considered wicked. Children no longer had their noses and ears perforated; hair was cut short. Often there was a public breaking of taboos.

Emphasis was placed on the abandonment of social distinctions, on the sharing of property and on the surrender of worldly wealth. Much emphasis was placed on democratic solidarity, symbolized in ascetic acts of renunciation and dedication to the new ethic. The cult members showed a new sobriety, piety, and strictness in their moral lives.

The break with custom itself helped to weld the devotees together in a new fraternity—they were bound by guilt and by being cut off from the old life. The ritual of publicly breaking the taboos was a powerful mechanism of social integration and a generator of much emotional energy.

Although in most cases the missionaries had withdrawn, the churches remained and were cleaned up or rebuilt and made the focus of the New Way, which was partly religious and partly social. If the cargo did not come it must be because of sin, hence the attempt to root it out by public confessions and public punishment. Thus a definite religious element is found in the cult.

From the Millennium to the Marching Rule. Since the Second World War, and particularly in recent years, the more hysterical and mythological elements of the Cargo Cults have given way to more concrete demands for representative government and social reorganization. New and saner leaders have emerged and have established contact with one another from island to island. There has thus arisen a political organization, expressing an embryonic nationalism and uniting scores of formerly separate and minute social groups and tiny island communities.

This trend found expression in what was called the Marching Rule, which was partly political and partly a campaign for moral reformation. The government arrested its leaders and in 1949 some 2000 of its members were in prison. Since then the government has gone a long way to meet the demands of the movement. More village councils have been set up and many of the local reforms established by the leaders of the Marching Rule have been recognized. Many of these reforms in village life had been long advocated on paper by the administration but were regarded as premature.

The whole movement is of significance because, while it increasingly desires independence of political control, it does not seek isolation from the cultural achievements of modern civilization or from its material advantages; these it strives for. The whole movement is progressive, not regressive. The order it looks forward to and works for is not the rejection of the present and a turning back to ancient ways, but a radical transformation of the present to carry it forward to a stage at which its benefits may be more widely shared and enjoyed.

THE ANTHROPOLOGIST AND CARGO CULTS

Since their appearance considerable interest in these phenomena has been taken by anthropologists, and a number of special studies have been made by investigators working in the Pacific. It has been noted that although these cults have sprung up all over the place in a variety of conditions, certain features are common to all.

They arise as the result of the activity of a *prophet*; they all manifest a particular religious form known as *apocalyptic*—that is to say, a sudden and dramatic end to the present order, and the miraculous arrival of a better state of affairs. Finally they all require (*a*) a condition of relative poverty and backwardness which stands in visible contrast to (*b*) the wealth, technical superiority, and comfort of the visiting military units which established bases on the islands during the war. This had occasioned surprise and excitement, and was seen, above all, as a manifestation of *power*. The key question was: *how to get hold of such power for themselves?* The prophet came with a supernatural answer to this question. He told them how to get this power.

It has to be remembered that all these societies were held firmly in the system so well described by Radcliffe-Brown and others as an example of structural functionalism. This closed, organic society is so hedged in by custom and taboo as to be largely unchangeable. Elsewhere, only the impact of a foreign power has disintegrated such societies. In this case disruption was *from within*. The prophet breaks the spell.

Professor Jarvie, in his book *The Revolution in Anthropology*, sums up the situation thus:

> We witness the breakdown of a closed society under pressures created by constant failures to explain things within its own system of religious magic and taboo. Their own magico-religious methods having proved powerless, they now try others.

The importance for sociology is that whereas existing Melanesian societies were accepted without question in all particulars—as we might put it 'divinely ordained'—now for the first time we see men deliberately questioning an age-old traditional society, destroying it, and themselves, and consciously and deliberately constructing another one. But still it takes the form of a religious revelation. There is a religious explanation of the whole situation and a religious solution; but in so far as it is a human construction, it is a move away from a closed society to an open one.

The cult cannot, in the form prophesied, prove successful. The cargoes do not come. But the adherents do not abandon the doctrine; they try other methods of achieving the conditions which will bring the cargoes. They try other prophets. If they still fail, this opens the possibility of criticism of the whole religious and apocalyptic solution of the social problem.

It has also been suggested that the Cargo Cult is a means whereby the Melanesians are projecting their political demands for the end of colonial rule into a religious form, this being the only explanation-form they know. Given new leaders, could they not be organized behind such a cause in a way that is not magico-religious, but politico-religious?

FIELD STUDY NO. XIII—ADOLESCENT PROBLEMS IN SAMOA AND AMERICA

Margaret Mead was one of the first anthropologists to apply anthropological knowledge to psychological and social problems, and to carry out an important piece of field-work among a primitive people with the express purpose of seeking light on the problems of American youth.

The anthropologist, as she points out, realizes more than most people the tremendous role played in an individual's life by the social environment in which he is born and reared. So many aspects of behaviour are not essential expressions of an unchanging human nature, but are the results of cultural and environmental pressure. Thus when we consider the psychological problems of adolescence, we must ask ourselves how much these problems are due to 'growing up' and how much they are due to *growing up in Western civilization.*

In order to solve this problem Margaret Mead decided to go to a different civilization and make a study of human beings under different cultural conditions from those in her own country. She decided, moreover, to choose a simple people, whose society had not attained the complexity of our modern world. The community she decided upon was Samoa, a South Sea island about 13° south of the equator, and here, because she herself was a woman, she proceeded to investigate the development of adolescence among these Polynesian girls. She concluded that the method of child training was very different from that in America, but this was because the pattern of Samoan society was different from ours, and the children were being conditioned for it.

Life in Samoa. She immersed herself in Samoan village life; she learned the language and customs. She participated in the activities of the women and gained their friendship.

She was impressed by the fact that the Samoan system of bringing up the young did not cause repressions. There was little punishment; intense competition was not encouraged. There was much sexual freedom for the young adolescent, and church membership (the Samoans are Christians) is not required before marriage, as Christian sexual standards are not imposed on the young.

Therefore with few exceptions there was *no crisis in adolescence*; it was simply a period in which interests and activities slowly matured.

The girls' minds were perplexed by no conflicts, troubled by no doubts, beset by no remote ambitions.

To live as a girl with many lovers as long as possible and then to marry in one's own village, near one's own relatives and to have many children, these were a uniform and satisfying ambition.

Such sex experimentation was possible because in adolescence there was a period of non-fertility after the onset of puberty.

In What Ways is Samoan Life Different? Samoa offers a social environment for the growing girl which is different partly because it is primitive, and partly because it is Samoan.

Samoan life itself has not been radically transformed by modern culture and industrialization. It is still genuinely primitive but it has undergone some changes. Western control has considerably softened its more violent aspects. Cotton cloth is used, steel has replaced stone for tools, scissors and sewing machines are in use. But the Samoans still produce their own foods—breadfruit, taro, yams, and coconuts—by the old method. The head of the household no longer has life and death power over those who dwell in his hut. Punishment for unchastity no longer occurs as far as ordinary people are concerned. (Rules for the chief's daughters are stricter.)

Psychological Attitudes. Samoan life as we find it today is less exacting than our own. It is more casual, and no one plays for very high stakes. No one suffers for his convictions or fights to the death for special ends. Wars and cannibalism have long since passed away, and social crises and disasters do not occur here.

In personal relations, caring is slight. Children have many 'mothers' to look after them and do not care too much for any one person. Few have an exceptional capacity for emotion. Conflict and poignant situations are avoided.

Limitations. Perhaps the most striking way in which Samoan civilization differs from our own is in the number of choices each individual may make. We have innumerable decisions to make: there are competing religions, different standards of morality, different political parties, many different social groupings with different customs.

The Samoan girl has very few choices to make. There is only one religion, which nobody questions. Sex raises few problems. Everyone in the community agrees about sex—except the missionaries and even they are wise enough to turn a blind eye to adolescent sexual experimentation. The Samoan girl's life is free from the contradictions which vex Western youth, because her civilization is simple, homogeneous, and primitive.

Why No Psychological Maladjustments? We are now on the way to discovering why there is a lack of neuroses among the Samoans, while neuroses are prevalent in our society. The chief influence which makes for normal development is the early education of Samoan children. In Samoa we do not find the small family, closely guarded by the father and mother. Children are reared in households where there are a half-dozen adult women and a half-dozen adult men to take care of them. They do not sharply distinguish their parents. Children perform definite tasks from the time they are four or five years old. These are graded to their strength and intelligence, but are nonetheless really useful chores. The girl tends babies, carries water, sweeps the floor; the boy digs for bait or collects coconuts. Work consists of these necessary tasks, which keep the social life going, both for children and adults, and is not like our school tasks, which are unrelated to adult activities and the necessary work of society.

Recreation. Play includes dancing, singing, games, weaving necklaces of flowers, flirting, repartee—all forms of sex activity. But the distinction between work and play is conspicuously absent. The Samoan does not, for instance, consider work as something one has to do but dislikes, and play as something he wants to do, nor does the Samoan consider work to be the main business of adults and play to be the main concern of children.

Dancing is very important. It is almost the only way of showing off, of asserting one's individuality. It effectively offsets the rigorous subordination in which children are habitually kept. They become the centre of the group and are much praised. Each child is now a person with a definite contribution to make; for the dance, even when many dance together, is not co-ordinated and disciplined but highly individualistic.

Sex, Birth and Death. Margaret Mead was impressed by the children's familiarity with those aspects of existence which we tend to gloss over or conceal from children. In a Samoan village nothing can be concealed, and secrecy, ignorance, guilty knowledge, and erroneous speculation are absent. The children know all that there is to know about disease, death, corruption, sexual intercourse, and labour. To them, as to their elders, birth, sex, and death are part of the natural, inevitable structure of existence.

Upon this acceptance of the physical facts of life the Samoans build, as they grow older, an acceptance of sex. This, however, is not a matter for romance. The Samoans have a low level of appreciation of personality differences and a poverty of conception regarding personal relationships, and to such an attitude the acceptance of promiscuity undoubtedly contributes. The Samoan girl never tastes the rewards of romantic love as we know it, but neither does she suffer from our neuroses.

The blurring of individual differences and strong personal interests also minimizes jealousy, rivalry, emulation, and those social attitudes which arise out of discrepancies of endowment and are so far-reaching in their effects upon the adult's personality.

Samoa and the West. Whether or not we envy the Samoans for their free existence, a study of their way of life must affect our attitude towards our own problems. Our ways are not inevitable, not the only ones, but have grown as part of our history. We may well examine in turn our own institutions, thrown into relief against the practices of other simpler and very different communities, and it may be that, weighed in the balance, we may sometimes find them wanting and sometimes find fresh insights in the carefree lives of more primitive peoples.

Sex and Temperament in Three Primitive Societies is a study of three different tribes in New Guinea. Here Professor Mead found three different types of dominant personality and three different types of sex relationships. Among the **Arapesh** there was no aggression: men helped to look after the children. Men and women were gentle and sensitive, both sexes being very much alike in personality. Among the **Mundugumors,** on the other hand, men and women grew up to be aggressive, jealous, individualistic, and violent. The women did most of the work, while the men carried on rituals and hunted. The third tribe, the **Tschambuli,** was largely run by the women, while the men were idle playboys.

The material drawn from these groups vividly demonstrates the flexibility of human nature and the fact that many of the temperamental characteristics usually assigned to each sex are not inherent but are determined by the particular culture.

FIELD STUDY NO. XIV—CAN HUMAN NATURE CHANGE?

One of the most important of anthropological studies was Margaret Mead's report on her return to New Guinea after an absence of twenty-five years. The people she visited on both occasions were the Manus, a community of a few thousand fisherfolk, living in houses built on piles in the sea. *Growing Up in New Guinea* describes the Manus as she first found them; *New Lives for Old* records the vast changes she observed on her second visit.

THE MANUS OF NEW GUINEA

The Manus as They Were. The Manus were a commercially-minded, money-loving (their money consisted of dogs' teeth and shells), rather surly, puritanical people. They were practical, quick to understand machines, hardy, disciplined from childhood, prudish and clean in physical functions. They were fanatically industrious, conscience-driven, competitive, and enslaved by their preoccupation with trade, work, and debt. They were censorious and insensitive. Shouting and anger were their main vices.

The Manus had a curious system whereby an older man financed a younger man when the latter wanted to marry, providing him with the considerable amount of "money" necessary to pay the bride-price and meet other heavy forms of expenditure. The young men thus got heavily into debt and would work hard for years to clear themselves. But after being thus exploited, they themselves became ruthless traders, first to put an end to their dependence and then to become, themselves, the sponsors for the next generation of young men.

Growing Up. Margaret Mead took special note of the relationship between child training and adult life in New Guinea. The children of the Manus were brought up without cramping inhibitions. They were as gay, spontaneous, unacquisitive, generous, and friendly as might be desired. But their fathers were acquisitive and quarrelsome and the happy, carefree children were to be speedily transformed to the behaviour pattern of their elders.

It would appear that the harried, complicated, commercial world of their elders did not exist for the children. (They never played at adult activities as do the children in communities where the adult world is more acceptable to the younger generation.) Did they perhaps sense their elders' dissatisfaction with the heavy burdens of a distorted culture and ignore it as long as possible?

Possibly this very free type of child training, which made the children active, energetic individuals, helped to prepare the way for the radical changes which followed the Second World War. Potential forces for change already existed. The typical personality was independent, alert, energetic, and able to accept new techniques. At the same time there was a deep dissatisfaction with the restrictions of society. The way to change was paved by the type of upbringing which produced dynamic individuals.

Adult Corruption. The Manus were a very individualistic people, every man jealous of his property, rights, and privileges. They all felt that they were on the treadmill of a tyrannical system which drove them and oppressed them. They were unloving and intolerant individuals, getting little pleasure from the lives they led.

Religion entered their lives not to ease their burdens but to increase them. Each house had its own guardian ghost, the spirit of the most recently dead male. The ghost sent misfortune, sickness, and death in punishment for sexual laxity, economic faults, the breaking of the taboos, or any failure in word, gesture, and behaviour to conform to strict tribal etiquette involving whole categories of relatives.

Many observers of these people, and students of Margaret Mead's books, came to regard the Manus as permanently cast into this mould and deeply imbued with a rather unpleasant kind of ineradicable 'original sin'.

The Process of Change. But these traits were not ineradicable any more than their pattern of economic and social life was something final and permanent. Irresistible forces were at work everywhere in Melanesia. The Manus could not escape them.

The special character of the Manus made them excellent policemen and they became the mainstay of the police force. Here they manifested considerable powers of self-discipline as well as the ability to discipline others; they were at the same time independent and self-confident. However, not all their officers noted how hostile they were, beneath an orderly exterior, to all Europeans and how sensitive to white affronts. They learned much from their contact with the white man, and when the waves of unrest associated with the Cargo Cults swept over them, many of them became the natural leaders of a movement that desired, initially, to secure for the people of New Guinea the commodities which the whites, particularly the Americans, enjoyed in such profusion; secondly, to assert their personal dignity as against subjection to Europeans; and thirdly, to secure some real measure of political independence.

Under the influence of a former Manus policeman this movement became something much more—a campaign for the reformation of custom, character, and economic life. Villages were removed from the sea and rebuilt on land; inland tribes came down to the shores; the tribes were banded together, gardens and fishing were shared. Quarrelsome people given to endless raids and counter-raids, alliances and betrayals were welded into one people. The old marriage customs— expensive, onerous, and really inimical to a happy marriage relationship —were revised to do away with their burdensome financial demands. The dominance of the older men, which largely depended on this, was broken. Kinship observances were discarded and new forms of clothing introduced.

New Minds, New Men. The result was not only the strikingly new appearance of the village and people, but a new morality, a new way of life.

It was clearly seen by their leaders that partial change, or even slow change, would not do. They must either go forward as a group or fall to pieces. So they burned their religious, social, and political boats completely. They moved fast because they changed the entire pattern nearly all at once—houses, customs, ceremonies, social organization, laws— making up the new pattern out of all they could assimilate from European and American examples.

The change in their character was remarkable. They became friendly instead of harshly competitive, relaxed and unworried instead of anxious, oppressed, and harassed. They became a singing, laughing people. Husbands and wives and mothers and fathers could meet and greet one another without the absurd prohibitions of the past. They wore European clothes and scrupulously washed them. They learned the Western way of working regular hours and had time for leisure. There were committees, meetings, and votes which the people seem to enjoy. Even the ghosts seem to have been driven off.

In the 'new way' anger and quarelling became the vices to be avoided at all costs—vices which had almost completely spoiled the sexual side of marriage. Now the pleasures of peaceful love had been discovered.

If this appears somewhat idyllic, we must remember that it was only a new *beginning*. It remained to be seen whether the new traditions could be consolidated. Even more important, was the question of whether the economic basis of the new society was properly established—or was the new pattern of behaviour grafted on to a declining subsistence economy and an indentured labour system. Should not the next step be a reconstruction of the economic life to provide the necessary foundation for the reformation of manners and ideas? Whatever the answers to these questions in the course of time, Margaret Mead has shown how changes in social and political organization, in religious beliefs and world views actually result in changes in the personalities of those who experience them.

SUGGESTED FURTHER READING

Beattie, J., *Other Cultures*. Routledge & Kegan Paul: London, 1964.

Belshaw, C. S., *The Great Village*. Routledge & Kegan Paul: London, 1964.

Barnett, H. G., *Innovation: The Basis of Cultural Change*. McGraw-Hill: London, 1953.

Bohannan, P., *African Outline*. Penguin Books: London, 1966.

Elkin, A. P., *Social Anthropology in Melanesia*. Oxford University Press: London, 1953.

Firth, Raymond, *Elements of Social Organization*. Watts & Co.: London, 1951.

Firth, Raymond, *Social Change in Tikopia*. Allen & Unwin: London, 1951.

Fortes, Meyer, and Evans-Pritchard, E. E., *African Political Systems*. Oxford University Press: London, 1940.

Fortune, F. R., *Sorcerers of Dobu*. Routledge & Kegan Paul: London, 1932.

Hailey, Lord Malcolm, *An African Survey*. Oxford University Press: London, 1939.

Hogbin, H. Ian, *Experiments in Civilization*. Routledge & Kegan Paul: London, 1939.

Hogbin, H. Ian, *Social Change*. Watts & Co.: London, 1958.

Jarvie, Ian C., *The Revolution in Anthropology*. Routledge & Kegan Paul: London, 1964.

Junod, H. A., *The Life of a South African Tribe*. Macmillan: London, 1962.

Lévi-Strauss, C., *The Scope of Anthropology*. Cape: London, 1967.

Marquand, Leopold, *The Peoples and Policies of South Africa*. Oxford University Press: London, 1962.

Mead, Margaret, *New Lives for Old*. Gollancz: London, 1956.

Schapera, Isaac, *Migrant Labor and Tribal Life*. Oxford University Press: London, 1947.

Sundkler, B., *Bantu Prophets*. Oxford University Press: London, 1964.

Worsley, Peter, *The Trumpet Shall Sound, A Study of Cargo Cults in Melanesia*. McGibbon & Kee: London, 1968.

CHAPTER TWENTY

THE ANTHROPOLOGIST AT WORK

Mankind in Perspective. The anthropologist and the archaeologist, in tracing the evolution of human culture from the horizon of our human forebears to the dawn of civilization, present a picture of the species lifting itself from the status of a mere animal to a radically new way of life, a way destined to win mastery and to exert a powerful and extensive control over the natural habitat.

Moreover the study of the simpler forms of social life reveals, more clearly than any attempt to unravel the complexities of contemporary life, the existence of **social pattern** and of **functionalism.** This means that every society is a whole and that any special activity, such as religion or government, must be understood in the context of the whole pattern of social life of which it is part. Thus all the actual institutions, attitudes, and customs of a society must be so related to one another that the social life can be perceived as a set of interconnected parts, as a whole.

The anthropologist tries to show, by comparing one society with another, the common features of institutions as well as the differing features in each society. He thus seeks to show the function played by, say, religion in *all* human societies. Going further, he may be able to show a dynamic order in social life, patterns which are common to all societies of the same general type and patterns which are universal.

The Value of Small-scale Study. Primitive societies are particularly useful as a subject for study because they exhibit the characteristics of a large society in a simplified form. Such activities as those comprised under art, religion, manners, law, custom, government, sex, and family are all present in primitive society, even if the words for them are lacking and their demarcation from one another is less distinct.

The difference in scale has immense value. It allows the observer an objective view of the whole, which is practically impossible in our own immensely complex modern life. It throws the articulation of the parts into relief. This gives us a real opportunity to conduct an objective analysis of social forms, as controllable and as demonstrable as a study of chemical interactions.

The application to contemporary life is twofold:

1. It may help us in dealing with primitive communities with which we are in contact today, and which we are radically transforming or disintegrating by the pressure of our more advanced technology and political development.

2. It may provide us with the material with which to think about human behaviour in our own society, to consider the ways in which people act, individually and collectively.

This difficult task is greatly helped by a preliminary study of the structure of primitive society.

Understanding the Primitive. Anthropology makes for a sympathetic understanding of other peoples, and especially those over whom we have come to exercise some kind of guardianship or other form of influence in their transition from savagery to civilization.

Universities are now providing training in anthropology for those intending to work in such fields, and are responsible for much important research. Anthropologists are employed in various capacities by the government of the United States, and by the United Nations.

Every person—colonial administrator, missionary, diplomat—called upon to live in contact with a society very different from his own needs the outlook and understanding of anthropology. Otherwise difficulties are bound to arise which may become acute, creating misunderstanding, fostering racial or social prejudice, and even compromising the cause of peace.

The light which is thrown on the race question by both physical anthropology and general anthropological studies, is of particular importance for dispelling prejudice largely based on ignorance. There is no biological evidence to support views of racial superiority. Men may look very different but they are all of the same species. *There are no inherent differences of mental capacity or personality which are associated with race differences.* No form of intelligence testing has ever refuted this.

Men of other races are not really discriminated against on these grounds. They are discriminated against economically and politically, often by the establishment of privilege over government, ownership of land and mineral rights. This is then justified by rationalizations of a racialist kind.

> These stereotypes are due to ignorance, and sometimes ignorance affords political or moral advantage. It does so where it provides a ground for maintaining an elite, or justifies a system of economic exploitation.
>
> (Beattie, *Other Cultures.*)

Of course under these conditions differences of an environmental origin do arise—poor health, lack of education, unwillingness to work for the benefit of others, degenerate habits. Delinquency can be created by inferior conditions and an under-privileged status. But anthropology affirms that these differences are not inborn but acquired.

On the other hand anthropology cannot declare that every culture is as good as every other culture. Whatever the evils of Western culture, the advance in technology (and agriculture, health, transport, house accommodation, and all the other amenities of civilization) brings undeniable advantages.

Sound anthropological knowledge would, in the past, have prevented many mistakes which have obstructed the well-intentioned activities of district officers and even provoked wars. In Ashanti two wars were fought largely because, at the time of the Ashanti campaigns, the British did not know the significance of the Golden Stool of this people, which was believed to contain the soul of all the inhabitants of Ashanti.

Anthropology helps in the understanding of bride-price and its economic and social importance; in looking for unexpected repercussions of administrative action; in understanding the native attitude to land. Thus the Kikuyu of Kenya had no idea that they had actually sold all the most fertile land in the country to British settlers, so that they could be and were legally evicted from it. Anthropology helps the administrator to have respect for native customs. What may appear to us to be a simple or trivial habit that may be ignored is often so related to the deepest feelings as to invite serious conflict if scorned.

New Ways, New Motives. Clyde Kluckhohn has pointed out that innovations do not necessarily create motivations corresponding to those in Western culture. On the contrary innovations may have a depressive effect on the incentives that previously existed.

There may be general agreement that economic development is desirable, yet people may be slow to respond. The relationship between their present standards of consumption, their incomes, and their future prospects may be such in their eyes as to offer too little inducement to improve production materially or to alter radically their technical methods.

Preferences for the social aspects of the customary working patterns, for the distribution of daily and seasonal leisure time in such a way as to give full scope for existing recreations, may stand in the way of a common-sense reorganization of social life.

What is the best way to present advice on agricultural methods, for instance? A bare scientific presentation is quite useless. Undoubtedly the most important consideration is that nationals from the new states should themselves be trained to take the responsibility of change, and for people themselves to *want* and *accept* the advantages which science offers them.

ANTHROPOLOGY AND SOCIAL CHANGE

Anthropology is of special importance in relation to the great social changes now proceeding in the backward areas of the world.

The Duke of Cambridge, brother of Edward VII, once declared that 'any change, at any time, for any purpose, is highly to be deprecated'; nevertheless change is inevitable and irresistible. The question is not how to prevent it, but how to control it.

It can be disruptive to the extent that whole groups become reservoirs of delinquency and criminality, or completely lose a zest for life and commit race suicide.

Even education and Christianity may not produce among a primitive people an acceptable imitation of a modern Christian but a chaotic individual not rooted in any definite way of life.

The anthropologist should be able to help here; indeed his assistance is indispensable in developing initiative and a sense of responsibility in those who must ultimately take control of their own destiny.

Anthropology and Human Rights. Unfortunately anthropology may be gravely misused in dealing with primitive peoples. It may become little more than an instrument for carrying through policies which it is not asked either to formulate or approve. It may be used to guide propaganda, or as a powerful weapon in the armoury of psychological manipulation.

The trusteeship principles of the United Nations and the professed aims of the great powers, which still exercise control over vast areas of Africa and other parts of the world, express the desire to protect the rights and interests of the native peoples whose territories are being developed. Stress is laid on enlisting their co-operation, on developing native society, on the need for a democratic foundation as the ultimate basis for these communities.

These professions and intentions have not, however, always been accepted at their face value and have even been challenged too often as only 'a moral cloak hiding the nakedness of economic exploitation and strategic intention' (Raymond Firth, *Elements of Social Organization*). Anthropologists give no support to any grading of primitive peoples as 'lesser breeds without the law', but on the contrary offer scientific grounds for regarding all men as potentially capable of full human development. They may be said, therefore, to further the general acknowledgment that it is not compatible with human dignity that one man should be either the political vassal of another or that he should be his economic chattel.

FIELD WORK

Anthropology is no longer based, as it was a hundred years ago, on travellers' tales speculated upon in the studies of philosophers who have never seen the societies they theorize about.

Today all serious workers are expected to visit, live among on informal terms, and be able to converse with, established communities in distant parts of the world. This has been successful not only in penetrating the veil of a radically different ideology but in establishing a profound sympathy and respect for primitive peoples. There is no other way of achieving the objectivity and disinterestedness which are so essential for getting at the real facts, and which cannot even be known as facts unless they are sympathetically understood.

One of the most exciting of these discoveries, which often disconcerts specialists in 'government' in our universities, is the existence of stateless communities, which possess government but not *a* government. It was only field-work, like that of Evans-Pritchard among the Nuer, that enabled us to understand how societies lacking any form of specialized political authority could possibly work. But it did successfully demonstrate that we can have an ordered society of a considerable size without the government and authority of chiefs.

Finally, a close acquaintance with primitive peoples may dispel the commonly held view that savages are ferocious, cruel, and war-like. Anthropologists are not pessimistic about warfare. Destructive behaviour is not a necessity for human life. Warfare was unknown during the earlier part of the Neolithic Age in Europe and during the whole of the Palaeolithic period. Organized warfare was unknown in aboriginal Australia and in many parts of the New World. It took civilization to show men how to exterminate his fellow man on a racial scale.

SOCIAL CHANGE IN PEASANT COMMUNITIES

Within recent years, and particularly since the end of the Second World War, a great change has come over social anthropology. It is becoming increasingly difficult to find mere survivals of simple food-gathering communities, almost untouched by civilization. The first reaction of anthropologists was one of intense regret, accompanied by still more determined efforts to put on record customs and attitudes too soon fated to disappear. But a wiser and more helpful attitude is emerging. This phenomenon surely is not so much a crisis as an opportunity *and a responsibility*. Social change is irresistible; here it is happening to those very peasant communities which anthropologists know most about. The transformation of whole peoples in Africa, the Pacific, the East, and South America is taking place *now*, before our very eyes. Should not anthropology find here a theme of absorbing interest?

The changing structure of native society also has political consequences—it is accompanied by social unrest, nationalism, and violent reaction against Western influence. Primitive peoples are taking over new tools, new crops, new processes, and new garbs; but this has involved a profound internal conflict, as new values supersede or struggle with the old, and new institutions conflict with old methods of organization.

New Tools, New Men. When a primitive community begins to use steel axes, bicycles, and sewing machines, it is foolish to imagine that these will serve as mere accessories to a culture otherwise unchanged. In the first place, these things have to be bought with money, and subsistence economies are not money economies; secondly, the new gadgets change the minds of those who use them. The potato and the pig, when introduced among the Maori of New Zealand, radically altered the economic structure. They reduced the amount of labour put in on other crops and on hunting; they gave commoners a chance to earn higher incomes and elevate themselves on the social scale.

New Markets, New Supplies. Once these new tools and many other useful articles, including dress materials and ready-made clothes, have created a demand and the native sets to work to earn a cash income, necessary market relations are created in the search for means of disposal of what can be produced locally, while for Western industrialism an expanding market develops. For over half a century, as labourers on sugar and copra plantations, the people of the Solomons have helped to supply our Western demands for raw materials. The effects on their economy and community life have been profound.

But as soon as the natives begin to work for the white man, the native community ceases to be self-sufficient and is drawn into a system which it cannot control and which takes charge of its entire life. Should the price of primary raw materials drop by two-thirds, as it does in a severe world crisis, or should new synthetic products replace them, the community is faced with ruin.

New Demands—Economic and Political. Human demands are insatiable. Once a community is exposed to full contact with the West and given a taste of our consumers' goods, they want all they can get. Not only cars, trucks, and bicycles appear, but plumbing and electricity, and then the demand expands to include roads, schools, doctors, and medical clinics. Who is to provide them? Who is to pay for them? The ultimate result may be a new political consciousness—the search for the kind of political machinery best calculated to help primitive people achieve their aims.

The Native as Wage Labourer. Perhaps the most drastic change that has come over the primitive village has been the migration of its younger men to the mines and plantations in search of a cash income to make their demands effective.

South of the Sahara some 3,000,000 Africans, in a sparse population, are employed in wage labour. This involves absence from the native village, often many hundreds of miles away, for about three and a half years. Forty-three per cent of the younger men are away from their homes earning money in this way.

This raises urgent problems: the children lack a father's care and authority; the younger women remain unmarried; the men return with new ideas to find the village as before; this results in family squabbles and conflicts with the elders. The whole pattern of native life is in disintegration.

Natives and the Land. In many parts of Africa, in particular—but similar changes are taking place everywhere—the whole land system on which the structure of society depends is breaking up.

In Kenya, which is 80 per cent desert, before it achieved independence, the White Highlands, a healthy, fertile area, were 'bought' by 3000 well-to-do British settlers, mostly ex-officers and members of the aristocracy. From these areas the Kikuyu were excluded, except as wage labourers. This area covers some seven million acres. The average density of population was two Europeans to the square mile, while in the Kikuyu native reserve it was 283 per square mile.

In the territory of Uganda there were very few white settlers, but the problem emerged in another form. Here the rights of the chiefs, which originally were purely administrative and to the benefit of the tribe, became proprietary. They were made landowners, and the people were their tenants. Then as commercial crops became important (coffee, tobacco, cotton), the chief became simply a receiver of rent with no duties and no responsibilities. He was free to charge what rent he could exact and dispossess his tenants when he wished. Thus the chiefs themselves had entirely revolutionized native society and, together with certain commercially successful Africans, established an aristocracy of wealth.

ANTHROPOLOGY AND WESTERN CIVILIZATION

It was an altogether new extension of anthropology when the methods of work and the achieved results of field anthropology were turned for the first time on our modern Western civilization. Self-knowledge is always a painful thing and not everyone was too happy about this. Would it not be better to keep to primitive tribes and their interesting ways? But no one has ever succeeded in limiting scientific inquiry to what is safe. Man's love of truth is insatiable, and if more light and truth can break upon the contemporary scene through applying to it the lessons we have learned abroad, there is nothing that can prevent that light from dawning.

This task has already begun. We are now in a position to investigate the pattern of a modern industrial community—its folkways, its religious organization, its taboos and ceremonials, and its pattern of family relationships.

Such a study, however, can no more remain the study of a static system than can the study of native life in modern Africa. Wherever we turn today we find a world in transition and old social patterns in kaleidoscopic change.

Within the last 150 years we have seen an advanced technology that has radically modified Western civilization so that new men, new ethical values, new institutions and even, though often clad in the old forms, a new religious attitude, have appeared.

In this newest and most virile of modern cultures we find an intense consciousness of the diversity of its cultural origins and of racial differences; we find, as in no other social system that has ever flourished before, a supreme emphasis on technology and wealth. There is also a strong belief in education and science, even if not all the results of intellectual inquiry are entirely welcome—a grave contradiction here. Along with the courage and self-reliance of the pioneer—the frontier spirit—there is quite an unusual degree of personal insecurity and also an uneasy consciousness of a growing discrepancy between the ideology of a nominally Christian democracy and the highly competitive and materialistic aims of what is now being called 'the Affluent Society'.

In some parts of the world, particularly America, agriculture is sometimes threatened with problems of overproduction, which most certainly never troubled primitive man. Often there are problems of soil erosion and exhaustion like those which vex the African. Even an ever-expanding industry looks forward uneasily to a period in which its products may no longer be in such great demand as they are now, and when foreign markets may diminish their requirements. These factors make for anxieties, phobias, and other symptoms of maladjustment which the anthropologist as well as the social psychologist must consider in our day. Already the study of anthropology is proving to be of great value in understanding ourselves.

This is the keynote of these concluding chapters—not merely the sympathetic understanding of others, valuable though it may be, but the far more difficult task of critical self-examination in the light of anthropological science, the task of understanding ourselves in an age of transition.

SUGGESTED FURTHER READING

Keesing, F., 'Applied Anthropology in Colonial Administration' in *The Science of Man in the World Crisis* (edited by Ralph Linton). 1945.

Kluckhorn, C., *Mirror for Man*. Harrap: London, 1950.

Mair, L., *Studies in Applied Anthropology*. University of London Press: London, 1957.

Tax, S., *Horizons of Anthropology*. Allen & Unwin: London, 1965.

Glossary

A

ACCULTURATION—The process by which culture is transmitted through contact of groups with different cultures, usually one having a more highly developed civilization.

AGE CLASS—Age Group, Age Set. A social-status level, which may be an organized association, including all the members of a tribe who are of a given age and sex.

ALBINISM—A deficiency of pigmentation of the skin, eyes, and hair. It is a hereditary trait, but can appear suddenly, owing to a chance modification of a gene.

ALPINE—A division of the Caucasoid race originally inhabiting East Central Europe and Asia Minor. They are brachycephalic (broad skulls) and have broad faces with sharp, square jaws, brown or black hair, and olive complexions.

AMULET—A small object, charm, or talisman which the wearer believes will protect him from danger, supernatural and magical; hence a good-luck charm.

ANIMATISM—In effect, another term for *mana*; belief in non-material supernatural essences or powers which inhabit material objects.

ANIMISM—A belief in individual spiritual beings, probably originating in the concept of *mana*, or in a spiritual and non-personalized quality which is believed to be present in the universe. It involves carrying over to *things* the attitudes and procedures used in dealing with people.

ANTHROPOID—An animal having the characteristics of the primate sub-order consisting of man, true monkeys, and apes. (*See* Pithecoid.)

ANTHROPOLOGY—The general term for the science of man: the cultural, social, physical development and behaviour of man throughout his history. The general term includes the special terms: physical anthropology; human evolution (the science of fossil man); archaeology (prehistory); cultural anthropology; social anthropology; linguistic anthropology.

ARCHAEOLOGY—The branch of anthropology that is concerned with the historical reconstruction of cultures no longer extant.

ARTIFACT—Any construction of the human hand—e.g., a wheel, jug, axe, arrow, loincloth.

ASSOCIATION—A general term for social groups in defined relationships; e.g., for such patterned groups as families, clans, clubs, classes, secret societies.

AUSTRALOPITHECUS—A genus of fossil hominoid found in South Africa.

B

BARBARISM—A classification of culture possessing primitive agriculture or domesticated herds but not metalworking or writing.

BARTER—The direct exchange of one kind of goods for another, with no employment of money.

BLOOD MONEY—Financial compensation paid to the relatives for certain cases of homicide.

BRACHYCEPHALIC—Having a comparatively broad skull, with a cephalic index (q.v.) of more than 81.

BRIDE PRICE—The wealth transferred by the kin of a groom to the kin of his bride in compensation for their release of claim to the children that are produced in the marriage.

BRONZE AGE—The period in cultural history, beginning in Babylonia, from 2500 to 3500 B.C., during which bronze implements were made. It carries with it settled life, a food surplus, and the beginnings of urban life.

BUSHMEN—Members of the Bushman–Hottentot pygmy population. Food-gathering groups in South Africa. They possessed a characteristic art of rock painting.

C

CANNIBALISM—Using human flesh as either a symbolic or regular food. It is often linked with ceremonials having religious significance.

CAPSIAN—A late-palaeolithic culture in North Africa. It is a *blade* culture with a characteristic art, as seen in certain cave paintings in Portugal.

CARGO CULTS—A fanatical movement which arose in certain Pacific islands, anticipating the miraculous arrival of cargoes of valuable goods for the natives.

CARMEL—The fossils found in the Mount Carmel (Palestine) caves date from the third interglacial period. The skeleton is heavy, the neck short. A possible cross between *Homo sapiens* and Neanderthal man.

CASTE—A hierarchical system of social control (for example, in India), with each sub-group assigned a ranked status, depending on its origin and religious strictness.

CAUCASOID—A racial group centring around the Mediterranean. Light skins, narrow to medium-broad faces, straight or wavy hair, body hair, eyes blue to brown. It includes the Dinaric, Nordic, Alpine, and Mediterranean subgroups.

CAVE MAN—The popular cartoonist's conception of anthropology; the famous misconception of Neanderthal man as brandishing a huge club and dragging his female captive to his cave.

CEPHALIC INDEX—The ratio between head breadth and head length. If these are equal the index is 100. A broad skull (brachycephalic) will have an index of 81 or over; a long skull (dolichocephalic) will have an index of less than 75.

CHIEF—A leader in a social organization on a low technological level. Sometimes the position is inherited.

CIVILIZATION—A degree of fairly advanced culture, in which the arts and sciences; as well as political life, are well developed. It should be characterized by social classes, specialization, cities, mathematics, and writing.

CLAN—Membership in a clan depends on kinship through one parent. It is often exogamous (q.v.). It provides mutual security, government, marriage regulations, religion and ceremonies, property regulations, and social control. Some authorities require not only a rule of descent but also a definite place of residence or locality and social integration.

CLUBS—Groups specifically organized for the pursuit of special interests and therefore not based on kinship. Most frequently these are for men only, and in New Guinea and elsewhere elaborate club-houses are constructed. (*See* Secret Societies.)

CORE—A piece of flint (or other stone) from which flakes have been struck to make implements. Either the core or the flake or both could be used as such an implement.

COUNCIL OF ELDERS—Among primitive food-gathering communities, the older men of recognized status and experience constitute an authority, with no legal status but very influential, which keeps the peace and decides on ritual procedures, hunts, and migrations.

COUSIN, *cross*—The child of a parent's brother or sister *of the opposite sex*, e.g., the child of the sister of the father.

COUSIN, *parallel*—The child of a parent's brother or sister of *the same sex*, e.g., the child of the father's brother or the mother's sister. Often not permitted to marry, although cross cousins may do so.

CRO-MAGNON—The western European population (Caucasoid) associated with the Aurignacian and other late-paleolithic cultures. Tall, large cranial capacity, high forehead, prominent chin. Among the first and best-known types of *Homo sapiens*, dominant during the last half of the fourth glaciation.

CULT—The ritual observances involved in the worship of, or communication with, particular supernatural persons or objects or their symbolic representation. A cult includes the collection of ideas, activities, and practices associated with a given divinity or social group.

CULTURE—All that is socially transmitted in a society, including artistic, social, ideological, and religious patterns of behaviour, and the techniques for mastering the environment.

CUNEIFORM—A writing method of antiquity, characterized by wedge-shaped signs, at first impressed on clay tablets.

D

DANCE—The most ancient art expression and major recreation of primitive man. A co-operative group art often of religio-magical significance. (*See* Ghost Dance.)

DIFFUSION—The method by which a part of culture—e.g., an institution or invention—spreads to other areas. It may occur through migration or borrowing. In an extreme form diffusion was regarded as more important than any other factor in the growth of cultures.

DINARIC—A European Caucasoid racial group originating in Yugo-slavia (Dinaric Alps). Large convex nose, long face, and round head.

DOLICHOCEPHALIC—Skulls which are long in proportion to their width, having a cephalic index of less than 75.

DRYOPITHECUS—Miocene ground-dwelling and erect apes, one group of which may have evolved into man.

E

ENDOGAMY—The rule that requires a person to marry within a specific social group of which he is a member.

ENVIRONMENT—The totality of the external conditions and influences that affect man, including such natural factors as rainfall, climate, and vegetation, but also the location of a society in relation to other societies.

ETHICS—The study or discipline which concerns itself with judgements of approval and disapproval, or as to the rightness and wrongness of actions, dispositions, or ends.

ETHNIC—Referring to a group distinguished by common cultural characteristics—e.g., a linguistic group like the Bantu of South Africa.

EVOLUTION—A continuous development, distinguished by each stage growing out of the one before. Biologically it refers to the appearance of more advanced forms of animal and plant life from simpler forms. Anthropology traces the development of man from simian ancestors. It is also applied to the development of human institutions from simple to more complex.

EXOGAMY—The rule that requires a person to marry outside a specific social group of which he is a member.

F

FAMILY—The key institution in society, consisting of one or more women living with one or more men and their children. A socially approved sex relationship and various rights and obligations characterize the family.

FAMILY, *bilateral*—A family tracing its descent from both parents, as, for example, in Britain today.

FAMILY, *extended*—A family consisting of a series of close relations along either the male or female line, usually not along both. A woman, her husband, their children and her married daughter, with her husband, would be one form of an extended family.

FAMILY, *joint*—Several related families in one household. Labour is pooled and all are responsible to the same authority.

FAMILY, *maternal*—A family in which relationships are counted through the woman. It consists of a woman and her male and female descendants.

FAMILY, *paternal*—A family in which relationships are counted through the father.

FETISH—An object which is supposed to have supernatural potency, perhaps because of association with a spiritual being.

FETISHISM—The doctrine that objects and persons may be possessed by spirits that are not their own souls, or a religion emphasizing the use of fetishes.

FLAKE—An implement made by removing flakes of flint from a large piece of core and using the flakes as tools.

FOLKLORE—The common orally transmitted traditions, myths, festivals, songs, superstitions, and stories of all peoples. Most folklore consists of survivals which continue to have functional value.

FOLKWAYS—The totality of widely observed traditions in a society, the breach of which is punished informally.

FOOD GATHERING—Obtaining subsistence by hunting and collecting fruits, berries, roots, moss, fungi, insects, fowl, or fish. It is the simplest form of economy.

FOSSIL—Plant or animal remains, or the impression of plants or animals, preserved in rocks or earth.

FUNCTIONALISM—A theoretical approach to anthropology that emphasizes concern with the part each unit within a culture plays in the total existence of that culture.

G

GENETICS—The study of the process of inheritance, involving basically, the laws formulated by Mendel in 1856 and their subsequent elaboration and development.

GLACIATION—A thick layer of snow and ice, covering large parts of the earth. Early Europe was covered by four ice ages. North America also had four major glaciations. These ice ages began, respectively, 600,000; 500,000; 250,000; and 120,000 years ago, with the last reaching its terminal period about 20,000 years ago.

GYNOCRACY *or* GYNECOCRACY—A society in which women are the rulers.

H

HEADMAN—A leader of a tribe or similar group who does not have precisely specified authority, but depends largely on personal influence.

HEREDITY—The totality of biological traits transmitted by the parents and determining the individual's capacity for growth and development.

HIEROGLYPHIC—The stylized picture of ancient Egypt that later became a script. Some signs stand for sounds and some for ideas.

HOMINID—A primate who belongs to the group of human beings.

HOMINOID—Primates including all forms of man extinct and living; *Australopithecus*; and the anthropoid apes.

HOMO SAPIENS—The species to which all extant human beings belong. First found in the upper palaeolithic.

HYBRID—The offspring resulting from the mating of two persons from different geographical areas with different gene structure for pigmentation, hair form and colour, eye colour, etc.

I

IDEOGRAM—Signs representing ideas, qualities, actions, and sometimes objects. The original simple picture signs lose their pictorial features for the sake of speed in writing or drawing them.

INCEST—Sexual or marital relations between two persons so closely related that their marrying is prohibited. They need not, however, be blood relations in some societies.

INITIATION RITES—The transition and attendant ceremonies, such as ordeals and rites, involved in passing from one status to another, especially those whose purpose it is to induct the young person into the full status of an adult. May also refer to obtaining membership of a secret society.

INTICHIUMA—A Central Australian ceremony, the purpose of which is to supply food and other necessities through certain magical activities apportioned to the totem groups.

INVERTEBRATES—Animals without backbones or skulls.

IRON AGE—Period covering the 2500 years before historic times, during which iron tools and weapons were used.

J

Joking Relationship—An institutionalized pattern of privileged familiarity or joking between persons of specific social statuses.

K

Kinship—The social recognition and expression of genealogical relationships. Kinship is not only actual but may be based on supposed ties of blood.

Kula—A circular system of exchanging goods by voyages from island to island, found in New Guinea.

L

Levirate—The practice of requiring or permitting a man to marry the widow of his brother.

Lineage Group—A group resulting from descent reckoned either from the father's or the mother's line. Whereas in a clan relationship it is assumed, in a lineage group it must be demonstrated, i.e., the actual relationship must be specific and known.

M

Magic—The techniques of coercion by making use of belief in supernatural power. Sympathetic or imitative magic supposes that an action (e.g., a spell) committed upon something that stands for a person or a thing (e.g., a wax image) will have the desired effect upon the actual person or thing.

Mammal—Belonging to a class of vertebrate animals suckling their young, breathing by lungs, possessing body hair and a four-chambered heart. They are warm-blooded and must nourish the foetus by a placenta.

Mana—A non-individualized supernatural force, independent of supernatural persons, responsible for the effect of magic and for unusual qualities having power for good or evil.

Marching Rule—A comparatively recent native movement in the Solomon Islands (Pacific), and in the Admiralty Islands of New Guinea, demanding a form of self-government and taking direct action to secure this. Strict codes of behaviour are drawn up and villages are rebuilt on modern lines. The movement is anti-European in spirit.

Marriage, *matrilocal*—Marriage in which the married couple reside with the wife's family or kin group.

Marriage, *patrilocal*—Marriage in which the married couple live in the husband's community, or the wife settles in the home of her husband.

MEDICINE—Technique used to cure disease or alleviate pain, but extended to fetish objects and magical methods.

MEDICINE MAN—The popular early name for an American Indian who treats the sick or has special powers. Medicine men also exist in other primitive societies. Some practice magic or act as intermediaries between the world of spirits and the members of the community.

MEDITERRANEAN—A racial sub-group which includes many Sicilian and southern Italians. Short, square face, dolichocephalic.

MISCEGENATION—Race mixture through marriage. There is no biological evidence of any resultant deterioration; in fact hybrid vigour may occur.

MONGOLOID—In physical anthropology, a racial group centring round the Pacific Ocean. Its characteristics include straight black or dark-brown head hair, skin colour from saffron to yellow brown, medium-broad face, brown eyes, nose with low bridge, sparse body hair. The group includes the Malayan, southern and northern Chinese, Mongolian, Siberian, Eskimo, and American Indian sub-races.

MONOTHEISM—Belief in a single deity, believing that the cosmos is a unity, with one God who created and ordered all.

MORALITY—The doctrine or the practice of moral duties. The codes, conduct, and customs of individuals or of groups.

MORES—Behaviour patterns that are accepted, traditional, and slow to change. The breach is punished more severely than the breach of folkways.

MUTATION—A spontaneous change in the genes of some individuals, bringing about new hereditary effects.

MYTH—A narrative, usually of a religious nature, which is generally fixed by tradition, and which is closely related to a ritual (as, for example, a fertility ritual).

N

NEANDERTHAL—The most widely distributed and most numerous of palaeoanthropic men. Some 100 skeletons have been found.

NEGROID—One of the major racial groups of mankind. Some of its characteristics are slight body hair, small ears, black head hair, curly or woolly, brown to black eyes, nose with low bridge, brown to black skin. This race includes Forest, Nilotic, and Oceanic Negroes.

NEOANTHROPIC MAN—Referring to the type of man that has persisted into recent times.

NORDIC—A supposed northern Caucasoid racial group, whose existence is not accepted. Straight nose, light hair, blue eyes. Cephalic index less than 80. Concentrated in Scandinavia.

NUMINOUS—The awe-inspiring quality of any object of worship, rite, or holy place.

O

OATH—A promise or affirmation, usually calling on a divine authority to punish the oath taker in case of perjury.

ORACLE—A person specially able to obtain guidance from supernatural agencies; or a technique with sacred objects and special rites which secures supernatural guidance.

ORDEAL—A technique of trial in which the accused submits to a dangerous or difficult task. It is assumed that supernatural powers help settle the dispute or test the accusation.

OSTRACISM—Temporary banishment by popular decision.

OVERLAP—In racial distinctions, when a characteristic predominant in one group is also found, though not to the same extent, in another group. This is true of dark and light skins, hair and eye colour.

P

PALAEOANTHROPIC MAN—A hypothetical type of early man that no longer exists. Often used of Neanderthal man.

PAPYRUS—A writing material used in ancient times. It came from a plant that grows in marshy places, notably in Egypt.

PASTORALISM—A culture marked by a subsistence technique centred about the herding and husbandry of domesticated animals.

PHONOGRAM—A symbol representing a phonetic form.

PICTOGRAM—A written symbol representing an object of which it is a complete or simplified conventionalized picture.

PILTDOWN MAN—British fossil-like structure formerly believed to be of second interglacial period, but now known to be a fraud and a hoax.

POLYANDRY—Marriage in which a woman can have more than one husband at the same time.

POLYGYNY—Marriage in which a man may have more than one wife at the same time.

POLYTHEISM—Believing in and worshiping several gods.

POTLATCH—A ceremonial giving away or destroying of property to enhance status. Practised among the Kwakiutl Indians of the Pacific Northwest.

PRIMATE—The order that includes man, the great apes, monkeys, tarsiers, and lemurs.

R

RACE—A major division of mankind, with distinctive hereditarily transmissible physical characteristics, e.g., the Negroid, Mongoloid, and Caucasoid races.

RELIGION—A system of beliefs and practices that formalizes the conception of the relation between man and his environment. It embodies the idea of a supernatural and of personified supernatural forces.

RITES OR RITUAL—A set or series of acts, usually involving religion or magic, with the sequence established by tradition.

S

SANCTIONS—Anything which persuades a man to observe or refrain from a given mode of conduct. Sanctions may be social pressure, legal threats, or the fear of God.

SEANCE—A meeting for the reception of communications from the departed.

SECRET SOCIETIES—Special groups within a tribe with secret membership and activities. They may be concerned with war, religion, witchcraft, and similar pursuits. Membership commonly limited to those of one sex. There are usually several grades for initiates.

SHAMAN—Originally a Siberian medicine man, but the word is now used to describe a medicine man in any primitive society.

SLAVERY—One person's legally owning and controlling another and denying him freedom of action or movement. Almost always it has an economic basis, the slave taking part in agricultural or other labour or in domestic work.

SOCIAL CLASSES—Groups within a society, distinguished by their social and economic level from other groups. Such characteristics as age, occupation, and birth have been used to differentiate classes.

SORCERY—Using magical power for causing disease or some other evil.

SORORATE—The practice whereby a younger sister marries the widowed husband of her deceased older sister.

SPELLS—Incantations; words sung, chanted, recited for magical purposes.

STATUS—Comparative prestige rank in a community. It comprises both rights and duties.

STRATA—Beds or layers of rock as arranged in series in the crust of the earth. Also used to describe levels of society.

SYLLABARY—A table of written characters, each of which represents a syllable.

T

TABOO—A restraint or prohibition placed against certain acts, words, things, which, if violated, leads to an automatic penalty inflicted by magic or religion.

TECHNICS—The types of tool, mechanism, and associated method used in production.

TOTEM—A totem is an object toward which members of a kinship must have a special mystical relationship and with which the unit's name is associated. The object may be an animal or a plant.

TRIBE—A social group, usually with a definite area, dialect, cultural unit, or unifying social organization. It may include several subgroups, such as villages.

V

VERTEBRATES—Animals possessing backbones, skulls, and limbs. They include fish, amphibia, reptiles, birds, and mammals.

W

WITCH—A person believed to have supernatural powers to do evil and cause sickness. Often supposed to be associated with a particular physical condition, detectable by autopsy.

WITCH DOCTORS—People who have the power to detect witches and cure a bewitched person. They profess to be able to look into the future, escape harm, transform themselves, and accomplish superhuman tasks.

Index